Senior
Moments

A book for seniors and those who love them

Jacqueline D. Byrd

Byrd & Byrd, LLC
Bowie, Maryland

Senior Moments:
A book for seniors and those who love them
Jacqueline D. Byrd

First Edition, May 2005

Printed in the United States of America.

Author photograph © Perry Price
Cover Design by Gina Addison
Mom photos by Mark Uehling

Information in this book is not intended to serve as a substitute for legal advice, which should be based on attorney review of each individual's personal facts and circumstances. Contact the National Academy of Elder Law Attorneys (NAELA)— www.naela.org—for a list of elder law attorneys in your area.

www.byrdandbyrd.com

For information and orders, address:

Jacqueline D. Byrd
14300 Gallant Fox Lane, Suite 120
Bowie, Maryland 20715
jbyrd@byrdandbyrd.com

ISBN 0-9769545-0-8

9 780976 954507

For Toby

With love and gratitude for all of it.
"The only dream that mattered has come true…"

Contents

Suggested Reading for Dealing with a Difficult Parent
When You Need More Help
    Share Eldercare
    National Family Caregiver Support Program
    Is an Emergency Response System Right for You?
    Adult Day Care
    Geriatric Care Managers
    In-home Care
Nursing Homes
    When Is the Time Right for a Nursing Home?
    Adjusting to When a Loved One Goes into a Nursing Home
    Tips for Visiting a Loved One in a Nursing Home
    Paying for Caregiving
Hospice
    What Is Hospice?
    Choosing Hospice

Foreword

Aging is more visceral than cerebral. It is a process involving physical, mental and emotional change and the beginning of the imposition of limitations on one's everyday life. Being a good lawyer begins with understanding the client, not just the law. In *Senior Moments* Jackie Byrd shows why she is one of America's outstanding elder law attorneys. She is more visceral than cerebral. She feels the aging process in her gut.

Yes, Jackie covers all of the usual legal topics and covers them well. These include issues pertaining to age discrimination, elder abuse, neglect and exploitation, guardianships, health care decisions, health care quality issues, independent living options, nursing home options, Medicare, Medicaid, and other public benefits, as well as estate planning, including wills and living trusts, powers of attorney, and all the other necessary documents. But Jackie goes well beyond the bare legal issues and puts them in the context of the aging process. She also covers the human side of aging, such as caregiving, medications, drug abuse, drinking problems, and driving an automobile. Jackie even touches on Alzheimer's disease and some of the many problems involved in coping with family members afflicted with this disease. She talks about raising grandchildren and avoiding scams and fraud, coping with prescription drug costs and using and misusing credit cards.

Jackie's treatment of these and many other issues is done with compassion and understanding and her tribute to her own mother is moving.

Compassionate thinkers like Jackie are different from the rest of us. She sees what we overlook. Her compassion ferrets out information that our intake forms cannot begin to illicit. Jackie's work is both moving and informative. This is a book that's hard to put down.

Tom Begley
Moorestown, NJ
December 2004

Preface: What Is Elder Law?

Because many people ask me the same question, I think it is a good topic to explore and discuss. If you combine this country's legal system with issues of aging, says Charlie Sabatino, the result is a complicated mess of rules and regulations that often takes an attorney to unravel. Elder law has evolved to deal with the growing elderly population and their unique and often complicated financial, medical and legal needs. You can think of elder law as an expanded version of estate planning.

Sabatino, assistant director of the American Bar Association's Commission on Law and Aging and past president of the National Academy of Elder Law Attorneys, says, "Elder law goes beyond the usual after-death planning for disposition of property to more important lifetime issues, such as dealing with quality of life during your last decades."

Planning is the focus of elder law, Sabatino says. It includes taking steps to preserve independence for as long as possible and appointing an advocate in the event of incapacity. In the case of married couples where one ill spouse may require institutionalization, planning takes on the added aspect of providing sufficient funds for the healthy spouse left at home.

Most of the time, elder law and conventional estate planning take place in different settings. First of all, most conventional estate planning takes place during non-crisis.

Though some event may have precipitated the desire to plan (birth of a grandchild, planning a trip out of the country, health problems, etc.), normally a client is not in crisis when he meets with an attorney to make a will. On the other hand, elder law cases almost always arise in a crisis setting. Either there has been a sudden traumatic occurrence (stroke, fall, etc.) or a family has finally decided that they must respond to a deteriorating situation arising from some sort of dementia.

In most estate planning contexts, it is the client himself who contacts the attorney. This means that the client usually has the information from which the plan is to be prepared. The nature of the attorney/client relationship is very clear. In most elder law consultations, however, it is the children or the spouse of the person with the impairment who initiates the contact.

The goals of elder law and conventional estate planning are quite different as well. In estate planning, the goal is to conserve the estate and pass it to the next generation in the most tax- and cost-efficient means possible.

The goal in elder law is more convoluted. While asset preservation is one goal, in many cases it may be necessary to dispose of assets during a lifetime, or it may be necessary to spend the assets to pay for types of care not covered by government programs. While taxes are always a concern, sometimes it may be necessary to enter into transactions that will generate tax liability because there is a greater good that must be attained, such as paying for care for the chronic illness of the elder individual. The client and the planner in an elder law setting are always faced with the overriding problem of long-term care costs (often now as much as $6,000 or more per month). These costs must be measured against the tax or financial costs of a particular transaction or the client's natural instinct to preserve assets.

Communication between the elder law attorney and other advisers is extremely important. This will lessen overwhelming confusion in an already stressed situation.

Elder law attorneys tend be compassionate as well as knowledgeable. They are aware of the importance of small things, such as printing documents in larger type, providing hearing-assisted devices in their offices and designing conference rooms to accommodate wheelchairs. Elder law attorneys often work with geriatric care managers or other eldercare specialists to identify services available in the community and to suggest financial alternatives, such as long-term care insurance, for their clients' medical needs while safeguarding their assets. And most will make house and facility calls to meet with clients.

What sets elder law attorneys apart from other attorneys is that their focus is on the older client and how best to assure that client's quality of life during his or her final years, not just on the division and disposition of assets left behind. America's growing elderly population is a key factor behind this emerging legal specialty. There are now more than 33 million Americans 65 years old or older that represent nearly 13 percent of the population. People over 85 comprise the fastest growing segment of this group. Improvements in health care and medical technology mean that more people are living longer, but often with chronic illness that may require expensive long-term care.

Additionally, many families are scattered across the country. Today's elderly person cannot always count on having a family caregiver close by. As a result, many people are taking advantage of new laws that allow them to determine the types of medical treatment they want at the end of their lives and appoint someone to make medical decisions when they are not able to do so.

As a generalization, lawyers are not noted for their kindness or their warm, fuzzy attitudes. Indeed, much of their ability to be successful and victorious for their clients in our litigious society depends on their ability to fight tough and go for the jugular. But elder law attorneys are chipping away at this stereotype.

Myra Gilfix, an elder law practitioner in Palo Alto, California told *Time Magazine:* "I like dealing with human beings, with individuals. I always wanted to do people law. I am not a fighter."

Growing old can be very tough. And it gets tougher as time passes. We start to lose our spouses and our friends. The popular culture becomes foreign to us. We do not understand the music, the TV shows, the way younger people dress, the choices they make or the language they use. Every day there are losses to face. Every day there are struggles with illness and potential incapacity.

Kate Mewhinney, a clinical professor at Wake Forest University School of Law, told *Time Magazine,* "We had a woman here this week who said, 'I wake up in the middle of the night worrying about if I have to go into a nursing home.' She's 79 and

---

Anyone can call him or herself an elder law attorney, so where do you go to find a qualified one? The National Academy of Elder Law Attorneys (NAELA) is a terrific source. Its Web site lists elder law attorneys by geographic location. The organization also offers a directory of its members. Local bar associations and the AARP also direct seniors or their families to appropriate attorneys. See Resources section for NAELA contact information

■ ■ ■

very healthy. She said, 'I really worry. Will I lose everything? Will I lose my home? Where do I stand in terms of Medicaid?' Fortunately, we can give her some advance information."

It is important to find an attorney with whom you feel comfortable because these issues are very personal. You will be talking about family relationships and problems, sickness, your deepest beliefs regarding end-of-life decisions and other matters close to your heart. Additionally, you may be working with the attorney over a long period of time. Plenty of people are interested in the wealth of older people, but they are not always looking out for older people's best interests.

For more information on elder law, see the Resources section at the end of Chapter 1.

Introduction

You know those terms that spread like wildfire from one end of this country to the other—and everybody somehow knows what they mean? Some of them come from advertising, such as "Where's the beef?" Some of them come from TV shows, such as "Is that your final answer?" Then, there are some whose origins remain a mystery.

Nevertheless, if you are above 40, and just as you start to say someone's name you forget it, then you know what a "Senior Moment" is. More and more people are smiling, scratching their heads and saying "oops—Senior Moment" and all listeners know what they mean. Thus, the name of the column I began writing for the local newspaper, *The Bowie Blade-News*, in Bowie, Maryland. For purposes of the column, Senior Moments means more than just momentarily forgetting a name. The column has included many topics surrounding the multiple issues and challenges of the aging population, and of those who care for them.

You've read the statistics regarding how quickly this country is becoming "senior" as the Baby Boomers move into middle and old age. But what you may not have known is that the average caregiver in this country is female, age 47, the mother of children and also works full time! My very first "Senior Moments" column promised to provide readers with information for that typical caregiver and for the recipients of her care.

And, so it began. For seniors, we have covered issues such as age discrimination, elder abuse, neglect and exploitation, guardianships, health care decisions, health care quality issues, independent living options, nursing center options, Medicare, Medicaid and other public benefits, wills and trusts, planning for possible incapacity, Powers of Attorney, technology issues and more.

For care givers, we discussed many of the issues a caregiver confronts with an aging parent or other loved one—what is involved in a contested guardianship, what a "springing" power of attorney is, things that are "need to know" regarding long-term nursing home, Medicaid, and when a nursing facility is more appropriate than assisted living. We've discussed communication issues between generations, where to go for help, what to do when you need a break, who will "care for the caregiver," and other similar topics.

This book is, essentially, a compilation of published columns, the major goal of which has been to provide information, web sites and other sources to assist seniors and their caregivers in the ongoing challenges of life. It is my sincere hope that the information shared through the weekly columns, and now in this book has and will enhance the lives of senior adults and those who love them.

In her wonderful book, *Another Country—Navigating the Emotional Terrain of Our Elders,* Mary Pipher wrote that good mental health is not a matter of being dependent or independent, but of being able to accept the state one is in with grace and dignity. "The trick for the younger [family] members is to help without feeling trapped and overwhelmed," she said. "The trick for older members is to accept help while preserving dignity and control. Care givers can say, 'You have nurtured us, why wouldn't we want to nurture you?' The old must learn to say, 'I am grateful for your help and I am still a person worthy of respect.'" Lofty goals. I hope that these discussions will encourage and assist all of us as we strive to reach them.

1
The Role of Caregiving in Modern-day America

"All progress is precarious, and the solution of one problem brings us face to face with another problem."

—Martin Luther King Jr.

According to the U.S. Department of Labor, the "oldest old," or those aged 85 and older, are currently the fastest growing age group in this country. There was a time when you were lucky to find even one birthday card in the Hallmark store for someone turning 100 years old. Now, you may have six or seven choices among cards created for someone reaching the century mark.

All that helps explain why a survey by the National Alliance for Caregiving and the American Association of Retired Persons (AARP) found that in 22.4 million homes in the United States—nearly a quarter of households—someone was caring for an older relative or friend.

Most people over age 50 have at least one living parent. Other surveys suggest that today's Baby Boomers, adults born between 1946 and 1965, likely will spend more years caring for a parent than for their children.

1

Most caregivers are glad for the opportunity to return some of the nurturing and love that was freely given as they grew up. Nevertheless, the responsibility of caring for an aging parent while trying to keep up with career and family is emotionally stressful and difficult to afford. Our best efforts are frequently accompanied by frustration and feelings of ignorance and inadequacy. Caregiving can take a heavy toll emotionally, physically and financially. How do we make life and death decisions for the people who gave us life?

When we are in the midst of a crisis, it is difficult to think rationally and almost impossible to put all the pieces of the challenge together quickly in effective ways. However, we can gain a huge advantage by educating ourselves in advance about financial and legal issues, health and fitness for the elderly, community resources and support and other resources now available.

Caregiver preparation tips from Jacqueline Marcell in her book *Elder Rage or Take My Father...Please! How to Survive Caring For Aging Parents:*

1. *Plan ahead. Talk to your parents while they are still healthy to learn their preferences for medical care and to assess their financial situation. Be sure they have signed legal and health-care Durable Powers of Attorney.*

2. *Act the minute you see signs of dementia. Get the person to a geriatric psychiatrist. Find out about medications that can control aggression, depression and dementia and can possibly slow the dementia.*

3. *Change your own behavior so you can cope with the situation more objectively and less emotionally. "Get yourself into a support group," Marcell advises, "so that you get help from other people who have gone through it."*

■ ■ ■

There are many resources that can assist you with the transition. (See the Resources section at the end of the chapter.) One such resource is a magazine called *Today's Caregiver*. It has current information on what options are available for out-of-home care. Another great resource is of course AARP. Many AARP articles focus on how to face the conflicting responsibilities of caregiving while still doing well on the job.

Look locally. Some hospitals, nursing homes or adult day care programs have volunteers that provide afternoon or evening relief for caregivers. A licensed health-care aide can also provide simple assistance with daily activities at home. Aides can be found through home health agencies or independent providers.

If you are caring for an elderly parent or other loved one, you are not alone. But remember, the most effective planning is undertaken before a crisis. Ask yourself whether you and your parents are sufficiently knowledgeable about available public and private community services. Do you feel you have the knowledge necessary to decide among home care, assisted living, continuing care retirement community, or nursing facility care options? Do you understand the differences between Medicare and Medicaid programs and their relevance to your family's plans? Are you aware of long-term care insurance and what to look for in selecting an agent and a policy? Are you aware of your asset protection options in the event of the need for long-term home care or nursing facility care?

Caregivers, be proud of yourselves. You are demonstrating that the words of love you have professed over the years are honest and true. You are showing your devotion in an extremely caring and meaningful way. The ancient Iranian religious leader, Zarathushtra, taught "Doing good to others is not a duty. It is a joy, for it increases your own health and happiness."

Touch Is Important

I recently read about the importance of touch in the life of an elderly person. I never really thought of it in this way, but the book Fourteen Friends' Guide to Eldercaring *points out that "After a long, close marriage filled with physical affection, a recent widow [or widower] may go for weeks, even months, without being touched by another person."*

It is difficult to overestimate how important a touch can be in the life of a nursing home resident, for instance. A hug, a pat on the shoulder or hand squeeze can bring great comfort and encouragement. That is one reason pet therapy has been so successful. A nuzzled pet nuzzles back.

Perhaps the lack of touch in their lives could be why elderly people often ask to take someone's arm. They may be concerned about falling, sure, but they also enjoy the sense of physical closeness to another person. Indicating that you would like to take the arm of a handsome stranger is a socially acceptable way to ask for it. And he does not even have to be handsome; he is certain to appreciate being needed.

Along those same lines, the elderly rarely get to be around, or even see, babies and younger children. My mother was once in a nursing center and an assisted living facility for five months. When my grandchildren, two-year-old triplets, were taken to see her, the other residents were enthralled, encouraged and invigorated by the toddlers and their antics. If you have thought about helping your own children develop a sense of giving to others, one of the best ways is to take them to visit and spend time with the elderly. It helps your child learn to be comfortable with people of a variety of ages, and in today's very busy world, to give one's time to a senior could be the gift he or she will appreciate more than anything else.

■ ■ ■

Perhaps no one really knows or can truly appreciate what you do. But you know. And that is sufficient.

Suggested Reading for Dealing with a Difficult Parent

In 1982, Grace Lebow and Barbara Kane combined their psychiatric and geriatric training and founded Aging Network Services, a social work care management agency dedicated to helping older people and their families. Both are psychotherapists specializing in grief and loss and are trained in clinical social work. They have written a very useful book for caregivers titled *Coping With Your Difficult Older Parent: A Guide for Stressed-Out Children*. The book aims to help those who find themselves needing help with complicated parental caregiving situations.

Lebow and Kane say that well over half the adult children coming to them for psychotherapy are in a state of stress over their "difficult" parents. The children, they say, use the word difficult not so much because of the physical burdens of caring for parents in a state of decline, but because of the emotional drain of trying to help parents who are hard to help.

While helping grown children, many of whom had been distanced geographically or emotionally from their parents but were obligated to step in, Lebow and Kane realized there was a gap in the literature available on eldercare. They noticed many excellent books on eldercare in general, but observed that not many books addressed the parent with so-called difficult behaviors. Additionally, most books about people with difficult behavior patterns or problem personalities address how to treat those problems, not how to help friends and loved ones deal with those difficult personalities. And last, this type of literature scarcely mentioned older people at all, because, as the book's introduction notes, "older people with difficult personalities rarely seek therapy."

Questions on the book's back cover can help you quickly see whether you think it would be of value to you. "Do you have an aging parent who blames you for everything that goes wrong? Cannot tolerate being alone, wants you all the time? Is obsessed with health problems, real or imagined?"

Lebow and Kane have identified 40 behaviors as "difficult" and listed them in a questionnaire. When grown children go to Aging Network Services for the first time, they are often asked to complete this questionnaire. They are amazed to see how well their parent's behaviors match those in the questionnaire. Some are surprised and relieved to discover there are many other parents just as difficult, or even more difficult, than their own— and they are even more relieved when they learn that there are things they can do to help both themselves and their parents. This questionnaire is at the beginning of the book and should not be skipped. It gives you a way of comparing your parent's behavior with a range of problem behaviors. The book also gives practical tips and sample dialogues for some of the most troubling situations.

In my opinion, the book's greatest value is in helping the grown child realize the truth about who has the greatest capacity to change. After all, as the book says, a difficult person often does not even realize how others perceive him or her. It may well look to that person as if you and everyone else have a problem. This book helps you to feel more compassion for your parent and, at the same time, be able to live your own life without being at the mercy of your parent's behaviors. Reading the book, you learn to re-channel your energies from the fruitless task of trying to get your parent to change to the more productive goal of learning practical ways of coping with your parent as he or she is.

See Resources for how to find this book.

When You Need More Help

Share Eldercare

Eldercare is not an easy job. Most jobs are less difficult when they can be shared. However, sharing eldercare is especially hard because of the various personalities of family members and the depth of emotions involved. Although everyone involved may be well-meaning, there are as many opinions about how to handle each situation as there are individuals.

The concept of sharing, even without involving eldercare, is a difficult one. Why then should we assume that caring for the aging parent of several children should be a seamless and continuously loving proposition? From my experience in elder law, I can assure you that it is not. I have worked with siblings who cross the spectrum from those who clearly love each other but are disappointed that things are not working out as some of them had hoped, all the way to siblings who can barely tolerate one another. In either situation, it can be very hard to accomplish those goals that are important for the aging parent whose condition requires decisions and cooperation among family members.

Sadly, some of these sibling problems have been caused by the parents themselves. Sometimes the person being cared for has always been extremely difficult and has left severe emotional, and occasionally physical, wounds for the children to deal with. Perhaps the parent has encouraged sibling rivalry by choosing a clear favorite child through the years. Perhaps the parent has always been angry and cruel or has recently become so because of illness or similar circumstance. Whatever the case, caregiving time necessitates that the family members work together insofar as possible. It is healthier for everyone involved.

In *As Parents Age: A Psychological and Practical Guide*, Joseph Ilardo stresses that all responses to the parent's aging must be taken into account— those of the parent, the adult child and the siblings. If the feelings of all parties are not taken into account, they will "interfere with the healthy process by which we prepare to say goodbye."

The ideal way to handle your elder's future care needs is for all the siblings to get together before a crisis or emergency arises. You could work out a reasonable plan to meet various contingencies for when Mom or Dad is no longer able to remain independent.

If your elder is in relatively good health, please consider organizing such a meeting with your siblings and perhaps other family members. The advantages to this approach are many. You have the opportunity to address important caregiving decisions without the emotional reactions to a crisis that may cloud everyone's judgment. Everyone can get a full understanding of issues that may arise in the future. Everyone will get a chance to consider how to respond to future caregiving needs in ways that best fit their abilities. Even more important, if the aging parent is able to communicate his or her wishes, you can determine what solutions would be preferred.

Chris Adamec has written a Macmillan Lifestyle Guides book called *The Unofficial Guide to Eldercare*. Here are some steps the book suggests to make such a meeting go smoothly:

- Hold the meeting in or near your parent's home, since the decisions you will be making are on your parent's behalf. Make it as convenient as possible for the elder to fully engage in the process.

- Prepare an agenda of issues ahead of time and provide written copies to all participants at the start of the meeting. This will help keep the discussion focused. The agenda should include a possible budget, scheduling issues, care needs and options, living arrangements and emergency planning.

- Ask a geriatric care manager or therapist to attend and work with your family during this meeting. This is useful because the subject of such a meeting is inherently emotionally difficult for many families and an objective third party can often defuse tensions. Moreover, a professional in the field of eldercare will be able to provide on-the-spot, authoritative answers to questions that arise in the course of the meeting.

In the book *Fourteen Friends' Guide to Eldercaring*, a lengthy section on sharing caregiving provides the following advice: "Early on, make a list of all areas where help is needed. Acknowledge what are essential requirements and what are added niceties. Determine and assess how each caregiver is willing and able to participate. You cannot expect someone with a full-time job to handle the daytime doctor appointments, and you do not expect someone who lives an hour away to make daily visits. Each caregiver's tasks may be different and not necessarily equal."

Eldercare 911, by Susan Beerman and Judith Rappaport-Musson, has a very useful section that helps caregivers organize to handle mild cognitive impairment (MCI). In the elderly, MCI can be a result of many things: beginning stages of Alzheimer's

Memory Enhancement Tips

1. *Post a large calendar in a prominent place and fill in doctor appointments, birthdays and other important dates. This can remind a mildly impaired parent of important occasions and give her a sense of control. One of the most disappointing and frustrating situations to an ill or aging person is to lose control over the whens and wheres of their lives.*

2. *Place a sign on the inside of the front door reading "Lock this door" or "Do not lock this door" to help remind a mildly impaired person to perform, or not perform, these important safety steps.*

3. *Install a telephone with extra-large, lighted numbers programmed for use by pressing the photo of the person your elder wants to call. This will relieve your loved one of the need to remember telephone numbers. Check with your local Alzheimer's organization or telephone equipment company to locate this and other helpful equipment.*

4. *Reframe or label photos with identifying notes, such as "Norm and me in Acapulco," and label photos with the names of grandchildren, nephews and nieces.*

5. *Place a basket in plain view for your loved one to drop keys, eyeglasses and loose change in the same spot every day. This helps alleviate some of the problems of misplacing these items. You can put a sign on the basket for even more help.*

6. *Place a notepad by the telephone and in the kitchen for to-do or grocery lists. At the top of the pad, put in dark letters what the pad's use will be. Black ink on white paper is the best contrast and easiest to see.*

■ ■ ■

disease, stroke or a typical infection with a rise in white blood cells. It may also just be a fact of life that never progresses further.

As a senior issues columnist, and a caregiver myself, I have found caregiving to be much like being a first-time parent. No classes are given to teach you how to do it right. The book's preface notes that caregivers are battling centuries-old expectations: "This timeless status quo includes the inherent assumption that even though you have no medical or gerontological training, you will know when, how and how much to intervene, how to manage insurance benefits, how to evaluate nursing homes, how to cope with Alzheimer's disease and how to resolve a host of other new and life-altering caregiving dilemmas." Of course, this assumption also holds that you will "find time to continue nurturing your children, being a good spouse, working on your career and maintaining your own personal time and space."

The authors suggest creating a system helpful to your mildly confused loved one by thinking about your own life experiences—what do you do with your house keys so they are easy to locate? How do you find your important messages and remember your appointments?

The information in *Eldercare 911* is practical, problem-solving and very useful. The book includes chapters on just about everything you need to know about being a caregiver, including a section on whether you are the one who should be doing the job. It includes a helpful list of caregiver organizations and resources, along with a glossary of terms used frequently in the eldercare community.

The best news, say the authors, is that experts in every walk of life, including the government, the business world and the clergy, are studying the needs of family caregivers and trying to devise systems to ease their burdens.

National Family Caregiver Support Program

Do not forget that caregiving can be shared with agencies outside the home and family. County Departments of Aging can refer you to adult day care centers and senior centers in your area, along with a multitude of additional resources. Remember that very few people can read minds! Be specific in asking for and in offering help. Friends and neighbors may be able to help if you ask. Keep a list of people willing to back you up when you are unable to do your usual elder caring. This list will increase your peace of mind.

A National Family Caregiver Support Program (NFCSP) has been established by Congress. This program released funds to the states through area agencies, and funds were awarded for innovative grants and projects designed to test the effectiveness of caregiving programs across the nation.

NFCSP calls for all states, working in partnership with area agencies and local community service providers, to supply some basic services for family caregivers:

- Information to caregivers about available services
- Assistance to caregivers in gaining access to the support services such as individual counseling, organization of support groups and training of caregivers to assist them in making decisions and solving problems
- Respite care to enable caregivers to be temporarily relieved from their responsibilities, including in-home care, adult day care and institutional respite on an intermittent, occasional or emergency basis
- Supplemental services, on a limited basis, to complement the care provided by caregivers, such as home

modifications, assistive technologies, emergency response systems, equipment, supplies and transportation

The practice of family caregiving contributes $196 billion annually to the nation's health care system. This is more than the amount spent on formal home care ($32 billion) and nursing home care ($83 billion) combined. Family caregiving significantly reduces costs to Medicare, Medicaid and private payers, and it is appropriate and long overdue for the government to begin official support in this area.

The NFCSP statute requires states to give priority consideration to persons in the greatest social and economic need and to older individuals providing care and support to persons 18 and under with mental retardation and related developmental disabilities.

See Resources for caregiving support organizations and information.

Is an Emergency Response System Right for You?

Emergency response systems, worn as a necklace or bracelet with a panic button that connects into a central system can be a great help for the 65 percent of seniors who fall each year or for the many who suffer a stroke or heart attack. Besides potential injury, there is also stress and anxiety for seniors and family members who realize that such occurrences are possible.

Emergency response services, when signaled via a panic button or voice command, are geared to respond immediately to a pre-agreed routine. They access a computer file for the patient/client and follow procedures to contact paramedics and designated neighbors, family, friends and health care professionals. They try to communicate by voice with the client

Book Offers Advice on Dealing with a Disaster

The American Red Cross has a guide to help seniors plan ahead for possible disasters. The guide, Disaster Preparedness for Seniors by Seniors, contains space for recording emergency numbers, tips for creating a disaster plan, supplies to have on hand and safety tips regarding grandchildren. The guide was written by seniors who experienced a two-week power outage after an ice storm in New York. They realized that a little advance preparation would have spared them many of the hardships they had to endure.

■ ■ ■

through strategically placed microphones in the home. In addition to contacts on file in their computer, they have medical history that can be shared with paramedics before they are dispatched.

An emergency response system may not be suitable for everyone. At a minimum, the user must be able to reach the panic button and push it for it to work. Additionally, users need to be willing to wear the bracelet or necklace at all times. A senior has to remember and understand that they are not to push the button when they are feeling lonely or isolated and need company, but only to push it at a time of crisis.

Seniors with physical limitations preventing use of a panic button may need an entirely different system. Those with dementia or memory problems may not be able to use the system even if it is in place.

If you decide an emergency response system could work for your loved one, you need to begin the process of deciding which model and type is the most appropriate option for your circumstances. First, check with the Better Business Bureau to determine whether negative complaints are on file about the system and company you are considering.

If your family determines that a medical emergency response setup is not a good option, how else can you address concerns about possible injuries due to falls? The frail elderly and those at risk for debilitating episodes should receive instruction to try to prevent falls in the first place and to minimize the degree of injury they suffer. Ask your general practitioner to refer the patient to a physical therapy practice for instruction on balance, coordination and learning how to fall. Additionally, many senior centers, area Agency on Aging offices and other geriatric programs offer classes for seniors to learn how to fall so they are less likely to sustain a serious injury. Some offer exercise classes to improve balance.

Finally, ask your physician or pharmacist to examine medication regimes periodically to see if they are likely to cause fuzzy-headedness alone or in combination, and if so, ask if any can be cut back or eliminated. Assistance devices such as canes or walkers might be a good idea. Evaluation and proper instruction in the use of such aids should be undertaken by a professional trained to make such assessments. Perhaps your home can be modified to reduce the chance of accidents; installing grab bars in the bathroom is easy and very effective. Even just adding better and stronger lighting can be of significant help to someone whose failing eyesight contributes to accidents.

See the Resources section for related information.

How to Pick an Emergency Response System

Questions to ask an emergency response system company:

Does the company provide the service itself or does it use a third party to perform some functions?

Is the company's response center dedicated only to this mission?

Does the company train its own response center personnel?

What types of data are held in the main computer?

Are such data made available to mass-marketing companies?

Does the company maintain a list of all your contacts, along with multiple ways to reach them?

Does the company keep accurate medical profiles with facts, past history and medications?

Are the medical records in a format that can be easily conveyed to paramedics?

Does the company's equipment have self-diagnostic checking capabilities?

Is an equipment check performed at least once a month?

Is equipment waterproof (wearable in the bath or shower)?

Does the company have two-way communication capability?

Does it work with or without a phone being picked up?

Is the equipment UL listed as a medical alarm?

Is the service portable, that is, will it work in another state or area if the wearer makes a short trip?

Some companies will require a large initial fee and a long contract for their services. What are the financial requirements for the company you are considering? What are your options for termination of the contract?

Adult Day Care

Adult day care centers are a caregiving option that can be a wonderful solution, especially when your loved one is somewhere between independent living and an assisted living facility.

Many seniors must live with their adult children or other relatives who are often absorbed with full-time jobs, after-school activities for their own children and the demands of ordinary life. Adult day care centers can give the caregiver a breather while providing a nourishing and fun-filled time for the senior. The centers offer a variety of programs and activities such as fitness classes, education discussions, classes through nearby community colleges, intergenerational activities and special events outings. In most cases, participants can be transported to and from their home in the center's van.

In my work with seniors and their families, I find that adult day care centers often provide just the perfect niche for giving needed assistance and yet allowing a senior adult to meet the overwhelming first-choice goal of every senior—to be able to remain in their home, or the home of their choice, rather than going to an assisted living or nursing facility. If your family member or loved one is socially isolated or seems depressed, is frail, impaired or experiencing mild confusion and is dependent on you for care or activities, an adult day care center may be just the right solution.

Many adult day care centers are fully staffed with a medical team to provide support for participants and caregivers. Baptist Senior Adult Ministries (BSAM) day care centers each have a registered nurse to administer and supervise medications, monitor blood pressure and check weight. Additionally, the centers have a geriatric-trained social worker who works on behalf of the participant and the family and who acts as a liaison between the family and community resources. There is a program coordinator with a degree in recreational therapy and/or a related field and an activity staff that implements individualized therapeutic care plans through daily activities.

The League for Excellence in Adult Day Centers (LEAD) is an alliance of nonprofit adult medical day care center providers serving Maryland and Washington, D.C. They have published a wonderfully informative booklet called *Selecting A Quality Program: A Consumer's Guide*.

In Maryland, all adult day care centers must be licensed by the Department of Health and Mental Hygiene. The booklet, however, provides measures of quality that go beyond mere licensing requirements, and is beneficial for any state. The authors advise you to visit several centers and make an appointment to talk with the social worker, director, nurse or other professional staff to discuss your relative's needs and interests. You will be looking for not just the highest quality of care, but for a program that is the best fit for your family member.

The booklet divides your possible questions into eight main categories:

1. Physical environment
2. Nursing and social work services
3. Activities
4. Nutrition
5. Transportation
6. Personnel
7. Administration
8. Finances

Under these main categories, the booklet advises you on what you should expect and provides lists of what you should ask and observe. For instance, under physical environment, there is a paragraph about the licensing regulations in the state. It also advises you to go "beyond basic safety issues, [to] look at the environment with an eye toward the emotional impact it may have on your family member. The fanciest facility can feel foreign and forbidding if adequate accommodations to meet the physical and emotional needs of its users have not been made." Some questions to consider include:

- Do they have handrails wherever needed?
- Are all spaces well lit?
- Is there a lot of natural light?
- Are there cues for finding restrooms and activity rooms?
- Is staff using the environment to promote independence?
- Are there provisions for privacy when needed or desired?
- Are there spaces where small groups can engage in simultaneous activities?
- Are displays and decorations age-appropriate, suggesting respect for the adulthood of participants?

Many adult day care centers have monthly caregiver support group meetings. Here caregivers can share and learn along with others in the same situations. They can pick up tips, solutions and the latest information regarding their own situation.

Under certain circumstances, Medical Assistance is available to help pay for adult day care. Also, some grant funding is available. Both types of assistance require written verification of income.

Geriatric Care Managers

The explosion of the aging population has resulted in changes, adjustments and advancements in the way the country provides eldercare. Among many pleasant developments in the past decade is the advent of geriatric care managers (GCMs). Their stated purpose is to "promote the advancement of dignified care for older adults." Sometimes arranging for a GCM or some other neutral third person to mediate, arbitrate and facilitate the best course of action for the elder needing care is the wisest thing to do. GCMs do not usually charge a fee until the family has mutually agreed upon a course of action.

GCMs can be the caregiver's eyes and ears by arranging and monitoring services and providing regular updates by phone or serve as a source of information about community resources and the process of setting up and paying for services. GCMs can arrange family meetings and help build strong support networks.

Having a GCM can be a wonderful solution when you or someone you love needs help with performing household chores, paying bills, taking medication, coordinating medical care, addressing legal concerns or obtaining social services. The GCM can meet the challenges of long-distance caregiving, put together a comprehensive plan for present or future needs, provide extra assistance during relocation or monitor your relative during your vacation.

GCMs are knowledgeable about local facilities for senior care and will work closely with you and your family to look at all of the options and make recommendations for your situation. They have the training and skills needed to develop rapport even with difficult clients. They know how to suggest creative alternatives and different approaches for dealing with the myriad challenges facing the senior and his family.

Most GCMs initially provide a home assessment and then create a recommended care plan based on the interview. A GCM can be a social worker, counselor or nurse. Their qualifications vary, but most have at least a bachelor's degree in social work, psychology, nursing, counseling or gerontology. Some have advanced degrees, and many have spent years in the field of gerontology and social services.

Basically, GCM services are broken down into four phases:

1. Conducting an assessment
2. Making a care plan
3. Arranging services
4. Providing ongoing care management

If a senior is living at home, the goal of a GCM is to set up services that will allow the individual to continue to live at home for as long as possible, at the highest level of independence. When services of this nature are being discussed, nearly everyone's first question is "How much will it cost?" Professional fees vary, of course, but average fees range from $75 to $165 an hour. Services can be short-term or ongoing. Some public and nonprofit agencies use a sliding-scale system based on income to set fees for the services.

The GCM Pledge of Ethics says, "I will provide ongoing service to you only after I have assessed your needs and you (or a person designated to act for you) understand and agree to a plan of service, the results that may be expected from it and the cost of service."

Unfortunately, Medicare and most health insurance plans do not cover the cost of care management at this time. However, some long-term care insurance plans will reimburse for care management services.

At this time, GCMs are not required to be certified by federal or state governments, but the National Association of Professional Geriatric Care Mangers has established standards of quality and a code of ethics for GCMs.

Five Must-Ask GCM Questions

If you are considering the advantages of a GCM, ask these questions during your interview:

1. Are you with a firm?

2. Are you a member of any national organizations such as the National Association of Professional Geriatric Care Managers, Children of Aging Parents, National Guardianship Association or American Association of Critical Care Nurses?

3. How many years have you been a GCM?

4. Can you provide me with client references?

5. What are your educational and professional credentials?

■ ■ ■

Some GCMs work in social service agencies that focus on seniors. Some work in hospitals, private care management agencies or adult day care centers. Some even work in the legal community, assisting the court with guardianships. There are some that work independently as well. See Resources for information on finding a good GCM.

In-home Care

A Family Caregiver's Guide to Planning and Decision Making for the Elderly by James A. Wilkinson is a very sensible book that will help caregivers gain information and tie up loose ends in areas such as housing, financing and available health care.

One of the more frequent questions asked of me is how to select good in-home health providers. Both caregivers and the elderly are almost always hopeful that the senior person can remain somewhat independent and in their home as long as possible.

Wilkinson's book gives useful information on this topic. It begins by advising caregivers to include the elderly person whenever possible in the hiring decisions. This helps eliminate any confusion in the senior's mind about why a professional caregiver is needed. It also helps clarify everyone's expectations and goes a long way toward ensuring that the elderly person will accept the provider and assist him or her in doing an effective job.

Gathering information is the place to begin. The book includes a "Home Care and Housekeeping Form" to clarify and prioritize the issues you need to address. Wilkinson offers advice for this step. The first step is to get organized—if hiring for home health care, talk to the senior's doctor about what kind of care is needed and for how long. Make a list of prospective providers and their phone numbers. Finally, make a list of questions to ask each provider (a list of possible questions is included).

Before making any calls, you will need the elderly person's Social Security number, his or her Medicare claim number, supplemental health insurance information, the doctor's orders and the care plan, if a hospital discharge planner has given you one. This information, along with conversations with the doctor, helps you succinctly state the exact services you need and for how long.

When gathering information, call first thing in the morning. By calling early in the day, says Wilkinson, you have the opportunity to share any information you get with the doctor, the senior and other family members the same day. Calling early also increases your chances of actually talking to the person you need. State your questions clearly, keep questions and answers short, keep the conversation moving and do not waste time trying to take down every detail during the conversation. Make sketchy notes and expand on them after you hang up. Use separate sheets of paper for each call and date them so you do not confuse the notes later.

Wilkinson cautions against making any commitments based on telephone conversations with a salesperson. He says, "Review the details of important documents, such as fee schedules and contracts, and talk to an elder law attorney before you commit to anything."

In-home service providers will come into the senior's home and, in some cases, into their lives and the lives of their families. They will become involved in the most personal and intimate aspects of everyday living. It is vital that they be carefully screened and monitored. In order for the senior to have the best possible care, writes Wilkinson, you have to hire the best possible caregivers.

The AARP also has checklists to help make an aging relative's living environment safer. Very often, a care recipient will resist changes of any kind in their environment. Usually, what is behind such resistance is nothing more than fear of the unknown. Respect and recognize that fear, understanding that these changes will be difficult for your loved one (and for you too). Start slowly and ask the care recipient to commit to try the service for a month. Reassure your loved one that these services will help to keep him or her safely at home in a familiar and comfortable environment.

See Resources for related information.

Nursing Homes

When Is the Time Right for a Nursing Home?

If you are the caregiver for a loved one, one of many perplexing questions is "When is the right time for the move to nursing home care?" What may seem like a simple question is actually part of an excruciating matter for everyone concerned. To the loved one who is ill, the right time may be never. On a very frustrating day for the caregiver, the right time may be this very minute. Is there, in fact, a right time?

In his book *Nursing Homes: The Family's Journey*, Peter S. Silin suggests that as far as the caregiving process goes, there is not really a right time. When we talk about the right time, he writes, we mean the right time for you, the caregiver—when you can no longer do it for whatever reason.

Everyone knows that emotional strength and the ability to handle heavy stress can vary from individual to individual. Silin says that, nevertheless, all caregivers are given both "warning signs" and "alarm signs." He maintains that if you do not pay attention to the warning signs, they become the alarms. Those are the times we find ourselves in crisis. The problem, he says, with waiting for the alarm to sound is that when you finally hear it, your options may be limited. For example, the nursing home you wanted may now have a waiting list, your finances may be stretched to the breaking point or your emotional reserves may be depleted. Under this type of crisis, physical and emotional risks are greater for both the loved one and the caregiver.

It is very important to plan and not panic. Silin gives some warning signs to help you assess whether your caregiving burden is about to become overwhelming.

- What about your own physical health? Is it beginning to suffer? Are you exhausted, not sleeping well at night and not eating properly? If so, you may not be able to provide the care that you should (and that you want to) provide—which in itself is a stress factor. You absolutely must seek help for your own well-being.

- What about your emotional balance? Do you find that you are crying more, feeling tearful about small things, feeling hopeless, feeling nothing—basically numb? These can be signs of serious depression.

- What about your loved one's health? If his or her health is beginning to suffer then he or she is at risk and needs different or better caregiving. What about bedsores? Rashes? Is your loved one eating, taking medications and sleeping as he or she should?

- Is safety becoming an issue? Is your loved one wandering out of your home, leaving the oven on or opening the door to strangers? Are you still physically able to provide care? Are you still strong enough to do the lifting and other required tasks?

- How about your temper? Are you feeling resentful, short-tempered or angry? These are all signs that the stress is getting to you. These feelings can lead to the caregiver becoming abusive.

- Are people, including your doctor, beginning to tell you it is time? Usually, says Silin, people on the outside notice the changes in you and in your loved one before you do. Because they do not carry guilt or other feelings, they can be more objective.

- Is your community or county able to meet your loved one's needs, or your needs, through the services it can provide?

- Silin poses an important last question for consideration in this area: Are you hiding the extent of your loved one's disability and your physical or mental state from your family and friends? Hiding something from family and friends means you are closing off your support network. It also may mean that you are trying to deny to yourself what you know to be true but do not wish to see—that your loved one needs help, and that you also need help.

All of the factors listed increase the risk to the caregiver and to the loved one being cared for. The paradox of needing to care for yourself before you can care for others is really true. If you allow the responsibility, pressure and stress to drive you crazy, what good will you be to the person who loves you and needs your help?

Silin says that if you answer "yes" to one of the questions, that it is a warning. If you answer "yes" to three or more, then this is an alarm. If you answer "yes" to six or more, he hopes your loved one is already in care or on a waiting list.

Adjusting to When a Loved One Goes into a Nursing Home

Recently, a client sobbed, heartbroken, as she explained to me that she had placed her mother in a nursing home. Although the decision was very difficult, it had been necessary. Like many others though, the woman was convinced she was a "horrible daughter" and had, in the end, totally failed her mother. One of the unfortunate realities of life is that sometimes, no matter how much we love someone, we cannot continue to take care of them. There may be a multitude of reasons for this, including financial constraints, physical space available or mental, physical and personality changes brought about by disease in the elderly loved one.

Placing a loved one in a nursing home is a difficult adjustment for all parties involved. The caregiver may feel a cornucopia of emotions ranging from relief to grief, while the elderly person may feel abandoned and angry.

During the original period of adjustment, maintain as much contact with your older relative as possible. Visit often. It has been my personal experience that the first few days are difficult for everyone, including facility staff. The care providers do not yet know the personality, likes, dislikes and needs of the new resident. The new resident, often ill and in pain, is in no mood to win friends and influence people. It is important to be around often to act as a buffer, and sometimes a translator, during this troublesome transition time. You will get to know the staff and they in turn will learn to recognize you. The nursing home's social worker can be particularly helpful as you and your relative deal with the emotions of this change.

If your older relative can go out, take him or her out for an overnight visit, a ride in the car or a meal in a restaurant. If he or she is allowed treats, bring fruit, ice cream or favorite snacks when you visit. If you think it will not be too upsetting, take your older relative to the old neighborhood to visit friends. Or better yet, offer old friends a ride to visit your older relative. If you are not available to take your elder out, arrange for a companion to take him out occasionally.

Keep your older relative informed and included when there are problems in the family. Ask for opinions and ideas about handling family issues. Both of you may benefit from seeking your older relative's point of view. Remember that part of feeling secure is feeling needed. Sometimes it can help to talk about your own feelings and let your relative offer you some comfort. Share family photographs and place some in the resident's room.

Encourage your older relative to reach out to other residents. For example, he or she might write letters for a resident or read to one who is blind. Doing something helpful for others is a time-tested way to keep depression and self-pity at bay.

Be sensitive to your older relative's feelings, especially on anniversaries, such as the death of a spouse, and on holidays. Do not forget occasions that are special to your older relative. Remember birthdays and holidays with a visit, phone call or gift.

Never, never argue —no matter how much you may want to speak up in self-defense or straighten out confused thinking. Try to talk about differences in feelings and without criticizing each other.

Call regularly. It is easy for people with busy lives to forget how boring and lonely it can be and how slowly time passes when one is not involved so directly in the hustle-bustle of life. Take books, puzzles, newspaper and magazines for your older relative to read and enjoy.

Involve the staff when you visit. Sharing stories and information about your older relative with staff members can help make their relationship with them more personal. When family members recognize and appreciate staff efforts, the staff members are motivated to meet an older person's special needs.

Tips for Visiting a Loved One in a Nursing Home

The fact that people are ill at ease and do not know what to say probably accounts for why many elders sit day after day in nursing homes with no visitors. Chloe JonPaul, a longtime Bowie, Maryland resident and active senior, has written a small but powerful book about how to truly take care of a loved one who is in a nursing home. It is titled *What Happens Next: A Family Guide to Nursing Home Visits*. She offers practical advice for overcoming feelings of awkwardness and ill ease so frequently encountered by visitors. Topics such as "Making Conversation" (not that easy to do if your loved one has Alzheimer's disease or some type of dementia), "Bringing Treats from Home" and "Taking Care of Yourself" will help people feel more confident about visiting an elderly loved one.

In the chapter "Things You're Bound to Hear," JonPaul jumps fearlessly and headlong into that most dreaded comment: "I want to go home." She states what we all know if we think about it—that this plaintive comment really means that the resident wants to go back in time to when everything was the way it was at its best. She suggests that there is no real need to respond to

> **Gifts to Bring on a Visit**
>
> *Here are some ideas for gifts you might consider taking to an ill friend or loved one: an assortment of greeting cards for the patient to send, stamps and stationery, hand lotion, hair spray, a small radio with earplugs, a favorite food, tapes of books, a small paperback book, word-puzzle books with extra pencils, lunch to be shared at bedside or playing cards. A really nice gesture would be to organize a small group of enough friends to play the patient's favorite game. It is always appropriate to call first to establish a convenient time for visiting.*
>
> ■ ■ ■

this statement because anything we say will be inadequate. The best thing to do, she says, is to give a reassuring hug and show in that manner that you understand.

There is a story in this section about when her mother's property was sold. She explained everything to her mother and reassured her that all of her personal effects were stored in JonPaul's house. Her mother, naturally, did not remember any of that and when she later asked about stopping by the house JonPaul reminded her that the property had been sold. She says that was a big mistake, as her mother became terribly upset. So the next time her mother mentioned stopping by the house she answered, "Okay, we'll do that one day soon." Eventually, her mother stopped mentioning the house.

So, what can you talk about when you visit a loved one in a nursing home, especially if the loved one has dementia? Everything, says JonPaul. You can relate news about family members, for instance. Even though you know you will repeat the information on a subsequent visit, who cares? If the information is new to your loved one at that moment, that is what counts.

If visitors are terribly bothered by the short-term memory losses and the necessity for repetition, they can give verbal cues. For example, JonPaul will say to her mother, "The word you want to remember begins with an M and rhymes with cherry." It does not work all the time, but it is amazing how often hints of that nature help the patient to remember. It becomes much like a game and pleases everyone. JonPaul suggests that we remember how when our children were toddlers they tended to ask the same questions over and over. That is the type of patience required.

A story in this section is illustrative of the humor and light-heartedness of the book, even though the subject matter is weighty. An aide who had been away on vacation returned to the room of an elderly person who had often played the rhyming game with her family. The elderly patient stared intently at the woman and then said, "I know you. You're Gail. And it rhymes with garbage pail!"

In addition to stories, suggestions and practical illustrations, the book contains lists of resources and books and a page to list important contacts. See Resources for more information.

Paying for Caregiving

I am often asked how much it will cost to provide caregiving. A large misconception exists that the government, through Medicare or Medicaid, will pay for the care of an aging relative.

Medicare, the federal insurance program typically for people age 65 and over, has very limited benefits to cover long-term care needs, in your loved one's home or in a nursing home. Medicaid, a state-funded program for people with minimal resources, sometimes pays for the costs of in-home care (through a waiver program), and nursing home care as long as the person meets the eligibility requirements. (See Chapter 3 on health care for more on this topic.)

Most costs associated with a chronic illness or disability are assumed by the family, the care recipient or private insurance, especially long-term care insurance. According to an annual family caregiver survey conducted by caregiving.com, about 50 percent of respondents spent at least $500 per month for services (home health, medications and supplies).

Many at-home care recipients depend on help from home health aides, trained professionals who assist with personal care, such as bathing and dressing, provide light housekeeping tasks, prepare meals and provide transportation. These types of aides can be hired through a home health agency or privately by the family.

According to the U.S. Labor Department, home health aides earn more than $8.00 per hour. The cost of hiring an aide through an agency is higher. Although hiring the aide privately may save money, you should be sure to check with your homeowner's insurance agent regarding insurance coverage. And you must be very diligent to comply with the IRS regulations about any tax implications. If you use an agency, you should choose one that performs background checks on their employees and screens for drug and substance abuse. Always have a back-up plan in case the aide becomes ill, quits or just does not work out.

Adult day care center prices are running at $40 per day and higher, depending on the services provided. Sometimes transportation is included in the cost. Meals on Wheels services are provided on a sliding fee schedule, depending on the recipient's income level.

The cost of room and board in a nursing home ranges from $50,000 to $75,000 per year in the Washington, D.C. Metropolitan area. The average length of stay in a nursing home is two and a half years. These days, many older adults use nursing homes for temporary stays for rehabilitation while they recover from a recent hospitalization or surgery. An assisted living facility, where the residents live in an apartment-like setting but can still receive assistance with personal care, tend to cost at least $35,000 per year. In addition to the cost of the room and board in nursing homes and assisted living facilities, care recipients also assume the costs of medications, supplies and personal care items.

Because caregiving is likely to be a long-term commitment, planning for the future is essential. Family members must consider the care recipient's financial resources, the emotional resources of all people involved and the resources available in the community.

Caregiving is one of the biggest challenges of the life in our aging population. Solutions to its problems may not be easy. Perfect solutions probably do not exist. Try to work through the problems. If one agency does not work, try another. Continue to ask for help. Keep an open mind about which services and organizations may be helpful, and accept help in whatever form it arrives.

See Resources for information on caregiving organizations.

Hospice

What Is Hospice?

A study conducted for the National Hospice Foundation found that Americans are more likely to talk to their children about drugs and sex than to talk to their elderly parents about terminal illness. One in four Americans said they are "not likely" to talk with a terminally ill parent about that parent's impending death. Often the terminally ill parent wants and needs to discuss end-of-life matters but is reluctant to cause additional stress for younger relatives. Because we are uncomfortable with such frank discussions and tend to avoid them, we often do not realize all the choices available to us for end-of-life care.

"Hospice," according to the Hospice Foundation of America, is a special concept of care designed to provide comfort and support to patients and their families when a life-limiting illness no longer responds to cure-oriented treatments. Hospice care neither prolongs life nor hastens death. Staff and volunteers offer a specialized knowledge of medical care, including pain management. The goal is to improve the quality of the patient's last days by offering comfort and dignity. Hospice deals with the emotional, social and spiritual impact of the disease on the patient and the patient's family and friends.

The term "hospice" can be traced back to medieval times. It was originally used to describe a place of shelter for weary and sick travelers returning from religious pilgrimages. It comes from the same linguistic root as "hospitality" or the Latin word "hospitium," meaning guest house. However, although many understand hospice to be a "place to die"—it is not just that. Although residence facilities are available, 80 percent of hospice care is provided in the home and in nursing homes.

Studies show that nine out of 10 adults would prefer to live the rest of their lives at home, avoiding hospitals and nursing homes if possible. Hospice care makes such a choice both possible and practical. Additionally, Medicare and Medicaid offer benefits that cover all or most hospice services. Most private insurance or prepaid health plans also provide some coverage for hospice care.

Hospice is considered to be the model for quality, compassionate care at the end of life. It involves a team-oriented approach to expert medical care, pain management and emotional and spiritual support expressly tailored to the patient's needs and wishes, and to family members and other loved ones as well.

The brochure *Understanding Hospice,* provided by Capital Hospice, points out that hospice care emphasizes each person's right to direct the course of care and supports patients in making well-informed decisions. Typically, a family member serves as the primary caregiver and helps make decisions for the terminally ill individual. Members of the hospice staff make regular visits to assess the patient and provide additional care or other services. Hospice staff is on call 24 hours a day, seven days a week.

Care and services are designed to provide in-home support and assistance to the patient and to the patient's family and friends. This help makes any perceived burden smaller and makes the situation more manageable and comfortable for all concerned. Staff generally includes physicians, nurses, home health aides, certified nursing assistants, social workers and chaplains who are available to make home visits according to patients' needs and wishes. This team works together to provide the best in pain and symptom management, along with emotional and spiritual support. Hospice can also access assistance from dietitians, physical therapists, speech therapists and other clinical specialists as needed.

Hospice care provides the patient with an individualized plan of care customized to his or her needs. The aggressive treatment of pain and the provision of emotional support allow people in the last stage of life to set their life in order, participate in conversations with family and friends and to settle any long-standing issues in their life. Hospice attempts to help people make the last chapter in life as meaningful as the earlier parts of their life.

Perhaps patients' families do not realize that they can advocate for the patient with the physicians and nurses for attentive and responsive pain management. Appropriate questions to ask providers caring for a patient with a terminal illness include:

- Have they assessed the patient's pain?
- What is the plan for managing pain?

Pain Management Is Part of Health Care

A continuing problem in the United States is the inadequate treatment of pain. In a recent medical study of end-of-life care, researchers found that five percent of all terminally ill patients who died during hospitalization "experienced moderate or severe pain at least half of the time during their last three days of life."

■ ■ ■

- Is round-the-clock pain medication appropriate in this case and, if so, is it being provided?

- If round-the-clock pain medication is provided, is there something provided for "breakthrough pain"?

- If the pain medication orders are written "as needed," ask if this is appropriate, or whether round-the-clock pain medication would work better.

- How often will the patient's pain level be assessed?

- Will responsive action be taken promptly if pain is present?

- Is a pain specialist available to consult, and will he or she be called in if good relief is not quickly forthcoming?

- Is the patient eligible for hospice care and, if so, can this be arranged?

Encouragingly, some state legislatures have mandated that patients suffering acute, chronic or terminal pain will be afforded a fundamental right of pain management in every health care setting.

Choosing Hospice

Did you know that there is more than one hospice? How can you be sure to choose the right one?

It is important to talk to people you trust who are familiar with hospice programs in your area. Resources for information about hospice care in our area include physicians, nurses and other health care professionals; social workers, clergy and other counselors; friends or neighbors who have had direct experience with hospice care; your local or state Office on Aging or senior centers; various medical and health-related Internet sites; and your local yellow pages or directory information.

Questions To Ask When Selecting A Hospice Program

❑ *How do hospice staff members, working with the patient and family and loved ones, honor the patient's wishes?*

❑ *Are caregivers given the information and training they need to care for the patient at home?*

❑ *What services are offered by the hospice to help the patient and loved ones deal with future grief and loss?*

❑ *Is respite care available?*

❑ *Are loved ones told what to expect in the dying process and what happens after the patient's death?*

❑ *What bereavement support is available after the patient dies?*

❑ *What is the role of the patient's physician once hospice care begins?*

❑ *How many patients at any one time are assigned to each hospice staff member who will be caring for the patient?*

❑ *What services do volunteers offer?*

❑ *What screening and types of training do hospice volunteers receive before they are placed with patients and caregivers?*

❑ *Do the hospice staff members regularly discuss and routinely evaluate pain control and symptom management with patients and caregivers?*

❑ *Do the hospice staff members respond immediately to requests for additional pain medication and after-hours emergencies?*

❑ *What will happen if care cannot be managed at home? What measures can the hospice take to ensure quality?*

❑ *Does this hospice program follow the NHPCO's Standards of Practice for Hospice Programs?*

❑ *What specialty or expanded programs does this hospice offer?*

❑ *How does the hospice meet the spiritual and emotional needs of the patient and caregivers?*

❑ *Is the hospice program certified and licensed by the state or federal government?*

❑ *What other accreditation or certification does the hospice program or its staff have?*

❑ *Are all costs of hospice care covered by the patient's health insurance?*

❑ *What services will the patient have to pay for out-of-pocket?*

❑ *Are any services provided at no charge?*

■ ■ ■

In addition, you can contact the National Hospice and Palliative Care Organization (NHPCO), which represents most hospices in the United States. Next, call or visit the hospice providers on your list. Talk with hospice personnel to find out what services are available from individual programs in your community.

Although it may be difficult, now is the best time to learn more about hospice care and to ask questions about what to expect. It is best for family members and caregivers to share their wishes long before the patient's condition becomes an actual concern. This can greatly reduce stress when the time for hospice care becomes apparent. By having these discussions in advance of need, patients—and caregivers—are not forced into uncomfortable situations for which they are totally unprepared. Instead, they can make an educated decision that includes the advice and input of their loved ones.

See Resources for hospice contact information.

Caring for the Caregiver

Coping with Caregiving

The average caregiver in this country is a 47-year-old female with a full-time job and children to raise. Although that mythical average caregiver's life must be unbelievably stressful, every caregiver—even the not average one—strives to conduct a life in addition to his or her caregiving responsibilities. For those who have not tried it, caregiving may seem simple. It could seem to be nothing more than a task born out of love and required by life.

However, in the same way that we cannot truly understand the grief of a parent who has lost a child and we cannot comprehend the heartbreak of a man or woman facing the death of a spouse until we have experienced those challenges ourselves, it is impossible to understand and truly sympathize with the kaleidoscope of care-giving responsibilities and emotions until life has required that we ourselves step up to the plate to try it. This knowledge has contributed to the enormous growth of support groups over the past several decades. Mental health professionals began to realize that one of the best therapies for an individual who is hurting is to talk with someone who has been hurt in the same way—and who has arrived triumphant on the other side of the valley with their life reasonably intact.

In order to remain healthy so that we can continue to be caregivers, we must be able to see our own limitations and learn to care for ourselves, as well as for others. I recently saw a client who has been a long-time caregiver. She told me that the single most important thing a therapist helped her to realize was that her mother's life is not her life. Her life revolves around her husband, her family, her activities, her job—and while it is sad that her mother's life requires the giving of care at this time, her mother's life is nevertheless still not her life. It is her mother's life.

Like most snippets of incredible wisdom, that one seems almost too simple. In trying to do the best job possible, caregivers very often forget that they even have their own life— much less that their own life needs to be tended to. In ways very similar to when we become a widow or widower, otherwise close friends begin to disappear and grow distant from the caregiver and eventually the caregiver is alone, without a support structure.

As a caregiver, we must take responsibility for locating support groups and talking with those who are in situations similar to our own. Dr. M. Ross

Tips for Family Caregivers

The National Family Caregivers Association provides these suggestions:

1. Choose to take charge of your life and do not let your loved one's illness or disability always take center stage.

2. Watch out for signs of depression and do not delay in getting professional help when you need it.

3. When people offer to help, accept the offer and suggest specific things they can do.

4. Educate yourself about your loved one's condition. Information is empowering.

5. There is a difference between caring and doing. Be open to technologies and ideas that promote your loved one's independence.

6. Trust your instincts. Most of the time they will lead you in the right direction.

7. Grieve for your losses, then allow yourself to dream new dreams.

8. Seek support from other caregivers. There is great strength in knowing you are not alone.

■ ■ ■

Seligson, a Florida psychologist, lists burnout characteristics. Burnout, he says, is "not like a cold—you don't always notice when you are in its clutches." He says that, like post-traumatic stress syndrome, symptoms of burnout can begin surfacing months after the episode. Some of the symptoms we might notice in ourselves, or that others who care about us might say

---

10 Caregiver Burnout Warning Signs

1. **Denial** *about the disease and its effects on the person who has been diagnosed.*

2. **Anger** *at the person you're caring for or at others, that no effective treatments or cures currently exist, and that other people don't understand what is going on.*

3. **Social withdrawal** *from friends and activities that once brought pleasure.*

4. **Anxiety** *about facing another day and what the future holds.*

5. **Depression** *begins to affect the ability to cope.*

6. **Exhaustion** *makes it nearly impossible to complete necessary daily tasks.*

7. **Sleeplessness** *caused by a never-ending list of concerns and "things to do."*

8. **Irritability** *leads to moodiness and triggers negative responses and reactions.*

9. **Lack of concentration** *makes it difficult to perform familiar tasks.*

10. **Health problems** *begin to take their toll, both mentally and physically.*

■ ■ ■

they see in us, are feelings of depression, a sense of ongoing and constant fatigue, decreasing interest in work, decrease in work production, withdrawal from social contacts, increase in use of stimulants and alcohol and feelings of helplessness.

Caregivers can use the following recommended strategies to avoid, cope with or ward off burnout:

- Consult professionals to explore burnout and caregiving issues.

- Attend a support group to receive feedback and new coping strategies and to understand that others face the same challenges.

- Vary the focus of caregiving responsibilities by rotating responsibilities with friends and family members.

- Exercise daily and maintain a healthy diet.

- Be fanatic about time for "quiet time" and meditation.

- Stay involved in hobbies.

- Try a weekly or monthly massage to relieve tension.

Remember: The best way to be able to continue taking care of those we love is to take care of ourselves. See Resources for caregiver care information.

Caregivers Have Rights Too

Stacey Matzkevich, a social worker and noted gerontologist in California, has a Caregiver's Bill of Rights. She maintains that caregivers have the right:

- To receive the knowledge, resources, training and support you need to be successful as a caregiver

- To acknowledge your own needs and to expect those needs to be met

- To enjoy a well-rounded and meaningful life that

includes family, friends, work, activities you love and time to yourself

- To seek and accept help from community, family, friends and support services
- To access quality services that treat you and the person you are caring for with dignity and consideration
- To be allowed to experience all of your feelings as a caregiver, from the moments of unexpected joy to those of anger and frustration
- To be part of a caregiving team rather than having to do it all by yourself
- To ask for—and receive—appreciation and respect for your caregiving
- To acknowledge that the unique gift of your time, energy and emotions has as much value as any caregiving task

Everyone is unique, with different emotional attitudes and approaches to life. Look again at the list above. Maybe we do have the right to be part of a caregiving team, but what if there are no other team members? Perhaps we can expect our own needs to be met, but what if there is truly nobody to meet them? We pretty much have to deal with life as it is handed to us.

There is more and more scientific evidence that a person who approaches life with an optimistic outlook is more successful and more apt to be mentally and emotionally healthy. If we focus on our rights, we are likely to feel sad and put upon. I present the rights list as a vehicle for thought. Take the ideas that may be helpful to you and let the rest go.

Caregiver Guilt

One of the most accurate descriptions of caregiver's guilt is in Mary Pipher's book, *Another Country: Navigating the Emotional*

Terrain of Our Elders. In the introduction, Dr. Pipher describes her mother's last illness: "That year, no matter where I was, I felt guilty. If I was with my mother, I wasn't caring for my own kids or my clients. If I was working, I was ignoring my family. When I was with my children, I thought of my mother alone in the hospital. I got depressed and crabby." I should think so. Dr. Pipher lived three hours away from her ailing mother, and she had a husband, two teenagers, a full-time job and a book contract to complete.

Dr. Pipher's experience is common. No matter what their particular combination of experiences and expectations, most caregivers fall prey to the "I am guilty whatever I am doing or wherever I am" version of the blues. This we all must fight. Guilt robs both the caregiver and the loved one. It saps your strength, moves you toward bitterness and resentment and finally causes you to tumble headlong into full-blown depression. You must learn to deal with it effectively—before it becomes a major problem.

In *The Complete Eldercare Planner*, Joy Loverde discusses the omnipresence of guilt in the life of a caregiver: "Guilt is the constant companion. No matter what you do, no matter how much you give, no matter what happens, no matter how much you know, no matter where you are—the guilt is still there. And it is painful." Loverde points out that when we have other types of pain, such as a toothache or a migraine, we do not just sit there. We get up and take medicine, or in some other way address the pain. We must do the same with caregiver's guilt. We must make a conscious decision to face it, manage it and diminish its negative impact on the overall quality of our life.

Mental health professionals recommend that one should determine whether a guilty feeling is valid. If it is valid, it is legitimate. When guilt is legitimate, it prods us to do better. Our response should be to move toward doing a little better than we were doing.

Legitimate guilt is our inner spirit's way of letting us know we should make amends when we do something hurtful—either on purpose or by mistake. In caregiving, you are certain to offend or hurt somebody somewhere sometime. It is part of the experience. It is important to accept responsibility for our misdeeds, say we are sorry and dust ourselves off to begin again.

False guilt is when we feel guilty for things over which we have no control; therefore false guilt is detrimental and unhelpful. When guilt is unwarranted, it causes stress and hampers our ability to make good decisions and give quality care. If you are visiting your elderly loved one but can stay for only a brief visit, ask yourself whether staying longer would truly prevent his or her unhappiness or just delay it. For instance, if you arrange to stay all day Saturday and, as you prepare to leave, your loved one says sadly, "Must you leave so soon?" you know that no matter how long you stay, the response will be the same. Therefore, you must not feel guilty when that comment comes. It is important to distinguish between legitimate guilt and false guilt.

In *Fourteen Friends' Guide to Eldercaring*, the authors write, "We must be able to distinguish between useful and legitimate guilt as opposed to guilt that is harmful and undeserved. The former can motivate us to get things done while the latter only serves to dishearten us."

When you are feeling guilty for things you are not doing, ask yourself, "Am I doing the best I can right now?" If you are doing your best, then refuse to accept the guilt. If you are not doing your best, try to move your focus from feeling guilty to taking action. Think about what you can do to reorganize, regroup and move toward your best.

A distressing truth about guilt feelings in the caregiver is that we feel guilty because we cannot make things better. We cannot cure old age or similar indignities. There is nowhere to hide from the truth that we may, in the not-too-distant future, be grieving over the loss of this loved one.

It is hard to think clearly when you are under a lot of tension or stress. Consider asking an outsider to help you figure out whether your guilt is realistic and find ways to cope with it. Friends, counselors, pastors and support groups can all be sources of help, comfort and guidance. Remember that what is important is ensuring the quality of care and meeting the realistic needs of the elderly. If this is being done, refuse to accept the guilt.

A wonderful book for both caregivers and older adults is *Self-Care Now! 30 Ways to Overcome Obstacles That Prevent You From Taking Care of Yourself* by Pauline Salvucci, a psychotherapist, trainer and teacher who works with a medical family practice where she counsels chronically ill individuals and family caregivers.

This little book explains the difference between selfishness and self-care in the clearest way I have come across yet. Salvucci writes that the confusion is because as a child we often translated messages that were intended to be about sharing, consideration of others and generosity into the belief that caring for ourselves would make us selfish, bad people. Although as adults we understand the difference, as kids it made us feel bad. This confusion has conditioned many people to feel unworthy of taking care of themselves. In this way, the concept of self-care has easily become identified and confused with selfishness.

Salvucci writes that "Selfishness means promoting your power, happiness and interests without regard for others. By contrast, self-care is the responsibility to take care of your physical, emotional and spiritual well-being."

Helpful Caregiver Web Sites

- The Web site **www.caregiver-information.com** offers basic and practical information for people caring for loved ones with Alzheimer's disease, stroke and brain injury.

- The **www.caregivers.com** site is an information and referral network for caregivers and seniors. It is most notable for its selection of search engines for housing, geriatricians, lawyers, care managers and hospice care.

- The National Family Caregivers Association is online at **www.nfcacares.org**. The site attempts to address the common needs and concerns of all family caregivers. On this site you can order a free Alzheimer Caregiver Survival Kit.

- The site **www.getcare.com** is designed to help you find information about long-term care choices and find the right option for you and your loved one.

- The site **www.caregiving.com** has a splendid array of articles, resources and advice for caregivers. You can ask specific questions of experts and order a newsletter.

- The Family Caregiver Alliance at **www.caregiver.org** is a resource for education, services, research and advocacy for caregivers and their loved ones.

Resources

General Caregiving Advice

Another Country: Navigating the Emotional Terrain of Our Elders by Mary Pipher (Riverhead Books: 2000)

As Parents Age: A Psychological and Practical Guide by Joseph Ilardo (VanderWyk & Burnham: 1998)

The Caregiver newsletter
Phone: (800) 672-4213
Address: Duke University Family Support Program, Box 3600, Duke Medical Center, Durham, NC 27710
Provides tips for caregivers, summaries of recent research and a forum for caregivers to share their thoughts, suggestions and experiences; cost is $10 per year.

Children of Aging Parents
Address: 1609 Woodbourne Road, Suite 302A
Levittown, PA 19057-1151
A national clearinghouse for caregivers and professionals, offering referrals, educational programs and support groups.

The Complete Eldercare Planner by Joy Loverde (Three Rivers Press: 2000)

Coping With Your Difficult Older Parent: A Guide for Stressed-Out Children by Grace Lebow and Barbara Kane (Avon: 1999)

Disaster Preparedness for Seniors by Seniors
Phone: (202) 728-6400 or (301) 559-8500
Call the Red Cross to order a copy.

Eldercare 911 by Susan Beerman and Judith Rappaport-Musson (Prometheus Books: 2002)

Elder Rage or Take My Father...Please! by Jacqueline Marcell (Impressive Press: 2000)
Web site: www.elderrage.com

A Family Caregiver's Guide to Planning and Decision Making for the Elderly by James A. Wilkinson (Fairview Press: 1999)

Fourteen Friends' Guide to Eldercaring by LLC Fourteen Friends (Broadway: 2000)

Third Age Enterprises
Phone: (410) 643-0394
Offers respectful, appropriate greeting cards for seniors.

Today's Caregiver
Web site: www.caregiver.com
Phone: (800) 829-2734
Call or visit the site to subscribe to this magazine.

The Unofficial Guide to Eldercare by Chris Adamec (Wiley: 1999)

Caregiving Organizations and Services

2003-2004 Services for Seniors and Adults with Disabilities in Anne Arundel County
Phone: (800) 492-2499
Call for this booklet of resources and help for seniors and caregivers.

Aging Network Services
Web site: www.agingnets.com
Phone: (301) 657-4329
Address: Topaz House 4400 East-West Highway, Suite 907, Bethesda, MD 20814
Offers nationwide help in selecting a GCM and other practical services for caregivers.

Baptist Senior Adult Ministries (BSAM)
Phone: (301) 669-0850
An adult day care facility in Bowie, Maryland.

Department of Aging
Phone (Anne Arundel County): (410) 222-4464
Phone (Prince George's County): (301) 699-2731
Offers referral services to adult day care and senior centers.

Federal Administration on Aging's Eldercare Locator
Phone: (800) 677-1116
Call Monday through Friday for information and a nationwide
assistance directory to help find resources for care.

The League for Excellence in Adult Day Centers (LEAD)
Web site: www.leadcares.com
Phone: (301) 883-4775
E-mail: SomersR@Keswick-multicare.org
A network of adult day care centers in the Maryland/D.C. area
that also provides a booklet called *Selecting A Quality Program:
A Consumer's Guide*.

LifeFone
Web site: www.lifefone.com
Phone: (800) 882-2280
An emergency response system.

Maryland Department of Aging
Web site: www.mdoa.state.md.us
Phone: (800) 243-3425
Provides caregiving support, and the site has useful information
and resources.

National Organization of Professional Geriatric Care Managers
Web site: www.caremanager.org
Phone: (520) 881-8008
Provides a nationwide searchable database of GCMs.

Visiting Nurses Associations of America
Web site: www.vnaa.org
Phone: (617) 737-3200
Provides home health care and information on providers
near you.

Nursing Homes

MyZiva: The Complete Nursing Home Guide
Web site: www.MyZiva.net
Offers comprehensive information on nursing homes.

Nursing Homes: The Family's Journey by Peter S. Silin. (Johns
Hopkins University Press:: 2001) Billed as *A Guide to Making
Decisions as a Family, Choosing a Facility, and Getting the Best
Possible Care*, the book is filled with information, resources, tips
for reducing stress and lots of practical information about
nursing homes, staff and moving day.

What Happens Next: A Family Guide to Nursing Home Visits by
Chloe JonPaul (Signature Imprint: 2003) Web site:
http://hometown.aol.com/cjp3931/myhomepage/business.html
Phone: (800) 819-6095

Hospice

Capital Hospice
Web site: www.capitalhospice.org
Phone: (888) 583-1900
A Washington, D.C.-area hospice organization that provides
services and information, including a booklet,
Understanding Hospice.

Hospice of the Chesapeake

Web site: www.hospicechesapeake.org
Phone: (301) 621-0686
Serves Prince George's and Anne Arundel County, Maryland and also has special activities available for children coping with loss.

National Hospice and Palliative Care Organization (NHPCO)
Web site: www.nhpco.org
Phone: (800) 658-8898
Represents most hospices in the U.S.; call or visit for hospice information or to find a member hospice.

Caring for Caregivers

Self-Care Now! 30 Ways to Overcome Obstacles That Prevent You From Taking Care of Yourself by Pauline Salvucci (Pauline Salvucci: 2001)

2
Estate Planning

Introduction to Legal Documents and Advance Planning

Taking the First Step

Make sure everything you need in the way of wills, trusts, powers of attorney and medical directives is taken care of. Too often, your wishes are never discussed with family and friends and never written down for future reference. Costly or painful losses can result from a failure to do this type of organization of your affairs. Stocks, bonds, bank accounts, real estate and insurance policy benefits may go unclaimed and be turned over to the state government.

"Billions of dollars currently sit in state treasuries because the rightful property owners couldn't be found. Millions of dollars worth of unclaimed assets are added to these coffers each year," says the NOLO Law for All Web site (www.nolo.com).

More personally, relatives or friends may not be notified, and valuable pieces of family history (whether an actual senti-

The Most Loving Gift You Can Give Your Family

According to Today's Caregiver *magazine, the most loving gift you can give your family is to put your affairs in order before a disaster or medical emergency occurs. Have the following information and documents in a safe and handy location:*

- *Bank account numbers and types of accounts, along with the location of the bank(s)*

- *Insurance company, policy number, beneficiary as stated on the policies and type of insurance (health, long-term care, automobile, etc.)*

- *Deed and titles to all property*

- *Loan and lien information (who holds them and if there are any death provisions)*

- *Social Security and Medicare numbers*

- *Military history, affiliations and papers, including discharge papers*

- *The will (inform your family where it is located)*

- *Any Living Will or other Advance Directives appropriate to your state*

- *Durable General Power of Attorney*

- *Instructions for funeral services and burial*

- *Special belongings you want to be given to others*

■ ■ ■

mental object or stories never before heard) may be lost forever. NOLO suggests some actions to take to make things easier for your family. Because such a task can be very time-consuming, it may be best to break it into manageable sections and take one part at a time. Start by thinking of broad categories, such as funeral plans (arrangements and whom to notify), insurance polices and important information about family history, including the location of photographs, heirlooms and other irreplaceable items. Include categories of bank, money market, mutual fund, pension and retirement fund accounts —you get the idea. You do not have to do it all at once, but make a list and start somewhere.

Then, think about organizing this information in a way that will help your family handle your affairs after your death. Once you get everything in order, it is extremely important to store it in a safe place. You could keep these papers in a fireproof metal box, file cabinet or home safe. The most important thing is to discuss your new records and information with members of your family and others who might be involved in handling your affairs in case of dementia, physical disability or death. You can prepare wonderfully specific and important directions, but they will be useless if no one knows where they are.

Important Questions to Think About

The purpose of an estate plan is to help provide for yourself and your loved ones in the future. Even if you feel your estate is modest, a will or other legal agreement such as a Living Trust, is necessary in order to ensure that your wishes will be carried out. A well- thought-out estate plan can save you and your heirs money by the possible reduction of estate taxes, probate costs and other legal expenses. Every adult should have a minimum of four documents: a will and/or trust, a Durable General Power of Attorney, a Health Care Power of Attorney and a Living Will.

Questions to Ask Before Making an Estate Plan

Do you have all your important personal documents together in a secure place?

Do you have basic legal documents that direct what happens to your assets when you die?

Do you have basic legal documents that ensure that someone you know and trust will make personal decisions and handle your financial and medical affairs in the event that you are unable to do so?

Do you have all your financial records on hand, in some order, and up to date?

Do you have a resource, such as an attorney or accountant, in the event you require professional advice or assistance?

Are you receiving all the public and private benefits to which you are entitled? If not, do you know when and where to apply for them?

Do you know how your assets are titled and why this is a crucial issue?

Do you have a sufficient amount of insurance or too much insurance?

Do you know which changes in your life will require you to do a review of your legal documents?

■ ■ ■

Advance Directives

How many of these terms do you keep hearing over and over: Advance Directive, Living Will, Health Care Power of Attorney, Durable Power of Attorney, Limited Power of Attorney, General

Power of Attorney? Who in the world knows what these mean? Why are they important? Which ones should you have?

In the past, most physicians acted in consultation with the patient's family to resolve issues of health care and end-of-life decisions. Now questions of possible legal liability, the geographic remoteness of many family members and other quirks common to today's world make such informal arrangements impractical, if not impossible.

With the exception of the Living Will, the documents listed above allow you to choose a trusted agent to act on your behalf when you cannot act for yourself. This need arises not only in life

---

Additional Questions to Think About From the NOLO Law for All Web site

Do you want a funeral or a memorial service? What type?

Do you want people to send flowers, or would you prefer donations to a charity? Which one (or others)?

Who do you want to be notified about your death and final services? High school and college friends? Immediate family or those you have never really met? Old military buddies?

Did you prepare a will or living trust? Where is the original?

Do you have a life insurance policy, pension, retirement account and/or annuity? Where are such documents stored?

Where do you have bank accounts? Do you have a safe deposit box?

Do you have stocks, bonds or money in mutual funds? Where are the records?

What real estate do you own? Where are the deeds?

■ ■ ■

and death matters, but also any time an individual is unable to make or express decisions about personal matters, medical care or possible institutional placement.

Powers of Attorney

A Power of Attorney is a legal document whereby you give another person (called an attorney-in-fact) the legal authority to manage your business and personal affairs. When the document is completely executed, the attorney-in-fact then has the authority to act on your behalf as your agent. It is important to think about what authority you want to give your agent and who you can trust to accept such a responsibility. You need to be cautious.

As Jason Frank, a noted Maryland elder law attorney, says "Be sure that ties of friendship or family relation do not cloud assessments of honesty, responsibility and general competence."

You want to delegate decision-making responsibilities to someone very reliable who has your best interests at heart. Among other things, your agent can continue to handle your affairs if you should become incapacitated. This requires a specific statement in the document that you want the agent to continue to act after your incapacity. This type of statement makes the Power of Attorney "durable." Many state legislatures have amended the Power of Attorney statute to create a presumption that any written Power of Attorney is a Durable Power of Attorney unless otherwise stated in the document.

You can also select when the Durable Power of Attorney will go into effect. It can start when you sign it or at some future time, such as if you become incapacitated. If you elect to make it effective when you become incapacitated, you must be very careful to clearly define in the document how it will be determined that you are incapacitated. One option is having two physicians, one of whom is your attending physician, certify that you are unable to make business decisions for yourself.

When you create a Power of Attorney that goes into effect only in the event of your disability, you have created a Springing Power of Attorney. A Springing Power of Attorney is like a Durable Power of Attorney, except that it "springs" into effect at some future time, such as your disability. You must include a clause in the document itself that says something like "This Power of Attorney becomes effective upon the disability of the principal."

All Powers of Attorney end when the principal dies, unless an earlier date is selected, which would make the document a Limited Power of Attorney. "Limited" means the authority given to the agent is limited to a specific transaction (selling a house, buying a car, etc.) or a specific time period or situation.

A Power of Attorney can be very specific or very general. Your agent can do anything that you would do if you were able and that is specifically permitted under the Power of Attorney document. A document that says "I give my agent the authority to do everything I could do" is, in fact, no authority at all. Powers should be granted in language that is as specific as possible. In many states such as Maryland, the powers of an attorney-in-fact are not defined by statute. Therefore, the agent's powers are limited by the wording of the document itself.

Unlike guardianship, a Power of Attorney is relatively inexpensive and does not require court oversight. A Power of Attorney is also far less complicated than a trust, which necessitates, among other things, that property be re-titled in the name of the trust. Creating joint accounts addresses some of these issues, but can cause possible tax liabilities and potential problems with creditors. Joint accounts are also a potential problem in planning for future long-term care needs.

Every Durable Power of Attorney should contain an indemnification clause. In other words, it should include language that provides for protection for the agent for exercising the powers described in good faith. Further, the document's language should promise to hold harmless any provider who honors the agent's decisions in good faith.

A very important provision of a Power of Attorney is naming your agent as your guardian, should the need arise. This avoids an expensive and long court guardianship proceeding in the event you become incapacitated. Unfortunately, there are no crystal balls to show us the future path of our own lives. Anyone over the age of 18 and legally competent can execute a valid Power of Attorney document. No matter how old you are, if you have a massive stroke or are made temporarily comatose by an automobile accident, it is too late to execute the document allowing family or friends to handle your affairs.

How can you choose the right person? The Commission on Legal Problems of the Elderly within the American Bar Association provides advice in this area. First of all you should choose someone who meets the legal criteria in your state. Your agent should be willing to speak on your behalf without hesitation. It should be someone who would be able to act on your wishes and separate his or her own feelings from yours. This person should know you well and understand what is important to you. Ideally, he or she should live close by or be able to travel to be at your side if needed.

This is a person who is willing to talk with you now about sensitive issues and to listen to your wishes. Your agent should be a strong person who would be able to handle conflicting opinions among family members, friends, professional and medical personnel and who could be a strong advocate in a situation with an unresponsive doctor or institution.

Business and/or Financial Powers of Attorney

Recently, some experts (often trying to sell something) have contended that Durable Powers of Attorney work only half of the time. It is true that some third parties such as the Internal Revenue Service and some financial institutions require their own documentation and forms in order for an agent to be named. However, most day-to-day institutions and third parties continue to accept valid Powers of Attorney. It is very helpful if the document is recent and, again, if the powers are granted in very specific language. These steps can increase the likelihood that third parties will accept the document and allow the agent to act on your behalf.

As the creator, you may revoke (cancel) the Durable Power of Attorney at any time by a signed and dated written revocation, physical

Book Offers Advanced Planning Help

The book My Parting Gift *was designed, according to the author, Albert F. Chestone, to "help families navigate the maze of information require-ments standing between family members and the survivor benefits to which they are entitled." The author, a former FBI agent who personally experienced these difficulties, set out to help others. In the book, you will find specific information on how to create wills and Living Wills, how to authorize organ donations and how-to's for a variety of needed legal documents.*

■ ■ ■

cancellation or destruction of the original document. You have the responsibility "to the extent reasonably possible" to notify any person to whom you have provided a copy of the document that it is now revoked.

Health Care Powers of Attorney

A Durable Power of Attorney for Health Care is an important advance directive that gives another person the legal authority to make medical decisions in the event that you are unable to make them for yourself. You can also use an advance directive to make an organ donation.

When you are choosing the person(s) to name as your health care agent and alternate, consider the emotional relationship between that person and yourself. Also, their geographic proximity and, most of all, the willingness of the proposed agent and alternate to follow your instructions. An agent is intended to "stand in your shoes."

On this issue, Jason Frank makes an interesting point in his book *Elder Law in Maryland* about a potential conflict between a health care agent and a financial agent. For example, says Frank, the financial agent may refuse to pay for medical treatment to which the health care agent consents.

As the creator, you may revoke (cancel) the Durable Power of Attorney for Health Care at any time by a signed and dated written revocation, physical cancellation or destruction of the original document, your oral statement to a health care practitioner or execution of a subsequent advance directive. You have the responsibility "to the extent reasonably possible" to notify any person to whom you have provided a copy of the document that it is now revoked.

A copy of any Health Care Advance Directive (e.g., Durable Power of Attorney for Health Care or Living Will) should be placed in your medical record. Also make sure that, if you go into a hospital, you take a copy to be inserted into your file. You should retain the original with your important legal papers, always giving a photocopy to the health care provider.

Free forms for executing a Durable Power of Attorney for Health Care are available at your local agency on aging, many doctors' offices, senior centers, nursing homes and hospitals. Remember that every state has different forms and also that they can be tailored so that they are in accord with particular religious, moral or ethical concerns.

You have the right to be in charge of your medical care. You can accept or refuse care based on your feelings and views about life and what is important to you. If you become ill and cannot tell others what you want, you will need other people to have knowledge of your wishes and to make decisions for you.

The state of Maryland has published an *Advance Directives Guide,* distributed without charge by the Department of Legislative Reference of the General Assembly and by the Office of the Attorney General. The guide includes free sample forms, with an explanation of each and a "Frequently Asked Questions" sheet. Many valuable resources are available for help with these issues, including sample advance directives. See the Resources section at the end of the chapter for more information.

Living Wills

A Living Will is a statement of your preferences about medical care in case of terminal illness or permanent incapacity such as an irreversible coma. This document describes how far you want your physicians to go in providing care when death is imminent. It further provides for carrying out your wishes about relief from pain. This can be included as a paragraph in your Durable Power of Attorney for Health Care or it can be a separate document.

It is important to note that in any individual situation where the patient is in a potentially terminal situation and the patient can be responsive, he or she will be asked if further treatment is wanted, such as resuscitation or other life-sustaining measures, regardless of any documentation provided by a Living Will. Even at the last minute of one's life, a patient can override any directives in the Living Will.

The required legal language of the Living Will and the Health Care Power of Attorney may differ from one state to the next. According to *The Unofficial Guide to Eldercare* by Chris Adamec, because health care providers are very cautious about incurring legal liability, you need to be very careful that your advance directives are in the form required by your state and are properly executed. He suggests that you seek legal advice rather than trying to do it yourself.

In Maryland, if a Living Will is written, it must be dated and signed by both the individual making the declaration and at least two witnesses. The Maryland Health Care Decisions Act allows an oral advance directive that must be made to a physician and witnessed by one individual, documented in the patient's medical record and signed and dated by the physician and the witness. The person making the advance directive must be a "competent individual." That means a person who is at least 18 years of age or who under Maryland law "has the same capacity as an adult to consent to medical treatment" and who has not been determined to be incapable of making an informed decision.

Everyone has personal priorities and spiritual beliefs, or the lack of spiritual beliefs, which will affect their medical decisions. This is especially true at the end of life with regard to the use of life-sustaining treatments. During the terminal illness of a loved one, families often have very tough choices. And after the death, family members can feel great guilt as to whether the right decision was made at the time. When people make their wishes known very clearly in advance this anxiety is eased for the family.

Many people do not realize that your medical directive can direct the kind of treatment you do or do not want. An advance directive is simply a written statement about your future medical care. You can say whether or not you want to be kept alive by machines that breathe for you or feed you. On the other hand, you can say whether or not you want aggressive treatment until nothing else is possible.

The important point is that you need to say something. Today's doctors are fearful of litigation, insurance costs and a hundred more things. If you do not have an advance directive and even one person interested in your care disagrees with others being consulted, your doctor may not honor your wishes for end-of-life care. An advance directive is a gift to family members and friends so that they will not have to guess what you want if you no longer can speak for yourself. It relieves them of the tremendous burden of trying to do what is "right"—for they can feel that what is right is to follow the plan you have laid out for them.

For each of us, the choices that we make with our families will be unique. There is no absolutely correct way or wrong way to choose end-of-life care.

The choices most typically made can probably be divided into three broad categories:

1. To seek a cure and prolong life at all costs
2. To prolong life with the use of artificial hydration and nutrition
3. To seek hospice care without artificially prolonging life

Briefly, the first option means continued treatment for the disease and its associated symptoms. The second one involves giving a person liquids and important vitamins through an IV or feeding tube. The third option, hospice care, focuses on providing pain management, comfort and emotional, social and spiritual support for the patient and their family members.

Talking about End-of-life Choices

Discussions about care wishes during the end of a life unfortunately often take place in the hallway outside the emergency room in the midst of a crisis. Therefore, these decisions are made under incredible stress. Additionally, family members may be making their best guess about what a loved one would want for end-of-life care, having never discussed their desires in advance.

Conversations about desires for end-of-life care can be very uncomfortable for us. We dislike thinking about our own mortality and that of our loved ones. This is normal. Avoiding these conversations and thoughts is a way of protecting ourselves from pain. However, it only postpones the inevitable and actually can make it harder on us and our family when we are faced with making such decisions at a time of crisis.

How do you know which end-of-life choice is best for you and your family? Kokua Mau, a Hawaii partnership of "individuals and organizations working with the general public and with the leaders of health care and government to improve how we in Hawaii are cared for at the end of our lives," has posted several questions on their Web site. These questions are a great tool to help you think about end-of-life care for yourself or to open up a discussion with loved ones.

The first is "What kind of care do you want for yourself if you are no longer able to make your wishes known, such as after a major stroke or bad accident?" A good way to get started thinking about this is to reflect upon the care that a friend or relative received at the end of their life. Is that what you want too? How would you change things? This is the question most fully addressed by the preparation of health care powers of attorney and living wills.

Second, "What are your greatest fears when you consider what the journey might be like at the end of life?" This is a very good question to ask ourselves first, before we even start a conversation with someone else. It is also a question that we might choose to take to our pastor or spiritual counselor for help and discussion. Knowing that we have faced this question—and conquered it—removes its power to frighten us and results in a wonderful sense of peace and well-being.

Third, "What do you hope for when you consider what the journey may be like at the end of life?" Thinking about and talking about how you imagine the last months of life to be may help you and your loved ones to create precious times together. My mother and her sister went to stay with their brother in his home the last week before he died. Hospice people were there, and my mom and her sister often think of the wonderfully precious and intimate visits they had with their brother during that week.

You must also actually get into the conversation with a loved one. First of all, you always need to ask permission to discuss this topic. Maybe you have been thinking about it, but the other person has not and they might be caught completely off guard.

Do you know about the little red light in your brain? It is the imaginary light that goes on in your head and causes you to think "Oops, this is not the appropriate time to say that" or "I can see Dad is tired and irritable now. I should not ask him if I can get a tattoo." If the time is not right, do not bring up the topic. Wait. There will be a better time. But even if you think it is the right time, do not start without asking permission, for just that kindness will help to assure your loved one that you will respect and honor their wishes. See Resources for more information.

Do-Not-Resuscitate Orders

Ambulance personnel do not have time to review advance directives and determine if they are legally binding. So, after completing your advance directive, you may have to take one more step if you want to avoid CPR (cardiopulmonary resuscitation) or other life support when an ambulance (911) is called.

Some people with serious and irreversible conditions do not want an emergency medical team to give them CPR if their heart stops. If this is your wish, ask how to get a DNR Order (Do-Not-Resuscitate Order) that will be respected outside of hospitals. These are also called Out-of-Hospital DNR Orders, Comfort-Care-Only Orders or other similar names. They usually require your physician's signature and your consent. You will get a special identifying bracelet or document that must be visible if you have a medical crisis. If the emergency medical team sees the proper bracelet or document upon arrival, you can expect to receive all necessary comfort care—but not life support.

Review and Update Your Documents

Advance planning for health care is always a work in progress. That is because circumstances and lives change. You could move. You could divorce. A decision-maker you have selected could move away or become unavailable. Your values and priorities may even change. As a sage remarked, "The world looks different when you're horizontal rather than vertical."

A question I am frequently asked is how often people should review health care directives that they have already executed. The American Bar Association suggests five times that you should definitely review your health care directives:

1. Before each annual physical exam
2. At the start of each decade of your life
3. After any major life change, such as a birth in the family, marriage, divorce, a further marriage and especially after the death of a loved one
4. After any major medical change, such as being diagnosed with a serious disease or terminal illness, or if such conditions worsen
5. After losing your ability to live independently

H.E.L.P., a California Health Care and Elder Law Programs Corporation, suggests that during a review of your health care directives, you check for the following:

- Is your decision-maker available, and able to be your advocate?
- Has your relationship with your decision-maker changed?
- If you stated feelings or views in the documents, are those still your feelings and views?

After a review, you should make a new advance directive if your old one no longer reflects your wishes. Ask about the proper way to cancel or amend your existing directive in your state. If you change your advance directive, it is important to notify everyone who has copies of your old medical directive forms. After you have made a new one, the American Bar Association suggests you do the following:

1. Keep the original copy of your health care advance directive and any other notes some place they can be easily found.
2. Give your chosen health care agent a copy of the directive plus any worksheets or notes. Make sure your agent knows where to find the original.
3. Give your doctor a copy of your directive. Make certain it is put in your medical record. Make sure your doctor will support your wishes. If your doctor has objections, you need to work them out or find another doctor.
4. Carry an advance directive wallet card with you.
5. If entering a hospital or nursing home, take a copy of your directive with you and ask that it be placed in your medical record.

There are organizations that register advance directives electronically and enable health care institutions to access them electronically. Additionally, some churches and synagogues keep advance directives on file for members. These are two options you might want to consider.

A similar service, MedNotice, provides what they call "secure, affordable" storage for and access to your advance medical directive. After registering, your PIN number is printed on an orange card that informs medical personnel that you have documents stored on the MedNotice system. Then, by entering your PIN number into the computer, health care professionals can gain access to documents from any Web-enabled computer anywhere.

The U.S. Living Will Registry electronically stores advance directives, organ donor and emergency contact information and makes access to them available to health care providers through fax or Internet 24 hours a day.

DocuBank® is also an electronic storage and access service for your advance directives (living will, health care power of attorney, and/or other health care document). When you store your health care documents with DocuBank® you receive a customized DocuBank® Emergency Card. If you are hospitalized, the hospital staff will then obtain your documents by fax by calling 1-800-DOCUBANK, and following the instructions on the back of your card. DocuBank® faxes your documents to the hospital right away.

Remember, an out-of-date will, trust, or other document is often no better than the absence of each. Update your estate plan regularly. Many occurrences can make it obsolete practically overnight, including changes in state and federal laws.

See Resources section for more information on these services.

Wills and Trusts

The Role of the Fiduciary

The dictionary defines a fiduciary as "One, such as an agent of a principal or a company director, that stands in a special relation of trust, confidence, or responsibility in certain obligations to others." The fiduciary of an estate is usually called an executor or a personal representative.

The American Bar Association has an informative pamphlet called *You Are the Fiduciary: A Handbook for Individuals Named as Executor or Trustee*, and many of the comments in this section are taken from that publication.

When someone dies, his or her assets need to be gathered, business affairs settled, debts paid, necessary tax returns filed, and ultimately assets distributed as the deceased individual (generally referred to as the decedent) directed. The person who is responsible for conducting these activities is the fiduciary. A fiduciary can be a "trustee" if the document distributing assets is a trust, or a "personal representative" if the distribution document is a Last Will and Testament.

Among the first things the fiduciary must do is read and understand the will or trust so that he or she knows:

- Who the beneficiaries are;
- What the beneficiaries are to receive and when;
- If a Trust, how many years the trust will be ongoing; and
- Who, if any, are co-fiduciaries.

The document imparts important information and directions to the fiduciary, such as which assets should be used to pay taxes and expenses, and it will usually list the fiduciary's powers in detail.

If you are working with a Last Will and Testament as the primary document, you must decide whether a probate proceeding is required. (See "Probate in Maryland" or check with the probate officer in your state or county.)

It is the fiduciary's responsibility to take control of all assets comprising an estate or trust. It is crucial to secure and value all assets as soon as possible. It is the fiduciary's duty to determine when bills unpaid at death should be paid, and then pay them or notify creditors about a temporary delay. In some cases, such as property or casualty insurance bills or real estate taxes, the estate may be harmed if the bills are not paid promptly. Most states require written, published notice to any known or reasonably ascertainable creditors. Actually, a fiduciary can be held personally liable for improperly spending estate or trust assets, and not having enough money remaining to pay bills.

The fiduciary is also responsible for a number of tax returns. First are the personal tax returns of the decedent, a federal estate tax return, if needed, and a state estate tax return, if needed. Since the estate or trust is also a taxpayer in its own right, a new tax identification number must be obtained and a fiduciary income tax return must be filed for the estate or trust as well. The fiduciary must be mindful of the fact that the estate or trust and the beneficiaries may not be in the same tax brackets. Thus, the good timing of certain distributions can save money for all concerned. Some tax preparers and accountants specialize in preparing these types of fiduciary income tax returns and can be very helpful.

Most expenses that a fiduciary incurs in the administration of an estate or trust are properly payable from the descedent's assets. These include funeral expenses, appraisal fees, attorney's and accountant's fees, insurance premiums, etc. Careful records should be kept and receipts should always be obtained, as the fiduciary is accountable to the court and the beneficiaries. Agreeing to serve as fiduciary is not a responsibility to be taken lightly.

Wills

Many people view a will as something nice to do but not necessary. If you have not written your own will, the state you live in has one written and in place for you.

I have seen the will prepared by the state of Maryland. (See the Illustration 1—Maryland's Last Will and Testament.) States have done well in trying to decide what some mythical average person might want. However, it does not seem to be what most real people want.

Perhaps you feel you are a person of modest means with a small estate, and that you do not need a will. This thinking can cause heartache and confusion for your family at the time of your death. The process of clearing everything up without a will is difficult and full of fees, bond requirements and frustration.

The American Diabetes Association says, "When you choose the route of over half of all Americans and leave no valid will, the state must intervene. You leave your heirs a legacy of neglect, confusion and waste at a time when they are least equipped emotionally and perhaps financially for such an inheritance."

I think the real culprit is probably procrastination. Many well-meaning folks intend to have a will done, but it turns out to be one of those things they never get around to.

Anyone who wishes a different distribution from that provided for you by the state, who wishes to select their own executor and who wishes to name the guardians for their minor children should have a will. In short, most people should prepare and sign a will, even if they are likely to adopt the average and standard answers as to most of the issues and questions.

Parents of disabled children have additional reasons to make a will. If no plans are prepared, the disabled child may be the recipient of an inheritance that he or she is incapable of managing, and that may interfere with, or completely void, the availability of crucial government benefits. If this is your situation, my best advice is to consult a reputable attorney as soon as possible to address these issues. All too frequently, we see family members bogged down in costly and lengthy judicial procedures because their loved ones never thought such basic planning was necessary.

In your will you can name your personal representative. This is the person who will have the responsibility of adminis-

Being of sound mind and memory, I, _____, do hereby publish this as my Last Will and Testament:

FIRST: If none of my children are minors, I give my spouse $15,000.00.

SECOND: I give 1/2 of the balance of my estate to my spouse and 1/2 to my children.

A. I appoint my spouse as guardian of my children, but as a safeguard, I require that he/she report to the Orphans' Court regularly and render an account of how, why and where he/she spent the money necessary for the proper care of my children.

B. As a further safeguard, I direct my spouse to provide to the Probate Court a Performance Bond to guarantee that he/she exercise proper judgment in the handling, investing and spending of the children's money, unless my spouse can prove to the court's satisfaction that such bond is not necessary.

C. As a final safeguard, my children shall have the right to demand and receive a complete accounting from my spouse of all of the financial actions with their money as soon as they reach legal age.

D. When my children reach the age of 18 years, they shall have full rights to withdraw and spend their respective shares of my estate, whatever the state of their maturity, and however they please. No one shall have any right to question my children's actions on how they decide to spend their respective shares.

THIRD: Should my spouse remarry, his/her next spouse shall be entitled to take a 1/3 share of everything my spouse possesses, including all that I left for him/her, including my life insurance, or a 1/2 share if there are no surviving children. The next spouse shall have the sole right to decide who is to get his/her share, even to the exclusion of my own children. The second spouse shall not be bound to spend any part of his/her share for the support of my children.

FOURTH: Should my spouse predecease me, I do not wish to exercise my right to nominate the guardian of my children.

A. Rather than nominating a guardian of my preference, I direct the Court to choose for me. If the Court wishes, it may appoint anyone who petitions the Court and claims to be interested in the welfare of my minor children.

B. If any child has attained the age of 14 years, the Court may appoint a guardian chosen by the child.

FIFTH: Under existing tax law, there are certain techniques available for minimizing death taxes. However, I prefer that my estate be used for governmental purposes, rather than for the benefit of my spouse and children. I direct, therefore, that no effort be made to lower taxes so that the government may benefit to the maximum extent permitted by my death.

SIXTH: Unless there is prior approval of Court, I direct that no funeral or burial expense in excess of $5,000 be paid from my estate.

IN WITNESS WHEREOF, I have set my hand to this, my Last Will and Testament.

Illustration 1. *Maryland's Last Will and Testament for Those Without a Valid Will (Maryland Institute for Continuing Professional Education of Lawyers, Inc.)*

tering your estate. And you can waive the requirement for a bond. Thomas Hart Hawley, author of *The Artful Dodger's Guide to Planning Your Estate*, says, "A bond is like an insurance policy that protects your estate if the personal representative disappears in your Ferrari Testarossa."

You should waive bond if you have complete trust in your chosen representative. This is important because bonds can be expensive, depending upon the size of the estate. Remember, if you die without a will (intestate) your representative will be appointed by the court, and bond may be required even if the court appoints one of your family members.

Not all property passes through your will. For example, property held in joint tenancy or, as in Maryland, by husband and wife as Tenants by the Entirety, passes immediately on your death to the survivor outside your will. Retirement benefits, life insurance and some investments that are payable at your death to a person you have designated will pass outside the will; so will bank accounts held in joint tenancy or in trust for another or assets held in a Living Trust. This, too, has its risks. If the joint tenant or the beneficiary of your life insurance dies before you or in a common disaster with you, this property will pass by intestate succession at your death.

Most wills contain a "simultaneous death" clause. If the will maker (testator) and his or her beneficiary die in a common accident or so close together in time that it is difficult to determine who died first, an administrative nightmare of double probate could ensue. Costs would increase, and property might not ultimately go to whom the decedent wished. Simultaneous death can also result in increased estate tax liability. Therefore, it is helpful to include a simultaneous death clause in your will and/or a provision requiring the beneficiaries to survive for a specific period of time before inheriting.

Lynn Loughlin Skerpon, Register of Wills for Prince George's County, Maryland, often speaks to organizations regarding wills. She understands how uncomfortable it is to think about our own mortality, but as Register of Wills, Skerpon is reminded daily of the repercussions of failing to plan for your family's future. "It does not get any easier as we get older," she said, "and it is a terrible task to take on when you have recently been diagnosed with a terminal illness."

Skerpon offers the following advice:

"Many people ask me, 'Why do I need a will?' I am of the firm belief that every adult needs a will. We have all heard horror stories about what happens when someone dies. Many of us have experienced it firsthand in our own families. To paraphrase a colleague of mine, it seems that many families go quickly 'from grief to greed.'

"To guarantee that your property passes according to your wishes, you must have a will. Even though you might think you do not own much, it seems that everyone owns something— your car, your retirement account, your final retirement or Social Security check. Most importantly, you may have minor children.

"If you die in Maryland without a will, it is the law of the State of Maryland, as administered by the Orphans' Court that governs how your property will be distributed. Did you know that if you are married, have minor children and die without a will, your spouse does not receive all your estate? Rather, your spouse receives half your estate and your minor children receive the other half. If you are not happy with this result, you should have a valid will to state how you wish your property to be distributed.

"If you and your spouse should both die as the result of a common accident, leaving minor children and no will, the Orphans' Court will decide who shall have legal guardianship of your children. As much as I respect the judges of our Orphans' Court, I still would not want them deciding who should be the guardian of my sons. That is a parental decision, best made by those who know and love the children, and who are most concerned with their future welfare.

"As a former practicing attorney, I know how frequently people put off making the difficult decisions that wills embrace. However, as Register of Wills, I am reminded daily of the repercussions of failure to plan for your family's future.

"Wills are not difficult to prepare. However, I urge all to see an attorney to have a will drafted. Do not try to draft a will on your own. Many legal technicalities must be met. Also, I do not recommend that you try preparing a will from a kit or off the Internet. These wills are designed for the most common denominator among all the states. Every state has its own rules and requirements for valid wills, and the kit or Internet will may not be valid.

"An attorney can help you through this process. There are many things you should consider, depending on the nature of your estate, family relationships and tax laws. Please make particular choices regarding your own family situation. Do not leave it to the laws of the State of Maryland to make those decisions for you.

"Can anybody make and sign a will that will be valid? In most states, the testator must be 'legally competent to make a will.' You should know that the law presumes that every person is sane and has the capacity to make a valid will. The burden of proving otherwise rests upon those who would challenge the will.

"Many wills contain a provision denying any inheritance to anyone contesting the will. Are these effective? It depends. In many cases, a provision that disinherits a will contestant partially or completely will probably be ultimately unenforceable if there is probable cause or some other level of evidence to support the challenge. On a practical level, in order to effectively prevent will contests, a will should probably provide for at least some reasonable inheritance for any person who might be expected to initiate a contest. Then, it can provide for the loss of that specific inheritance if that individual files a challenge."

See Resources for additional information on wills.

Probate in Maryland

Some people do not want to prepare a will because they want to avoid probate. If you are like most people, you probably do not have much of an idea what probate is. You have heard just enough to feel that it is not a good thing. "Probate"—meaning to prove—is simply the judicial process for the orderly distribution of an estate. *Black's Law Dictionary* says that probate is "a court procedure by which a will is proved to be valid or invalid." The dictionary goes on to say that current usage has expanded the term to "generally include all matters and proceedings pertaining to administration of estates."

What does not have to be probated in Maryland:

- Property held in joint tenancy or, in some states, property held as tenants by the entirety

- Life insurance proceeds (unless you named your probate

estate as the beneficiary or if all named beneficiaries predecease the insured)

- Assets such as retirement accounts (like IRAs) and government bonds that are payable upon death to a person you name
- Assets held in a living trust

Although these items are not probated, in some cases they are reported to the Register of Wills through the information sheet as a part of the probate process, and they are included in the total value of your estate for estate tax purposes. The rest of your property is most likely subject to probate.

A probate proceeding is most often started by the person you named in your will as your personal representative. If you never got around to making a will, just about anybody can start the proceeding, even one of your creditors. However, most courts would give preference to your spouse and your relatives for personal representative. If your will does not name a personal representative, or if you did not have a will, a judicial hearing will be held in order for the court to name a personal representative for the estate. This is an advertised, open hearing. It gives interested parties the opportunity to object to the proposed personal representative.

The person seeking to be your representative fills out probate forms provided by the county's Register of Wills office. As a general rule, I have found the clerks in the county Register of Wills offices to be friendly, helpful and knowledgeable. When the probate forms are completed, a legal notice is published in a local newspaper. This notice informs your creditors that they must file claims, if they have any, against the estate and informs the public of the date of the first hearing. The notice also must be sent to all interested persons, generally the beneficiaries named in your will as well as your next of kin who would inherit if there were no will.

If the statutory waiting time expires without a challenge, your Last Will and Testament will be admitted to probate, and letters of administration will be issued to the personal representative. These letters are your representative's written authority to act for the estate. Creditors have a limited time from the date these letters are issued to file a claim against the estate for money due (two to six months). If they do not file during that time period, they lose the right to collect the debt. According to Hawley's *The Artful Dodger's Guide to Planning Your Estate*, this cutoff of creditors' claims is an important benefit of probate.

Your personal representative's first task is to inventory the property of the estate and, if required by the Register of Wills, to have it appraised. These values are used on your federal estate tax return if one is required. These values also establish the new tax basis of all estate assets. As Hawley explains in an example, "The vacation cottage you purchased for $50,000 (your original tax basis) will get a new basis of $500,000; its value at the date of your death. Your beneficiaries, if they sell the cottage, will pay capital gains tax on only those sales proceeds over $500,000."

During probate, your representative receives all income, pays all expenses, invests surplus cash and generally manages your estate. He or she must also file your last personal income tax returns along with your estate's income tax returns. If your gross estate exceeds the amount of your personal exemption (this will increase to $1,000,000 by 2006), your representative must also file an estate tax return within nine months of your death. After the time for filing creditors' claims has expired and after any required tax returns have been filed, your estate can be closed.

The personal representative files an itemized final accounting in which all income and expenses, gains and losses of the estate must balance. The representative also requests approval of his or her fees and, if an attorney was used, the probate attorney's fees. These allowable fees vary from state to state. Family members are often likely to waive this fee.

Finally, your representative sets out how the estate will be distributed. Once the final accounting is approved, your representative will distribute your estate and his or her duties will be finished.

In Maryland, probate is not difficult. In a simple estate it frequently takes no longer than six months. Additionally, Maryland has a streamlined procedure for estates under $30,000. So please get to work on that will: You will feel better prepared, and I am sure your heirs will be grateful.

Revocable Living Trusts

Do you need a Revocable Living Trust (RLT)? I will rush in with the classic legal answer to every difficult question— it depends.

You do need to create a RLT if your circumstances, your goals and your financial state of affairs so indicate. Otherwise, you will probably be just fine with a will and Power of Attorney documents. If you are uncertain about these matters, an attorney or a financial adviser could help you decide.

Whereas a will is a matter of public record, RLTs are confidential. You may go to the office of the Register of Wills in your county and look at the will of any deceased individual. Information about assets and the addresses of beneficiaries are just some of the items that outsiders can glean from the will. But information about any property that has been placed within a trust and information about distribution from the trust at the time of death are not subject to public record. As a part of your evaluation of RLTs, you will want to consider how important this point is to you. One can understand why privacy in this area might be very important to certain public figures. However, it may not be as crucial to many of us average citizens.

A Revocable Living Trust (RLT) is particularly important if you own real property in another state. If an individual moves from one state to another, a will must conform to the laws of the new state. However, a RLT can be used in the new state or even left in the old state if post-death laws are more favorable there.

When an individual owns real property in more than one state and the property is transferred according to a will, it is often necessary to open a probate estate in each state where property is owned. Sometimes it is also necessary to appoint a personal representative, or executor, in that state. Therefore, the time and costs required to complete probate in your home state and probate in other states—called ancillary estates—are increased. If you have a RLT in place, the property will transfer according to the trust provisions. That property bypasses probate.

Another advantage of a RLT relates to possible future physical or mental disability of the grantor (the person giving assets to the trust). We must consider who will be in a position of management over our property in case of mental or physical disability prior to death; that is, who will be the trustee(s). A trust is very effective in allowing the assets to be managed and distributed in accordance with the grantor's wishes even when the grantor becomes incapacitated. The trust instrument usually anticipates the incapacity of the grantor by giving guidelines for determining incapacity and by naming successor trustees who can take over fiduciary responsibilities at the incapacity of the initial grantor.

Married couples with combined assets in excess of a million and a half dollars should seriously consider a RLT, as they may be able to save federal estate taxes by establishing a Credit Shelter Trust—a type of Living Trust.

Living Trusts cost more than traditional wills. Creating a RLT will most likely increase the number and complexity of documents that need to be prepared. Also, the trust requires additional steps to complete the planning cycle. In the case of a will, planning is finished once the document and any supporting documents are signed. The RLT must be funded. That is, all (or most) assets must be transferred into the trust's name, often a time-consuming process.

You can do a simple cost-benefit analysis by considering the question: Is the cost (today) of establishing a RLT significantly lower than the cost (at some future date) of probating my estate? Remember that the cost of preparing the trust will come from your funds, while the cost of probate will come from funds being paid to your beneficiaries.

If you decide to create a RLT, please remember that it is important to get the advice of a competent estate-planning attorney and a financial planner who can advise you concerning the complex legal and tax issues that arise at death. This is definitely not a do-it-yourself project.

Revocable Living Trusts vs. Powers of Attorney

A Durable General Power of Attorney makes provision for your business affairs to be handled in the case of your mental or physical disability. Now you may be wondering whether a trust is better than a Durable Power of Attorney for that purpose.

In his book, *Elder Law in Maryland*, noted elder law attorney Jason A. Frank writes that trusts are sometimes preferred to

Powers of Attorney because of the superior authority, durability and scope of discretion that a trust entails. A trustee, says Frank, has legal title to all assets comprising trust property, and this fact inspires a higher degree of confidence in the actions and decisions of a trustee as opposed to the attorney-in-fact (the agent) created by the Durable General Power of Attorney. "Since the creation of a trust involves a more extensive and sophisticated procedure and involves more explicit provisions, there are fewer potential doubts as to the nature and extent of the powers a trust conveys," he says.

Revocable Living Trusts vs. Probate

David A. Diamond, a California attorney, has a web site called The Trust Wizard (see Resources). He says that he recommends Living Trusts for the majority of his clients. His definition of probate is interesting: "Probate is simply a court procedure whereby a court-appointed personal representative performs three distinct functions: (1) inventory and appraise the decedent's assets, (2) pay the decedent's debts and taxes and (3) distribute the remaining assets to the decedent's beneficiaries."

Diamond says that after the death of the grantor/trustee, the successor trustee of a RLT performs the same three basic functions. He maintains that in reality, the only difference between probate and post-death administration of a Living Trust is that probate is supervised by the court. The court has a structured, formal system with rules for handling the administration of estates.

If you choose to create a RLT, remember that the informality that makes trust administration cheaper, faster and easier than probate is also an informality that could result in confusion, mismanagement, lawsuits and potential liability for the successor trustee. The successor trustee that you choose must be knowledgeable (or willing to learn) about the operation of trusts. The trustee must be well organized and committed to carrying out his or her fiduciary responsibility in strict accordance with the terms of the trust and trust law.

Supplemental Needs Trusts

Elder law attorney Elizabeth Weis of Wilmington, North Carolina asks us to picture this scenario: Lois's 45-year-old retarded son, Alan, had never held a job and had always lived at home. Lois loves him dearly, but her doctor has just told her that her cancer had spread, and that she has six months to live.

Though Lois knows that Alan and Janice, his divorced sister, will each inherit $120,000 when she dies, Lois worries about Alan's future. She does not want him to have to depend upon government assistance for his care and support. However, she does want to make sure that, if that were the best alternative, money would be available to supplement that assistance. She knows that her present will would not meet this goal.

Fortunately for Lois, the government allows estate planning that will enable her to execute a will that includes a trust under which Alan may receive government assistance for his care and support and still receive other support that supplements, but does not supplant, his government benefits.

This trust is known as a Supplemental Needs Trust and is, as are all trusts, an invisible container that holds assets. Lois could use such a trust to hold Alan's $120,000 inheritance and control its distribution. The government allows a Supplemental Needs Trust for one reason. Lois has no legal obligation to support Alan. She has every (legal) right to disinherit him.

To qualify as a Supplemental Needs Trust, the trust language must state that neither Alan, the government nor any court would have the authority to dictate to the trustee how to spend Alan's inheritance. Furthermore, the language must also forbid the trustee to use the money to pay Alan's creditors. Such a provision is called a "spendthrift" provision.

- The language of the trust must also state
- That the purpose of the trust is to supplement and not supplant government support for Alan
- Who will manage the trust (i.e., who will be the trustee)
- Under what conditions the trustee may distribute money
- When the trust will cease to exist
- Who will inherit the remaining money in the trust as remainder beneficiary when the trust terminates

The trust language should offer suggestions for discretionary distribution of the money in ways Lois believes would enhance Alan's lifestyle. Examples of such discretionary distributions might be the purchase of a VCR and a special chair that will allow for Alan's very large size or payment for someone to take him on excursions to his favorite fast food restaurant and travel expenses to visit his sister.

When such a trust is placed in Lois's will, it is revocable. Lois can change her mind about its existence by executing a new will or a codicil to her existing will. However, once she dies, the trust is irrevocable.

Gifting

If I were to choose the single subject that most readers, friends and clients are slightly confused about, it would be the subject of gifting and taxes. Currently, there is an annual gift tax exclusion amount of $11,000 (in 2004) per recipient. So what if there is a gift of more than $11,000 to a single recipient in a year? Who owes taxes? Anybody? Everybody?

First of all, a gift recipient never has to pay income taxes on the gift, no matter the size, because gifts are not taxable income. To quote John Fisher, tax attorney, "the blessed recipients of a gift never pay any tax."

Don't forget common sense, though. If you receive a gift, which is tax free to you, and you then put the gift (which is now your own asset) into an interest-bearing account, you will receive a Form 1099 for the income the gift generates and you will owe income taxes on the interest received, just as you would for any other account you've opened with your own funds.

The possibility of paying gift taxes rests on the giver, not on the receiver. The government does not want you to give all your assets away, willy-nilly, and then say there is nothing in your estate at your death for federal estate taxes. Therefore, in order to give attorneys and tax preparers meaningful work, the government has created elaborate and complicated rules for taxing gift-givers.

To understand the rules, you have to know that the government gives credits that can be applied to the amount of tax owed, thereby either eliminating or reducing the tax. This unified credit applies to both the gift tax and the estate tax. For tax year 2004, the unified credit that applies to your estate is $1.5 million. The unified credit that applies to your gifts is $1 million. The $1.5 million for estate tax purposes and the $1 million for gift tax purposes are called "applicable exclusion amounts." Simply put, the applicable exclusion amounts can be thought of as the amount of wealth that Congress and the IRS either allow a person to have—for estate tax purposes, or allow a person to transfer—for gift tax purposes, without creating federal estate tax obligations.

Here's the hard part. As discussed above, the $1.5 million for estate tax purposes is not a credit, but rather, the applicable exclusion amount, meaning the amount that is, in essence, not taxable. However, you cannot simply deduct $1.5 million from your taxable estate and pay taxes on the rest. That is way too easy. I suggest that you check with your tax adviser for direction and the rest of that story.

So, why is the $11,000 figure so important? Everyone seems to know that $11,000 gifts can be given to as many different people in any year as she or he likes with no tax consequences. Therefore, people think "you" have to pay taxes if "you" give away or receive more than $11,000 in a year. No, you don't. But interaction with the IRS is required. If the gift-giver gives any individual (except his or her spouse) more than $11,000 in a year, the filing of Form 709 is required.

Form 709 basically indicates "I gave $12,000—or whatever amount—to whomever during 2004, or the appropriate tax year." The IRS keeps that form and when you have gifted even $1.00 more than $1 million, you may owe gift taxes on that overage. The $11,000 is a very popular gift idea, because the IRS is only informed of gifts to any one person in a year that exceed that exclusion amount, so if you limit your gift-giving to $11,000 gifts, you do not have to report those to the IRS and they do not count toward the $1 million lifetime limit.

Finally, you need to know that when you make large gifts, even though you most likely will not be paying gift taxes, you are using up part of your lifetime exclusion amount. If you use up that amount prior to your death, then your estate may have to pay gift taxes, even if no tax is owed on your taxable estate.

By far the majority of us do not have to worry about paying gift taxes because we are not financially able to give away a million dollars in our lifetime. Neither do most of us have estates large enough to push the federal estate tax button. Actually, we are in the majority—only about 2 percent of Americans pay estate taxes, says the IRS.

So, if for some reason, you need to gift more than $11,000 to somebody in a year, and your estate will probably never be more than the $1 million applicable exclusion amount for gifts, then go to it. Gift with abandon.

You know what? This is about federal taxes. There's also a whole State Estate Tax thing. Oh, my aching head.

Beneficiaries

Just as having estate planning documents is important, so is thinking about your beneficiaries. Do you know exactly who are the beneficiaries on all of your life insurance policies, IRAs, 401k plans and other assets that will pass outside your will? When was the last time you even thought about such things? Is your beneficiary a former spouse? Is your beneficiary someone who has already died? Is it a child who has continued to disappoint you and perhaps refuses to grow up and accept responsibility? Is it a sibling with whom you are no longer close?

The designation of a beneficiary, just like estate planning documents, cannot be changed or revised after your death. Your family must deal with whatever is written on the beneficiary line at that time. I once heard of a situation where the agent on a Power of Attorney was a former spouse. The principal had been married to his new wife for more than 12 years but never took the time to update his documents and plans. What a mess that was.

If you die and there is no living person eligible to be a beneficiary, many companies (and the federal government) will pay the benefit according to an order of precedence not unlike intestate laws. You should contact each company with which you have signed such a document and ask for a copy of their order of precedence for paying benefits. While you are speaking with them, get a copy of your current beneficiary designation forms and a change of beneficiary form in case you need to name a new beneficiary. Keep a copy of your completed and most current designation forms with your important legal documents. This will be an incredible help to your family and loved ones after your death.

When people come to me to discuss their wills, I always suggest that they consider naming what we call a "catastrophic beneficiary." Did you know that if all your primary beneficiaries predecease you, by law your estate could go to distant relatives you do not even know about? Or, failing that, to the state?

After you have listed all the people you want to remember, ask yourself, "Now what if none of them is alive to receive it?" Then complete your plans by naming a final beneficiary— perhaps your church or your favorite charity. These are institutions that will live on for years to come.

If you know who your designated beneficiaries are and they are indeed the persons you want to receive any monies payable after your death, you do not have to do anything. If you know that you never designated beneficiaries on certain documents and you are comfortable with your company's order of precedence, you also do not need to do anything. But if you are not sure, you had best check it out. Otherwise, your loved ones may be in for a rude shock after your death when you can no longer do anything about the designations.

Other Legal Issues

What Is HIPAA?

The advent of the 2003 phase-in of the Health Insurance Portability and Accountability Act of 1996, more commonly known as HIPAA, is significantly impacting every one of us and our health care providers. Because of HIPAA, you should review and amend your health care directives now.

HIPAA was conceived mainly as a privacy vehicle. It was planned to allow you, the sometime patient, to decide who may have access to your medical records. Not only may you decide who can access your medical records, you must name this person, or persons, in writing. Otherwise, hospitals and health care providers may be assessed penalties for sharing medical information. Your Healthcare Power of Attorney should designate someone, or should state that your health care agent is designated as your personal representative for all purposes under HIPAA. Check with your favorite attorney to see what actions are appropriate for you because of HIPAA.

Let's set the record straight on some popular myths regarding the new HIPAA law, which applies to health care providers, health plans and health care clearinghouses.

Myth One: Your doctor's office cannot send your medical records to another doctor's office (such as a specialist) without your consent. Wrong. No consent is necessary for one doctor's office to transfer a patient's medical records to another doctor's office for treatment purposes, even under HIPAA.

Myth Two: A patient cannot be listed in a hospital's directory without the patient's consent, and the hospital is prohibited from sharing a patient's directory information with the public. Wrong.

The Privacy Rule permits hospitals to continue the practice of providing room number and other directory information to the public unless the patient has specifically chosen to opt out.

Myth Three: Members of the clergy can no longer find out whether members of their congregation or their religious affiliation are hospitalized unless they know the person personally by name. Wrong. The regulation specifically provides that hospitals may continue the practice of disclosing directory information to members of the clergy unless the patient has objected to such disclosure.

Myth Four: A hospital is prohibited from sharing information with the patient's family without the patient's express consent. Wrong. Under the HIPAA privacy regulations, a health care provider may disclose to "a family member, other relative, or a close personal friend of the individual, or any other person identified by the individual," the medical information directly relevant to their involvement with the patient's care, and also for purposes of payment related to the patient's care.

Myth Five: HIPAA mandates all sorts of new disclosures of patient information. Wrong. Under HIPAA, disclosure is mandated in only two situations: to the individual patient upon request, or to the Secretary of the Department of Health and Human Services for use in oversight investigations.

Myth Six: Patients may sue health care providers for not complying with HIPAA privacy regulations. Wrong. Amazingly, perhaps, HIPAA does not give people the right to sue.

Myth Seven: The media can no longer access vital public information from hospitals about accident or crime victims. Not totally true. Under HIPAA, hospitals may continue to make public certain patient directory information, including the patient's location in the facility and the patient's condition in general terms—unless the patient has specifically opted out of having such information publicly available.

Myth Eight: If a patient refuses to sign an acknowledgment stating that he or she received the health care provider's notice of privacy practices, the health care provider can, or must, refuse to provide services. Wrong. It is not that strict. HIPAA grants the patient a right to notice of privacy practices for protected health information and requires that providers make a good faith effort to get patients to acknowledge they have received the notice.

Myth Nine: A patient's family member can no longer pick up prescriptions for the patient. Wrong. Under the regulation, a family member or other individual may act on the patient's behalf "to pick up filled prescriptions, medical supplies, x-rays or other similar forms of protected health information."

An overarching concept of HIPAA is the "minimum necessary standard." The law provides that whenever a covered entity uses or discloses protected health information or requests such information from another covered entity, it must make reasonable efforts to limit the information to the minimum amount necessary to accomplish the intended purpose of the use or disclosure. In other words, they are not to provide more information—just the information necessary to accomplish the purpose or satisfy the demand.

You and I may authorize a specific covered entity to disclose medical information to anyone we want, including an advocate, a family member or someone else. To do so, we must submit a written authorization form to the covered entity. Under HIPAA, the person authorized to receive such information is called the personal representative.

See Resources for additional HIPAA information.

What Is Competence?

The question of competency frequently arises in an elder law practice. Sometimes court challenges are made to estate planning documents based on a contention that the person who executed the document was incompetent at the time of execution. Children call me, explaining that their parent is incompetent. Parents call me and say, "My son thinks I'm crazy!"

Exactly when is a person considered competent or incompetent to sign important documents? Interestingly, an older client may have different capacities for different functions, making them incapacitated for some purposes but not for others. In a 1994 *Fordham Law Review* article, Professor Peter Margulies listed six factors that are important in making capacity determinations:

- Ability to articulate reasoning behind a decision
- Variability of the client's state of mind
- Appreciation of the consequences of a decision
- Irreversibility of a decision
- Substantive fairness of a transaction
- Consistency with lifetime commitments

Therefore, depending on the complexity of the contract or paperwork to be signed, the required level of capacity may vary. In Maryland, an individual signing a Living Will or a Power of Attorney is required to understand the "purpose and effect" of the document to be signed. Mere confusion or the infirmities of old age do not, by themselves, make a person incompetent to sign a legal document.

A person (called the "principal") signing a Power of Attorney needs only to understand that an agent is being placed in charge of certain affairs and that this agent will handle those certain affairs on behalf of the principal. The principal must desire such an arrangement and must have at least a minimum understanding of what his or her affairs are and what the agent is likely to do. Some legal writers take the position that a person signing a Power of Attorney is without capacity only when the person is entirely without understanding.

In most jurisdictions, in order for a person to be considered competent to sign a will, he or she must:

1. Know the "natural objects of their bounty," the persons to whom they are leaving their estate
2. Know the nature and extent of their holdings
3. Be able to form a reasonable plan for disposition of their assets

It is generally believed that a higher capacity is required to sign a contract than to sign a Power of Attorney. In order to sell a house, buy a business or invest in the stock market, a person should really be competent 24 hours a day. Because of phenomena like sun-downing and the side effects of infections or medications, we know that many seniors, while competent most times, may not be competent every hour of the day. In fact, many people have periods of incompetence—distractions because of business pressures, a relative who is not well, money worries, a death in the family, etc. Being incompetent some of the time does not make a senior incompetent to execute the documents we are discussing during times of lucidity.

There are various mini mental tests available today for determining capacity. An attorney has a clear duty to assess a client's capacity to make decisions. A California court has held that an attorney fulfilled this duty when, based on his own observations and experiences with the client, he was convinced that she had testamentary capacity. I think most attorneys, especially elder law attorneys, assess the capacity of their clients based on observation and instinct on a daily basis.

A person who just had a massive stroke and is in a coma is not mentally competent to sign a Power of Attorney. If you wait until then, it is too late. I have an acquaintance who had a major stroke at age 42. I have friends who have been in car accidents and suffered brain damage while only in their twenties. Documents discussed here are important not only for the elderly, they are important for every adult, regardless of age.

Assessing Advisors

One of the ways to avoid many of the negative and frightening pitfalls surrounding aging is to plan in advance for as many events as you can. Of course, you need advisors to help you. But choosing advisors is in itself loaded with uncertainty and possible negative consequences.

Many of us needing legal, financial, retirement, accounting, estate, long-term care and similar planning services do not know how to find an advisor who is well qualified, honest and capable of providing the advice we need. Unfortunately, sometimes unqualified or dishonest people masquerade as expert advisors, and many of them provide substandard service or have hidden financial motives when they give advice to you.

When you are considering a new advisor, always ask yourself at least two questions: Does the new advisor have legitimate professional credentials? How does the new advisor get paid and by whom?

A wonderful Web site, www.help4srs.org, has developed a form called "Ask First!" (see Resources) to help you decide about a potential advisor. You can download the form free and use it to learn more about the person who wants to help you. If you are not that good with computers, you can write to H.E.L.P., a nonprofit information resource for older adults, and ask for free copies of the form.

When you have copies of the form, keep them handy. Ask any new and potential advisor to complete the form and disclose in writing his or her credentials and ways of being paid. Have him or her return the signed form to you before you do any business. At the same time, ask for and check the person's references.

The form is meant to be filled out by any person offering legal, financial, retirement, insurance, accounting, estate, long-term care or similar planning services. Questions include highest education completed, information regarding specialized credentials and relevant licenses. In addition, there are questions regarding whether the person is an attorney and whether he or she has a license to practice law. They are asked to complete the sentence "I will be paid in the following way (commission, fee, salary, etc.) by the named person or company in connection with the services I am offering to you."

If the potential advisor is an honest person, he or she will be glad to cooperate in this way. In fact, if the person is reluctant to complete the form or answer the questions, you should probably take that as a warning flag—and try to find out more about his or her credentials before paying them the honor of your trust.

Once the form is completed, you should review the person's written answers and look for missing or inconsistent information. You should check out the person's licenses and other credentials and any past complaints. If the person does not answer all the questions, if the answers make you uncomfortable, or if any answers do not check out, do not do business with this person.

Perhaps the very best way to look for the right legal, financial or medical advisor for you is to talk with friends and acquaintances. Word of mouth is sometimes the most reliable way to make a choice of this kind. If your friends have found the person to be honest, hard working and responsive, most likely you will receive the same kind of service. Remember, you are entitled to basically the information the H.E.L.P. form requests—whether you get it through a form or in some other way. You should find out in advance if the person offering planning services to you has legitimate professional credentials. You should find out in advance if the person has hidden financial motives. Be careful out there.

See Resources information on choosing an advisor.

Resources

Elder Law

Elder Law Answers
Web site: www.elderlawanswers.com
Explains Social Security, advanced planning and a host of other topics.

Elder Law in Maryland by Jason A. Frank (Michie: 1996)

Health Privacy
Web site: www.healthprivacy.org
Phone: (202) 721-5632
Address: 1120 19th Street NW, 8th Floor,
Washington, D.C. 20036
Information about health privacy and the law.

Maryland Senior Legal Hotline
Phone: (800) 999-8904
Legal help to seniors.

Metropolitan Maryland Office of the Legal Aid Bureau, Inc.
Phone (Prince George's County): (301) 927-6800
Phone (Anne Arundel County): (410) 263-8330
Offers local guidance with elder law issues.

My Parting Gift by Albert F. Chestone
Phone: (877) 823-9235
Helps guide you through end of life planning.

National Academy of Elder Law Attorneys
Web site: www.naela.org
Phone: (520) 881-4005
Address: 1604 North Country Club Road, Tucson, AZ 85716
Information and a directory of reputable elder law attorneys
and offers a booklet, Questions and Answers When Looking for an
Elder Law Attorney.

National Senior Citizens Law Center
Web site: www.nsclc.org
Phone: (202) 289-6976
Address: 1101 14th Street, NW, Suite 400,
Washington, D.C. 20005
Advocates for legislation for low-income seniors.

NOLO Law For All
Web site: www.nolo.com
Legal information and publications in plain English.

The Unofficial Guide to Eldercare by Chris Adamec
(Wiley: 1999)

Documents and Advanced Planning

Advance Directives Guide
Web site: www.oag.state.md.us/Healthpol/index.htm
Phone: (410) 576-7000
Maryland Attorney General Office of Health Policy
Development offers this brochure and more information on
advanced planning.

Aging with Dignity
Web site: www.agingwithdignity.org
Phone: (888) 594-7437
Address: PO Box 1661, Tallahassee, FL 32302-1661
E-mail: fivewishes@agingwithdignity.org
Popular sample advance directive document, Five Wishes.

American Bar Association Commission on Law and Aging
Web site: www.abanet.org/elderly
Offers advice and information on various issues such as using
advance directives to shape your health care.

The Artful Dodger's Guide to Planning Your Estate by Thomas
Hart Hawley (Adams Media Corporation: 2004)

Kokua Mau
Web site: www.Kokua-mau.org
Offers advice for talking about end-of-life decisions.

Life and Death Planning for Retirement Benefits by Natalie B.
Choate (Ataxplan Publications: 1996)
Web site: www.ataxplan.com
Provides estate planning information.

MedNotice
Web site: www.mednotice.com
Phone: (877) 776-3162
Provides online storage for your medical directives for access
during an emergency.

The Trust Wizard
Web site: www.trustwizard.com
Provides information about trusts and estate planning.

U.S. Living Will Registry
Web site: www.uslivingwillregistry.com
Phone: (800) 548-9455
Address: 523 Westfield Avenue, PO Box 2789,
Westfield, NJ 07091-2789
E-mail: admin@uslivingwillregistry.com
Stores advance directives, organ donor and emergency contact
information; accessible to health care providers.

DocuBank®
Website: www.docubank.com
Phone: (800) 362-8226
Address: Advance Choice, Inc, 109 Forrest Avenue,
Courtyard, Suite 100, Narbeth, PA 19072
Stores advance directives, organ donor and emergency contact
information; accessible to health care providers.

Your Way—A Guide to Help You Stay in Charge
Web site: www.help4srs.org
Phone: (310) 533-1996
Addresss: Your Way, H.E.L.P., 1404 Cravens Avenue,
Torrance, CA 90501
E-mail: yourway@help4srs.org

Other Issues

Ask First!
Web site: www.help4srs.org/articles/askfirst.htm
Phone: (310) 533-1996
Address: H.E.L.P., 1404 Cravens Avenue, Torrance, CA 90501
Provides forms to help you evaluate potential advisors.

Let the Choice Be Mine: A Personal Guide to Planning Your Funeral
Web site: www.funeralplanning1.com
Address: MCR, P.O. Box 1922, Sandpoint, ID 83864

3
Health Care

*"I believe in looking reality straight in the eye...
then denying it."*

—Garrison Keillor

It is important to be a good health care consumer at all stages of care. First, there are things you can do prior to choosing a medical provider. You can conduct your own search to determine if a physician has been disciplined or had claims filed against him or her.

You can visit the Maryland's Health Claims Arbitration Office to look through the Defendant's Index kept there for matters filed and arbitrated through that office. Additionally, you can refer to the latest edition of *America's Top Doctors: The Best in American Medicine* at your local library, use the American Board of Medical Specialists' searchable database of board-certified specialists or check the Board of Physician Quality Assurance for disciplinary records. "Board certified" means that a doctor has passed certain specific exams and is thus considered well qualified in that field of medicine. This is an important question to ask any doctor you contact. See the Resources section at the end of this chapter for more information.

One of the best ways to choose a physician is to ask your friends. Look around for someone who is doing very well after recent heart surgery, knee replacement and other events. Ask if they would recommend their doctor to others.

Medical Issues to Consider

Preparation and Thoroughness Are Keys to Good Care

Once you have chosen a physician, prepare carefully for your first office visit. Dr. Andrew S. Dobin, a board-certified geriatric physician in Maryland, gave a presentation once on how seniors can obtain the best health care. He said that in today's medical climate, everyone must take responsibility for their own health care, because no one but you really has the entire picture or, sadly, the time to care.

Dr. Dobin told seniors how to prepare for a visit to the doctor in ways that help the doctor help you. Because medical history contributes about 90 percent to any diagnosis, he suggested that, when an appointment with a new doctor is on your schedule, you call the doctor's office and ask them to send the medical history forms to you in advance. That way, you can take all the time you need to fill them out accurately. If past medical records and/or test results are available, you should take them to your appointment.

Additionally, it is very important to give complete information regarding the medicines you are taking. Some people tend to see several different doctors, and perhaps medicine prescribed by all of them. Dr. Dobin suggested that you make a list of the medicines, the dosage, how and when you take the medicines and the prescribing doctor's name. Keep this list in your wallet. This would be very helpful if you were in a car accident, for instance, and were taken to the emergency room.

On that same topic, if you do not take a certain medication as directed, be honest with the doctor about that. If you have forgotten to take your thyroid medicine for two weeks, the doctor may notice a low thyroid level in blood tests. He may then prescribe unnecessary medication. The doctor cannot read minds.

Dr. Dobin says that people are sometimes embarrassed and do not reveal their real complaint at the beginning of the appointment. Just as the visit is winding up, the patient will say, "Oh, by the way, since I'm here..." That little parenthetical statement introduces the real complaint. There is very little that doctors have not already heard. Not much will shock them. It is important to begin the visit with your major complaint or the real reason for your visit.

You should also be honest with the doctor about anything that may frighten you. If your mom died of a brain aneurysm, tell the doctor that you fear the same thing may happen to you. Maybe your best friend had knee surgery and died from a blood clot that traveled to the heart, and now you are afraid to have knee surgery. Tell the doctor. He or she can explain things or institute procedures to help put your mind at ease.

Preparing in advance for your visit to the doctor can save time and money because your time with the doctor will be more efficient. If your complaint, for instance, is headaches, think ahead of time and anticipate questions you will be asked. How long have you had these headaches? Be specific. Do not say "a while." When have you had them before—perhaps in times of stress, such as family illness or divorce? Are you under some stress right now? What makes the headache better? What makes it worse? Did any of your immediate relatives have these types of headaches?

Medicare has recently lowered reimbursement to doctor's offices. Physicians will probably react to this, as economics dictate, by trying to see more patients in less time. Therefore, it is very important to prepare in advance for your visit to the doctor and make every minute count.

Dr. Dobin said that recent changes in health care provisions include having a team of doctors and nurses at a hospital who see the hospitalized patient often and interact with the physician who is actually in charge of the patient. This bothers some seniors who may be used to having their own doctor stop by at least once a day when they are hospitalized. However, this change may result in better care because the team doctors are there when needed and can assess the situation and determine whether the doctor should be called. A patient will not be waiting hours for his or her own physician to stop in.

Always inquire as to whether the physician is board certified in the area of medicine that he or she practices. Verify who will be performing any surgery, especially in the case of a teaching hospital. If a resident is providing your medical care, ask to speak with an attending physician.

Be sure to follow up after your hospital discharge. You should always schedule your follow-up appointment before leaving the hospital or outpatient facility. Be sure that information pertaining to prescription medications, including side effects and interactions with other medicines you may be taking, is given to you in writing. Immediately report any problems or concerns to your medical provider.

Take care to avoid prescription errors. They are common and can occur at many stages of the process. Always ask your doctor why he or she has prescribed each medication and request an overview of dosing and potential side effects.

Make sure the prescription is legible and the pharmacist or technician can read the prescription from the doctor. Always verify before leaving the pharmacy with a prescription that it is indeed what your doctor ordered. Finally, be certain to follow all dosing guidelines including frequency and whether to take the medicine with or without food and drink, and always monitor yourself for possible side effects.

Nowadays most prescriptions (even refills) will be accompanied by a patient education leaflet that describes common uses, how to use the medicine, cautions and possible side effects. You should read this form carefully, keep it for future reference and reread the form with every refill because the information can change.

See the Resources section for more information on prescription drugs.

Planning Eases Transition from Hospital to Home

Discharge planning can make things less scary when seniors are leaving the hospital after a stay. Twenty years ago, no one ever heard of discharge planning. It is another one of those fields that has sprung up to meet the demands of a new health care environment.

We all know that because of insurance costs and complications no one stays in the hospital as long as they used to. Years ago, people stayed at the hospital until they were well enough to care for themselves at home. Today, the average length of stay is much shorter, and many patients require some level of assistance or support when they leave the hospital in order to recuperate fully and resume an independent lifestyle.

Discharge planning is an essential part of a patient's treatment, and facilities should include patients and their families in the planning in order to ensure the most successful outcome and a safe, comfortable return to home.

Ideally, planning should begin at the time of admission or even before a person enters the hospital if the admission is for an expected or elective procedure. For example, when discussing a procedure with your physician, make sure to ask what problems you may encounter following the procedure:

- Will you be able to shop and prepare your own meals?

- Will you require the assistance of a home health aide or a personal care attendant to assist you with taking care of yourself after you get home?

- Will you need physical therapy, assistive devices or other specialized care at home?

- Will you need someone to assist you with housekeeping duties, picking up prescriptions and accompanying you to follow-up doctor visits?

Unfortunately, many seniors do not request or accept the assistance of hospital discharge planners, believing that they can do it all themselves or that family and friends will be available to help them with necessary tasks. However, even the best-intentioned relatives and friends may not be available when needed or comfortable with helping someone after a hospital stay. This is probably particularly true if the help is needed for more than a day or two. Unless you are absolutely certain that you have secured all the assistance you will need, you should welcome the professional support and assistance that a discharge planner can offer.

Cost, of course, is always an important consideration and should be reviewed before agreeing to any service. This is a particularly difficult problem for people on a fixed income. However, discharge planning is an important component of good health care, and it is included in the cost of your hospital stay. Good planning could ultimately prevent readmission to the hospital, which, of course, would be more expensive for everyone.

Some health insurance plans will help pay for the home-based services that are set up for you, especially if they are medically necessary and are ordered by your doctor. The doctor's orders should be part of the discharge plan so that you are not responsible for trying to obtain documentation from your doctor after you get home.

If you are uncertain about which services are covered by your health insurance or by Medicare, the discharge planner can assist you with obtaining this information. Services that are helpful but not medically necessary may require you to pay privately or share in the cost of the service. If you really need assistance but are unable to afford it, be sure the discharge planner knows in advance. A discharge planner may be able to work with other community service groups to help you obtain the temporary assistance you need.

If you are nearing the end of a hospital stay and no one has met with you to discuss your care at home, you should request an appointment with the hospital's social worker or discharge planner. The more you educate yourself about being a patient, the better your health outcome will be.

Ten Common Health-related Mistakes

The Institute for Health Care Advancement (IHA) has identified the 10 most common mistakes older people make in caring for their health.

1. *Driving when it is no longer safe.* The elderly often associate mobility in a car with their independence, but knowing when it is time to stop driving is important for the safety of everyone on the road. Decisions about when to stop driving should be made together with a family physician because chronological age alone does not determine someone's fitness to drive.

2. *Fighting the aging process and its appearance.* Refusing to wear a hearing aid, eyeglasses or dentures and a reluctance to ask for help or to use walking aids are all examples of this type of denial. This behavior may prevent seniors from obtaining helpful assistance with some of the problems of aging.

3. *Reluctance to discuss intimate health problems with the doctor or health care provider.* Older people may not want to bring up sexual or urinary difficulties. Sometimes problems that the individual thinks are trivial, such as upset stomach, constipation or jaw pain, may require further evaluation and could be serious.

4. *Not understanding what the doctor said about health problems or medical treatment plans.* Typical complaints are "I could not hear the doctor, he mumbles" and "He told me what to do, but you know me, I cannot remember what he said." Reluctance to ask the doctor to repeat information or to admit that they do not understand what is being said can result in serious negative health consequences for seniors.

5. *Disregarding the serious potential for a fall.* Falls can result in fractures and painful injuries which sometimes take months to heal. To help guard against falling, the elderly should remove scatter rugs from the home and have adequate lighting in home and work areas. Seniors require more lighting than younger people. Seniors

should wear sturdy and well-fitting shoes and watch for slopes and cracks in sidewalks. Participating in exercise programs to improve muscle tone, strength and balance can also be very helpful.

6. *Failing to have a system or a plan for managing medicines.* Missed medication doses can result in inadequate treatment of a medical condition. By using daily schedules, pillbox reminders or check-off records, seniors can avoid missing medication doses. Because health care providers need to know all of the medicines that an elderly patient is taking, patients should maintain a complete list of all their prescription and over-the-counter medicines, including dose and the reason for the medication.

7. *Not having a single primary care physician who looks at the overall medical plan of treatment.* Health problems may be overlooked when a senior goes to several different doctors or treatment programs, and multiple treatment regimens may cause adverse responses. The patient may be over treated or under treated if a single physician is not evaluating the full medical treatment program.

8. *Not seeking medical attention when possible early warning signs occur.* Reasons for such inaction and denial may include lack of money or reduced self-worth due to age. These treatment delays can result in a more advanced illness and a poorer prognosis.

9. *Failing to participate in prevention programs.* Flu and pneumonia vaccinations are examples of readily available preventive health measures that seniors should utilize.

10. *Not asking loved ones for help.* Many elders are simply too stubborn to ask for help, whether due to an understandable need for independence or because of

early signs of dementia. It is important that elderly people alert family members or other loved ones to any signs of ill health or unusual feelings so that they can be assessed before the problem gets worse.

In an effort to help older Americans become less fearful of medical conditions and more empowered about their health, the IHA has published *What to do for Senior Health*, an easy to understand self-help medical book for seniors. See Resources for information.

NIH Web Site Provides Resources for Senior Health

The National Institutes of Health (NIH) has a Web site called NIH Senior Health that features topics tailored to the needs of older people. NIH Senior Health makes aging-related health information easily accessible for seniors, family members and friends seeking reliable online health information that is easy to understand. The site was developed by the National Institute on Aging (NIA) and the National Library of Medicine (NLM), which are both part of the NIH.

The site's design grew out the NIA's research on the types of cognitive changes that are part of the normal aging process. Changes in memory, vision, text comprehension and the speed of information processing can interfere with older adults' use of computers. Research indicates that older adults can effectively use computers if information is provided in a senior-friendly manner. The NIH extensively tested the site with adults aged 60 to 88 years to make sure it was easy for them to see, understand and navigate.

Senior-friendly features on this Web site include large print, short and easy to read segments of information and simple navigation. An audio function reads the text aloud, and the text can be made even more readable with special buttons for enlarging the text or increasing contrast.

New health topics are added to the site on a regular basis. Each topic includes general background information, open-captioned videos, quizzes and frequently asked questions. The American Geriatrics Society provides expert and independent review of some of the material on the site. Topics on the site include Alzheimer's disease, arthritis, balance problems, breast cancer, caring for someone with Alzheimer's disease, colorectal cancer, exercises for older adults, hearing loss, lung cancer and prostate cancer.

For the site's address, see the Resources section.

Keep Tabs on Your Medications

People 65 and older consume an estimated 30 percent of the drugs prescribed in the United States while comprising only about 13 percent of the population. Medications act differently in older adults' bodies than they do in the bodies of younger people. This is only one reason why it is so important for older adults and their caregivers to understand medications and use them correctly and wisely.

Electronic Pill Bottles Facilitate Health Care

The Pill Vial Alarm reminds you to take your medicine. The cap contains a tiny chip that beeps when it is time for your medicine. For an additional cost, you can have the cap play someone's voice—as in, "Mom, it's time to take your medicine!" or something similar. There are also pill organizers, medical watches (vibrating or sound), automatic tablet dispensers, medical alarm clocks, multi-alarms, countdown timers and medical jewelry. See the Resources section for where to find these items.

■ ■ ■

The book *It Takes More Than Love: A Practical Guide to Taking Care of an Aging Adult* by Anita G. Beckerman and Ruth M. Tappen recommends that caregivers or seniors themselves make a comprehensive assessment of medications taken, in order to ensure a complete understanding of why each medication is being taken. "It's possible to abuse and misuse medications without even knowing it," say the authors.

Problems can arise from the use of multiple medications. One of the ways these problems can begin is when each possible medical condition is considered a single problem that requires a single medical solution and each condition is treated by a different physician. If each physician prescribes medication for the singular problem for which he or she was consulted, a patient can end up with a lot of medicine. This can result in one drug being used to treat symptoms that are merely side effects of another drug. This cascade can cause even more health problems and significantly reduce an individual's quality of life. There is also the extra expense of the unneeded drugs themselves.

Seniors often buy over-the-counter remedies. It is only now starting to become widely known and understood that over-the-counter medications can interact or interfere with prescription medications. Additionally, one doctor may prescribe a medication by its brand name; another doctor may use the generic name. These medications will differ in appearance, and many older adults assume that they serve different purposes. Of course, taking both medications puts them at risk for overdose.

One strategy for checking medication is conducting an occasional "brown bag" survey with the primary care physician: throwing all medications into a bag and taking them to the doctor's appointment. List all the prescribed medications, over-the-counter medications and any medications borrowed from family and friends. Explain why the person is taking each medication. Note when and how often the person is supposed to take the medicine and how and where the medications are stored. Note whether the person takes more or less than the recommended or prescribed dosage and whether he or she has experienced any adverse drug reactions.

The doctor can review all prescription drugs, over-the-counter drugs, herbal remedies, vitamins and any other supplements that the individual may be taking. This exercise can help the physician discuss the risks and benefits of the different medications, identify potential problems and recommend the simplest, most appropriate regimen.

Dr. Geri R. Hall, associate clinical professor at the University of Iowa College of Nursing, advises that caregivers and seniors monitoring their own medications should keep the following questions in mind:

- Make sure you have a clear explanation of the purpose of each medication. It is okay to ask "Is this medication necessary?"

- Ask whether a new medication is being started at the lowest dose possible to achieve the required benefit.

- Ask if new medications can be introduced one at a time, if possible, in order to monitor effects more accurately.

- Ask if a new medication is meant to replace another one, so that the former medication should be stopped.

- Ask what are the desired treatment outcomes.

- Ask "How long might it be before we know if this medicine is effective?"

The medications assessment should include questions about the patient:

- What is the older adult's cognitive level (what or how much can he or she understand)?
- What is his or her ability to see and read labels?
- Does the older adult have the strength and muscle coordination to be able to cap and uncap bottles or pour liquid medicine?
- Can she or he swallow without difficulty?

With regard to ending current drug treatments, the caregiver or senior should not hesitate to question whether a drug is still necessary. Appropriate questions would include the following:

- What changes over what period of time can we expect if we end a treatment?
- If there are withdrawal symptoms associated with stopping this drug, how long might they last?
- How will these effects align with our overall treatment goals?

Should we end this drug treatment all at once or gradually?

I also recommend that older persons be seen at least once by a board-certified geriatric physician. The intent of the certification of physicians is to provide assurance that those certified have successfully completed an approved training program and an evaluation process assessing their ability to provide quality patient care in the specialty.

Drug Abuse

Recent studies show that, although we tend to associate drug abuse with young people, a significant number of older people are drug dependent. These seniors may be individuals who drank little or no alcohol in early life and never experimented with drugs. However, changes in health or lifestyle in later years have led them to abuse alcohol or other drugs as a way of managing sleeplessness or chronic pain. Drugs that are frequently abused or misused by older people are anxiety, sedative and antidepressant medications, narcotic analgesics and over-the-counter pain medications such as acetaminophen (Tylenol, for example) and ibuprofen (Motrin, for example). Dependence can occur more quickly than seniors realize, and efforts to discontinue the drug may prompt severe withdrawal symptoms.

When detected soon enough, seniors' drug problems can be treated successfully. In fact, some studies suggest that older adults respond better than younger ones to treatment programs tailored to their needs. Seniors do better in programs with an individual focus, flexible discharge rules and extensive mental health aftercare. It is important for family, friends, pharmacists, doctors and other health care providers to be aware of this possible problem and get their seniors any help they may need.

Drinking Problems

An article by Jane Brody in the *New York Times* is another reminder that even moderate drinking can have serious consequences for seniors. Because the body that is consuming alcohol at age 65 or beyond is not the same as the one that drank at 45, doctors say the effects of a given amount of alcohol can be greatly exaggerated in the older person.

As people age, they lose lean body mass, explained Brody, and acquire a greater percentage of body fat. This results in a decrease in body water. Since alcohol is soluble in water, not fat, a given amount of alcohol reaches higher concentrations in the blood of an older person. As a person ages, tolerance for alcohol declines, and the risks of excessive drinking rise. Blood alcohol levels in older people, said the *Times*, typically are 30 to 40 percent higher than in younger people who consume the same amount of alcohol. But, even at equivalent blood alcohol levels, older people are more likely than a middle-aged person to experience intoxication, cognitive difficulties and problems with balance and coordination.

Problems with balance and coordination? I visit nursing homes often, and I sometimes think that if no one ever fell down, nursing homes would be about half-empty.

Carol Egan, director of older adult services at the Henley-Hazeldon Center in West Palm Beach, Florida, says that although we like to think of Grandma and Grandpa in terms of Norman Rockwell and apple pie, the reality is often darker.

Addressing a Colorado Springs symposium on older adults, alcoholism and substance abuse, Egan said friends, family and physicians often do not pick up on this problem because "Mom and Dad never drank immoderately, and they don't do so now. The bodies of elders, though, metabolize alcohol less efficiently. It doesn't take an increase in drinking to acquire a drinking problem."

Memory loss, disorientation, tremors and depression are often normal to the aging process, and relatives and medical professionals are quick to attribute such symptoms to the onset of Alzheimer's Disease, Parkinson's, or some type of senile dementia. In her address, Egan cited a study by the National Center on Addiction and Substance Abuse at Columbia University. Four hundred primary care doctors were provided with symptoms of early alcohol addiction in senior women. With only the symptoms in hand, 78 percent of those doctors gave a diagnosis of depression. Only four even considered alcoholism.

A similar report by the American Medical Association says that part of the problem is getting doctors to accept that elderly alcoholics exist. The report suggests that doctors may deny that the patient has a drinking problem or be reluctant to make a diagnosis because they are uncertain about how to treat the disease or because they question whether treatment is likely to be successful with this age group. The British Royal College of Physicians suggests that as many as 60 percent of elderly people admitted to hospital because of confusion, repeated falls at home, recurrent chest infections and heart failure may have unrecognized and untreated alcohol problems.

The World Health Organization defines three types of elderly drinkers. Early-onset drinkers are those people who have a continuing problem with alcohol that developed in earlier life; late-onset drinkers are those who begin problematic drinking later in life, often in response to traumatic life events; and intermittent or binge drinkers are those who use alcohol occasionally and sometimes drink to excess, which may cause them problems.

The losses involved in aging, such as retirement, decreased social activity, isolation, loneliness, illness, pain and the death of loved ones, can lead to increased drinking. Families, caregivers and health providers should be alert to this possibility and ready to suggest avenues of help. The abuse of alcohol in conjunction with prescription drugs (which many seniors take in abundance) causes additional problems.

A Healthy Diet Can Reduce Blood Pressure

The foods we choose to eat greatly affect our health. The National Institutes of Health (NIH) recently released the results of a study that found that the combination of reducing sodium levels and following the Dietary Approaches to Stop

Hypertension diet (DASH) reduced blood pressure more than doing either one (the diet or reduced sodium) alone. The combination of the eating plan and a reduced sodium intake may actually help prevent the development of high blood pressure.

For a quick review, remember that blood pressure is the force of blood against artery walls. It is measured in millimeters of mercury and recorded as two numbers—systolic pressure (as the heart beats) over diastolic pressure (as the heart relaxes

Get Off on the Right Foot with a Fitness Program

The American Heart Association has a free 12-week fitness program. You get a workbook in the mail that is meant to help you start exercising, set goals and make healthy eating choices. There are recipes, stretches and activity sheets. See Resources for information on getting a copy.

■ ■ ■

between beats). Both numbers are important. Optimally, in general terms, people 18 years of age and older should have a systolic pressure of 120 and a diastolic pressure of 80. The higher blood pressure rises above optimal, the greater the health risk.

Blood pressure rises and falls during the day, but when it stays elevated over time it is called high blood pressure. High blood pressure is dangerous because it makes the heart work too hard, and the force of its blood flow can harm arteries. High blood pressure often has no warning signs or symptoms. Once it occurs, it usually lasts a lifetime. If uncontrolled, it can lead to heart and kidney disease and stroke.

High blood pressure affects about 50 million Americans—or one in four adults. It is very common among African Americans and older Americans. About 60 percent of those 50 years of age and older have high blood pressure.

The DASH diet had its beginning when scientists supported by the National Heart, Lung and Blood Institute (NHLBI) conducted two key studies. The first tested nutrients as they occurred together in food. This study's findings showed that blood pressures were reduced with an eating plan that is low in saturated fat, cholesterol and total fat, and that emphasizes fruits, vegetables and low-fat dairy foods. The diet also includes whole grain products, fish, poultry and nuts. The study showed that blood pressure reductions came fast—within two weeks of starting the plan.

"The combination of eating the DASH diet at a lower sodium level is a significant effect—equal to or greater than the result you would expect from treatment with a single hypertension medication," says Dr. Frank Sacks, chairman of the DASH-Sodium Steering Committee and associate professor of medicine at Brigham and Women's Hospital and Harvard Medical School. "However, the long-term health benefits of the low sodium DASH diet will depend on whether the American public is willing to make long-lasting dietary changes, including choosing lower sodium foods."

Like every healthy eating plan, the DASH diet is wonderful, but it only works if someone follows it. I am aware, as you are, of exceptions to that general rule. My grandmother, who never drank a drop of alcohol in her life, died of cirrhosis of the liver. No doubt you know people who smoked a pack of cigarettes a day for 50 years and are living well. I know thin people who eat very unhealthy diets and who have lived very long lives. However, by and large, we can make healthier choices and increase our life span and our health.

The DASH Web site suggests some ideas for getting started:

1. Change gradually. If you now eat one or two vegetables a day, add a serving at lunch and another at dinner. If you do not eat fruit now, pick one as a snack. Gradually increase your use of fat-free and low-fat dairy products to three servings a day.

2. Treat meat as only one part of the whole meal, instead of the focus. Include two or more meatless meals each week. Limit meat to six ounces per day (two servings). Three to four ounces of meat is about the size of a deck of cards.

3. Eat fruits or other foods low in saturated fat, cholesterol and calories as desserts and snacks. Use fruits canned in their own juice. Snack on unsalted pretzels, graham crackers, raw vegetables and popcorn with no salt or butter added.

See Resources for additional information about hypertension and DASH.

Vitamins May Reduce Macular Degeneration

Age-related macular degeneration (AMD) is an increasingly frequent tragedy of growing older. Statistics show that 1.7 million Americans age 60 and older have lost part of their vision before they are even aware of this dreaded condition.

A nationwide clinical study shows that a high-dose combination of vitamin C, vitamin E, beta-carotene and zinc, taken daily, can reduce the risk of developing advanced stages of AMD by as much as 25 percent. These supplements are not effective for people with early stages of AMD or for cataracts, but they are believed to slow the progression of AMD.

AMD begins with yellow deposits under the retina which can be detected in an eye exam. Although people with early AMD do not suffer vision loss, those with advanced AMD lose the sharp, central vision required for reading, driving and recognizing the faces of friends. Results of the study, which followed 4,757 participants ages 55 to 80, were published in the October 2001 issue of the journal *Archives of Ophthalmology*.

Daily dosages of the dietary supplements used in the study were 500 milligrams of vitamin C, 400 IUs of vitamin E and 15 milligrams of beta-carotene, all of which are antioxidants. The daily dosage of zinc was 80 milligrams, plus 2 milligrams of copper, which may be depleted by zinc.

Although these supplements are available without prescription, it is absolutely necessary to check with your physician before beginning such a regimen. These levels exceed those recommended by the Food and Drug Administration and might interact negatively with medicines you are already taking.

Arthritis

Dr. Marshall K. Steele of the Anne Arundel Medical Center, Annapolis, Maryland and the Orthopedic and Sports Medicine Center in Bowie, Maryland is a renowned orthopedic surgeon who specializes in the treatment of arthritis. Dr. Steele's top 10 list for dealing with arthritis included make sure you have a proper diagnosis, start an exercise program supervised by a physical therapist and lose weight.

Nearly 40 million people in the United States have arthritis—one in every seven people. It affects people of every age, but most often comes on as a person ages. The word arthritis literally means joint inflammation: "arthr" means joint, and "itis" means inflammation. There are many different types of arthritis and most are chronic—which means they may last a lifetime.

Among the "frequently asked arthritis questions" discussed by Dr. Steele was one that seems to be on everybody's mind these days: What about the effects of diet and/or nutritional supplements on arthritis? Dr. Steele said that although many assertions have been made concerning diet, none are proven except for the relationship between high protein and gout, which can cause arthritis. And, of course, eating too much causes weight gain, which is very bad for joints. As for nutrients, despite many wild claims, there is no evidence that cartilage can be regenerated by taking anything by mouth. However, Dr. Steele said, glucosamine and chondroitin may help to strengthen and protect cartilage that is already damaged.

Another common question revolves around the use of heat and cold in the treatment of arthritic joints. Some people swear by cold, some by heat. Dr. Steele explained that heat increases local circulation in the joint, bringing more blood to the area and making the muscles and other joint structures stretch more easily. Therefore, heat should be used prior to exercise or activity. It improves motion, decreases joint ache and helps you relax. Cold, on the other hand, decreases local circulation and reduces swelling. It should be used on affected joints after exercise. Cold is good for reducing pain and inflammation.

Although exercise may sometimes appear to cause pain, it is very important for arthritis sufferers. According to Dr. Steele, proper exercise will help nourish the cartilage, strengthen the muscles and prolong the life of the joint. Exercise with impact such as running or jumping is not good for joints, but both swimming and walking can be wonderfully helpful. In swimming, the buoyancy protects your joints from impact injury. The water resists movement, which is helpful for strengthening. Just walking in water is extremely beneficial, or you can join a water aerobics class. Walking is also an excellent form of exercise. Dr. Steele stressed that walkers should be sure to warm up and cool down by walking slowly before and at the completion of each walking session.

Researchers at Tufts University have developed a plan for reversing the effects of arthritis. The researchers looked at how strength training and other lifestyle changes may affect the symptoms of arthritis. Dr. Miriam Nelson, the lead researcher, said "Strength training is really important in arthritis."

In fact, a major risk factor for getting arthritis is muscle weakness. The Tufts study included four months of strength training three to four times a week and a diet designed to reduce inflammation. The diet emphasized fruits and vegetables, whole grains and certain types of oils, especially those rich in omega-3 fatty acids.

The results were dramatic. Those who followed the program had 43 percent less pain, 44 percent improved physical function and 71 percent improved strength. Researchers claim results show that this type of program will reverse the disease and the symptoms of the disease so that patients can function much better in their environment.

See the Resources section for more information on arthritis.

Heart Disease and Women

The U.S. Centers for Disease Control and Prevention (CDC) recently said that while women continue to have greater life expectancy than men, that gap is narrowing. Currently, a woman at age 50 has a life expectancy of 81.8 years, compared to

77.9 for men the same age. For women who are 65 today, life expectancy is 84.2 years compared to 81.3 for men.

Many people probably do not fully appreciate the startling impact of women's heart disease. Forty-one percent of all women die from cardiovascular disease. Women are ten times more likely to die from heart disease than from breast cancer. More women than men die from heart disease. A woman is nearly twice as likely as a man to die from a first heart attack. A woman's cardiac symptoms may be different from a man's. If you are a woman, you may want to pick up *How to Keep From Breaking Your Heart: What Every Woman Needs to Know about Cardiovascular Disease* by Barbara H. Roberts, M.D.

Dr. Roberts is director of the Women's Cardiac Center at the Miriam Hospital and associate clinical professor of medicine for the Brown University Program in Medicine, Rhode Island. The Miriam Center is devoted to the diagnosis, treatment and prevention of cardiovascular disease in women.

Her book is divided into three fascinating parts. Part one discusses cardiac risk factors and what a patient can do if she has them. Part two discusses new treatments for heart disease risk factors and heart disease itself and part three contains interesting facts about the past and future of medicine and, perhaps most important, advice on finding a doctor you can trust. The book is not a heavy medical textbook. It is reasonably short and easy to read, with plenty of food for thought and recommendations that are simple to follow.

See Resources for related information.

Laughter: The Best Medicine?

Thinking about that reminds me of the famous Abe Lincoln quote, "Most folks are about as happy as they make up their minds to be." I know this life is not always perfect, but it is definitely all we have for the present, so we might as well make up our minds to be happy. One day, we will probably look back on these as the "good old days."

Laughter has many positive physical benefits. Research published in various places seems to indicate that good, hearty laughter increases the release of endorphins in our brains. Endorphins are the body's natural pain killers. Michael Brickey, a board-certified psychologist, maintains a Web site called The Ageless Lifestyles Institute. He recently devoted some space to the effect of laughter on our sense of well-being. Our brain, he said, is like a muscle and, like all the muscles in our body, if we do not use it, we lose it. Humor is one of the most intellectually complex things we do, he said— and here is how he explained it: "To appreciate humor requires a good understanding of both the

Attitude Matters

The New England Journal of Medicine *recently reported results of a study about knee surgery. Researchers divided 180 people who had osteoarthritis knee pain into three groups. Two groups had arthroscopic surgery that uses miniature tools to wash or clean out the knee. People in the third group were led to believe they had surgery, but actually they just had tiny incisions made on their knees. All participants reported less pain and more function during two-year follow-ups. The study concluded, "Our study shows that the surgery is not better than the placebo." Doctors feel that improvements resulted from "patient expectations that surgery would make them better." It seems to go back to "mind over matter."*

■ ■ ■

culture and the language. Telling a joke also requires memory, timing, acting skills and a good sense of what is appropriate."

Other points he made were that laughing relaxes and tenses our muscles, giving us a mini workout. It gets our mind temporarily off problems and physical pain. Humor helps us turn past blunders and embarrassments into a good laugh. Laughter increases our alertness and helps us to not take ourselves and our problems too seriously. Best of all, says Brickey, it is free.

How can we make ourselves laugh more? Brickey suggests that you challenge yourself to tell a joke or share some humor with someone every day. Consider a dinnertime tradition of having family members share something humorous. We can look at one cartoon a day— and on the Internet you can have a daily joke sent to you.

The Association for Applied and Therapeutic Humor (AATH) is committed to advancing its knowledge and understanding of humor and laughter as they relate to healing and well-being. The AATH maintains a Web site that provides links to related resources and information about its annual conference.

Speaker and writer Patty Wooten is a proponent of laughter in managed health care settings, such as nursing homes. "Humor," she writes, "is a complex phenomena that is an essential part of human nature. Throughout the ages, anthropologists have never found a culture or society that was completely devoid of humor. A sense of humor is both a perspective on life—a way of perceiving the world—and a behavior that expresses that perspective. It is a quality of perception that enables us to experience joy even when faced with adversity, and to fully experience the joy that humor can bring we must share that perspective with others and join together in the laughter."

Wooten's Web site is very informative, and she provides a large amount of information regarding therapeutic humor for patients.

Barry Sultanoff, M.D., president of the American Holistic Medical Association, has written, "Laughing together can be a time of intimacy and communion, a time when we come forward, fully present, and touch into each other's humanness and vulnerability. By joining in humor and acknowledging our oneness, we can have a profound experience of unity and cooperation. That in itself maybe one of the most profound expressions of healing energy of which we are capable."

Steven M. Sultanoff, a Pepperdine University professor, has appeared on various PBS TV specials and on the Lifetime cable channel discussing such topics as " humor in the workplace" and "humor as an antidote to stress." Professor Sultanoff's work is to help people realize how humor influences health, reduces stress, provides perspective, improves communication, energizes, enhances relationships and generally makes people feel better."

Once again, it looks like it was said first in the Bible: "A merry heart doeth good—like medicine."

See the Resources section for humor-related resources.

Memory and Aging

Types of Memory Impairment

After age 50 the brain starts to shrink, and mental function declines. However, the severity and rate of the mental function decline will vary greatly from person to person. There are different stages of brain aging.

The first is age-associated memory impairment. This consists of occasional forgetfulness, primarily of new information such as

You can improve your memory and increase its efficiency. Dr. Barry Gordon, in his book *Memory: Remembering and Forgetting in Everyday Life,* offers the following tips:

1. Get a medical tune-up: deal with matters related to blood pressure, thyroid malfunctions, types of medication, depression, sleep, alcohol abuse, and vision and hearing impairments.

2. Exercise daily.

3. Pay attention to little things. For example, make a special note where you leave the car in the parking lot.

4. Repeat to yourself what you want to remember.

5. Use to-do lists, calendars, timers, Post-its™ and beeper alarms.

6. Ask your spouse or a friend to jog your memory.

7. Be consistent. Put things back in the same place all the time.

8. Associate what you want to remember with what you already know. A friend reminded me of an old trick: move your wedding ring to your right hand to jog your memory when you must remember something. If you do not want to change your ring, move something else from its usual position or put a rubber band on your right arm to trigger your memory.

■ ■ ■

names of people you recently met. This is considered a normal response to aging.

Second is mild cognitive impairment (MCI). MCI is manifested by severe or frequent memory lapses, such as repeatedly missing appointments, but no other mental impairment. Sadly, almost half of the people diagnosed with MCI develop Alzheimer's within three years.

Dementia, the third state, is manifested by severe cognitive decline marked by large memory deficits. Dementia is not a disease, but a symptom of a number of diseases, including stroke, substance abuse, head trauma and Alzheimer's disease.

Last, of course, is Alzheimer's disease, a progressive brain disease that initially causes mild memory loss and eventually destroys all cognitive functions, leading to death. Alzheimer's disease is responsible for about 50 percent of all dementia cases.

Remember, neurologists are increasingly recommending exercise and a healthy diet as key ways to stay mentally and physically fit. Lifelong learning, continuing social engagement and regular mental challenges can go a long way toward holding at bay the mental decline of aging. See Resources for more information on memory and dementia.

Strategies to Improve Memory

By refreshing one's use of these common memory strategies, Gordon says that older adults can work wonders in offsetting normal age-related memory skill loss.

1. *Pay attention.* Developing the habit of actively paying attention will relieve a lot of frustration. Your memory ability may be fine, but you may allow your mind to be on something else at crucial times. Stop. Look. Listen. It takes no more than a second to say to yourself, "My car is in lot A, row 5."

2. *Rehearse and repeat.* Information must be rehearsed to be placed properly in your long-term memory. Example: You are in the shower when you get an idea you wish to discuss with your spouse. You cannot make a note, and you do not want to forget that great idea. What should you do? You must rehearse by repeating to yourself the idea that you will discuss with your spouse.

3. *Chunk.* This is a rehearsal strategy. Most people have the ability to remember short lists such as in a phone number if they group, or chunk, the list items. Chunking will aid working memory. A 10-digit number such as 3013661755 can be remembered easily as 301, then 366, then 1755. Three chunks, not ten numbers.

4. *Use cues.* Two strategies can be used here. Visual elaboration is simply creating a mental snapshot to enhance a memory. Example: You are away from home and think of a phone call you should make when you return home. In addition to rehearsal, you can create a visual image. The visual image should be associated with a very familiar object. You may visualize a telephone hanging on your front door. When you see your front door, the sight will remind you of the need to make the call.

The second strategy is verbal elaboration, a simple and effective memory exercise for conceptual and abstract information. Some of the verbal elaborations you have been using throughout your life include acronyms, word associations and rhymes—PTA, "Spring forward, fall back" and "Thirty days has September."

5. *Get organized.* Once you have established fixed locations for medications, important phone numbers, valuable papers, useful tools, keys, wallets and glasses, you will minimize frustrating searches for a misplaced item. You can organize your medication needs by time and place to be taken. Medications taken before, with or after meals can usually be stored in the kitchen. Remember to plan for times you are not eating at home. Other medications such as eye drops, lotions and ointments located in other places in your home should be organized as well.

6. *Increase your use of external aids.* Keep all emergency and prospective information as visible as you can—appointment books, memo pads, things to be taken with you the next time you leave the house, etc. These aids will not help you if they are not in appropriate and easily accessible places. Also, use symbolic reminders—some version of the string around your finger. Use your imagination and invent some new memory aids.

7. *Mind your PQRST.* A five-step memory and learning exercise will help you organize text material written with too much fine print. Examples include automatic teller machines, programming a VCR, reading a new insurance policy or understanding the regulations of your IRAs or a pension fund. P stands for preview—skim the text to identify the main points. Q suggests that you create questions that identify the essential points you want to learn. R indicates rereading the material to be able to answer your previously generated questions. S requires that you study and understand the answers to the questions raised concerning the central ideas. T is to test yourself to be sure you understand the answers. For example, you want to program your new VCR, even though at first glance the directions seem written in a foreign language. Use PQRST. Reread and study the instructions until you feel you can perform the task. Test yourself by taping a program. With this method, it really is simple.

Program Helps Slow MCI

How are you with brain exercises? Would you quickly pick up that "DOCTOR DOCTOR" means paradox? That is just a sampling of the challenging brainteasers I tackled during a seminar about mild cognitive impairment (MCI). The seminar was conducted by Joyce Simard, a nationally known speaker, educator and geriatric consultant. Simard worked for such well-known folks as Manor Care and Marriott Senior Living before starting her own business.

MCI is a condition characterized by short-term memory loss and certain memory deficits, but not dementia. Simard said that people affected by MCI experience forgetfulness beyond what is normal for age and education but do not exhibit symptoms of dementia associated with Alzheimer's disease or other dementia illnesses.

In distinguishing MCI from normal forgetfulness, she said that normal memory losses associated with aging are characterized by momentary lapses, such as misplacing an item, forgetting someone's name or forgetting something on a grocery list. Memory loss associated with MCI is a more persistent and troublesome problem. People with MCI have much greater difficulty remembering a fact after a relatively short time, and they are likely to forget important dates and events repeatedly, while those with normal aging are able to retain significant information.

She pointed out several differences between MCI and Alzheimer's disease. She said that Alzheimer's disease invariably results in a gradual decline, eventually progressing to severe, debilitating dementia. However, not everyone with MCI will get worse, although many will. About 14 percent of people with MCI develop Alzheimer's each year. She stressed that family and caregivers treat each situation differently. With MCI we push reality, but in Alzheimer's, we "join them in their journey."

MCI is sometimes thought of as a transitional state between normal aging and dementia, "the in-betweeners," as Simard refers to them. A significant number of members of the medical and health provider professions believe that accurate and early evaluation and treatment of individuals with MCI might delay or prevent further cognitive decline, including development of Alzheimer's. With those ideas in mind, she developed the new Memory Enhancement Program.

Program participants are residents in assisted living situations who are showing signs of significant memory loss, but who are not yet ready for the structured environment of a secured special needs unit. The main goal of the program is to slow the progression of memory impairment. The program includes working with medical professionals to establish a beginning baseline of the resident's cognitive functioning level. Then an individualized plan is developed for each participant that includes components such as medication administration, education and information about memory-related drugs, a personal journal to record daily activities and personal thoughts and a personal calendar for key dates, events and physicians appointments.

Program participants will also receive a diet rich in brain-stimulating foods containing antioxidants. The seminar information packet included a press release from the National Institutes of Health about studies showing the benefits of eating those particular foods, especially blueberries, strawberries and spinach. In studies on rats, those with blueberry supplements came out on top in tests of balance and coordination. The group of animals that received eight-week-long diet supplements with fruit or vegetable extracts showed some improvement on key indicators of age-related decline. Further studies are needed to determine whether such a diet benefits humans and whether the positive effects are long-lasting.

Simard said we should avoid pressuring ourselves when we forget something. Although forgetting important things is frustrating, worrying about it can make it worse. Everyone should attempt to retain a sense of humor and a positive attitude. Additionally, it is important to wear your glasses and/or hearing aids so you can see or hear information clearly.

See Resources for Joyce Simard's Web site.

Dementia

What If It's Not Alzheimer's? A Caregiver's Guide to Dementia, edited by Lisa and Gary Radin, is a helpful book for those dealing with dementia. Lisa Radin and her son provided complete care for husband and father Neil Radin over a four-year period, and from that experience came their book.

Although the Radins are not physicians, other contributors to the book are specialists in their fields or have exceptional hands-on experience with dementia sufferers. As the book says, it was not that long ago that all dementia was considered a natural part of aging—in fact, nearly all dementias were lumped into a category broadly called senile dementia. Since then we have heard a lot about Alzheimer's disease, and now any time an older individual misplaces car keys or forgets an appointment, family members "are quick to conclude that their loved one is in the throes of Alzheimer's disease"—oftentimes not correctly.

As a matter of fact, the medical profession now distinguishes various types of dementias that also undermine cognitive abilities, and many of them are not associated at all with aging. One of these is called frontotemporal dementia (FTD). It was the dementia Neil Radin had. It is one of the largest groups of non-Alzheimer's dementias.

The book is divided into four major parts. Beginning with a discussion of the medical facts, part one defines and explores

FTD as an illness distinct from Alzheimer's disease. Part two focuses on managing care and daily routines, including nutrition, exercise, socialization, adapting the home environment and behavioral issues. Part three centers on caregiver resources, and the contributors identify professional and government assistance programs along with private resources and legal options. Part four stresses the need for caregivers to take care of themselves as well as their loved ones.

At the end of the Radins' book, several pages list helpful resources for information on adapting the home's environment, eating utensils and food thickeners, elder law attorneys, medical centers and organizations, Web sites and books. See the Resources section of this chapter for more FTD and dementia information.

Basic Memory Impairment

The brain's ability to store knowledge is still considered to be vast, although it is unclear exactly how vast. According to a study done in France, it is estimated that if we were fed 10 items of data every second for 100 years, it would only take up one-tenth of our brain's storage capacity. I guess we can think of our brains as vast computers with unlimited memory.

So, the problem associated with sensory and memory overload is not actually memory, but loss of focus. The more things we have to remember, the more likely it is that some will be forgotten. It's difficult to focus on each one individually with so many items of information cluttering our brains. "Activating memory requires concentration and practice," says Gordon Logan, a psychologist at Vanderbilt University in Nashville, Tennessee. "If your life is busy, applying steady concentration becomes challenging."

You are probably familiar with studies indicating that the time of day can strongly influence how well we are able to focus, and how well we are able to remember. Lynn Hasher, a professor of psychology at the University of Toronto, has found that adults older than 60 are generally much sharper in the early morning hours, but their attentions drift by the afternoon. Students in their 20s, says Hasher, appear to operate on a reverse clock and are highly distracted in the morning, but better focused in the afternoon. Even now, educators are finding that high school students learn better and retain information longer when their classes begin just one hour later in the morning.

Memory is divided into many types. Semantic memory is general knowledge, e.g., names of movies, authors of books, etc. Episodic memory includes recollections of personal experiences like how we spent last summer. Procedural memory is the more automatic how-to memory, such as knowing how to drive.

Studies have shown that it's usually semantic and episodic memories that are first affected by age and disease. Suggestions to help personal memory power include limiting drinking and smoking. Both habits degrade memory over time. Try associating new information with facts, songs, names or other things you already know. Memory sticks best, experts say, when it's encoded with existing memories. Focus and practice. Adding information to your mind in smaller bundles appears to be more effective than loading it up with lots of information at once.

Coping with an Alzheimer's Diagnosis

Sadly, there is no cure and, for now, no prevention for Alzheimer's disease. The Alzheimer's Association and other organizations, however, provide wonderful information and support for those with this disease and their families. They can help make coping with an Alzheimer's diagnosis easier.

First, learn all you can about Alzheimer's. Education empowers us, providing tools that help us contend with the slings and arrows of our daily lives. A good place to start, if you have access to the Internet, is to enter "Alzheimer's disease" in a search engine like Google or Ask Jeeves. You will receive a list of enough information to last you for a month of Web surfing. If you do not have access to a computer, the local library is a wonderful source for research. The librarians will have suggestions for where to start. The Alzheimer's Association also has information regarding local support groups.

You do not need to deal with this alone. Tell family and friends how they can help. Be honest. Be specific. Be appreciative. Furthermore, maintain those friendships that are satisfying and comforting and that are meaningful. You do not

Eating Right May Reduce Chances of Alzheimer's

Dr. Steven T. DeKosky, chair of the University of Pittsburgh's Alzheimer's Disease Center, outlined a hypothetical preventive regimen for Alzheimer's disease based on current promising lines of research. It included a daily dose of a multivitamin that includes folic acid; a B vitamin; antioxidants such as vitamin E; anti-inflammatory drugs such as ibuprofen; a low-fat, low-cholesterol diet that includes salmon, mackerel or some other fish high in omega-3 fatty acids; regular mental and physical activity; and aggressive and early treatment of hypertension, high cholesterol and other cardiovascular conditions. This regimen has not been shown to prevent Alzheimer's disease, but the research looks encouraging.

■ ■ ■

need demanding or judgmental friends. This is time to let them go.

Take care of your health. Do not put off needed medical care. Like everyone else, you need a nutritious diet, good rest and moderate exercise.

Try to accept feelings of sadness and anger without guilt. Feelings are not deeds, and you should not criticize yourself. Anyone would feel angry and sad confronting such a diagnosis. If you are able to, talk about those feelings with someone who will listen supportively and with sympathy.

Try to be realistic about what you can do. Decisions must always be based on your changing needs. It is difficult to find the thin line between trying to do too much and not trying to do anything at all. You do not want to overdose on the former, but you should not allow yourself to succumb to the latter. Remember that family members also may be confused about this issue, and sometimes do not know how to be helpful—whether you need encouragement from the sidelines or just a hug.

Do not hide. This is a disease, not a crime. Continue all the activities you love as long as you are able to do so.

Humorous things will happen. Greeting these with a laugh and maintaining your sense of humor as much as possible will be incredibly helpful. Laughter itself has a basic health benefit in that it increases our sense of well-being. All of us should laugh more.

Keep a journal. Research has shown that journaling is very effective for sorting out your feelings and coping with them. It also gives you a way to organize your thoughts and to keep track of changes.

Always maintain hope. Miracles can happen. Someone said, "I don't just believe in miracles. I expect them." Try to do the same. In my lifetime, the polio vaccine seemed to come suddenly, out of nowhere—and millions of children stopped dying from that dreaded disease. In this world, anything can happen.

After a diagnosis of Alzheimer's you may worry about the impact the disease will have on you and your family. Planning ahead is one way to deal with those fears. By participating in decisions now, you can determine the kind of life you want for the years ahead. You may be able to live independently and safely for some time on your own or with the help of a family member or hired caregiver. As Alzheimer's progresses, there may come a time when your daily care will require the skills of a health care staff. To make sure that your needs and preferences for care are understood, talk about the options available to you with a family member or trusted friend. The sooner you do this, the more likely you are to find those options with services you prefer.

Cost is always an issue. You may be worried about the cost of your future care and if you will have enough money to cover these costs. Discussing your immediate and future financial needs and goals will help protect you, the people who depend on you financially and the people who will care for you.

It is important to obtain legal advice and services. Take

Alzheimer's Screening

The Web site of the Medical Care Corporation offers a screening test for Alzheimer's disease. The test ends up costing some money, but you can gather a lot of information before you reach that point. The site says that Alzheimer's disease begins in the brain 30 years before the first symptoms appear and that people 40 years of age and older should take the screening test annually. See Resources for a link.

■ ■ ■

a family member or friend with you when you see your attorney, and make sure the attorney is familiar with issues surrounding Alzheimer's disease. Free legal advice may be available from the Legal Aid Bureau, the Area Agency on Aging or the Law Foundation. For Alzheimer's organizations and information, see the Resources section.

Communicating with Alzheimer's Patients

Talking to Alzheimer's by Claudia J. Strauss is a useful book for those with a loved one who has the disease. I have noticed that many of us seem to have this one thing in common—we are uncomfortable and unsure about what to say when we must interact with someone who has dementia or Alzheimer's disease. This book gives extremely practical information about what to say and, perhaps more important, how to respond to the questions nearly every patient asks—sometimes repeatedly. The book is full of examples of what to do and say, and what not to do and say.

I have observed that friends and relatives will tend to quit visiting family members with dementia because with each visit they are faced with the tearing down of identity and the terrible wastefulness of the disease. They become frustrated by attempts to communicate in any meaningful way. Betty Ransom, director of education and training for the National Capital Area Alzheimer's Association Chapter, says, "Visiting is clearly recognized as an issue...and some families become so disappointed and disheartened that they stop coming. This targeted, doable book helps people come to terms with what they can really do."

One of the most useful things about this very practical book is an index telling you where to look for answers to things patients with this disease often say. For example, if your loved one pleads, "Please take me home with you. I want to go home," the book provides a discussion about what to say in response. Some examples of similar comments from Alzheimer's or dementia patients include "Is that the door? Can you unlock it?" "Who are you?" and "I want to call my parents so they can pick me up."

Ms. Strauss's book is organized helpfully. It does not appear to be designed for reading cover to cover, but for picking up as a reference. The author is aware that families and loved ones of patients with dementia are perplexed about many things before, during and after a visit. She walks the reader through each situation, suggesting helpful coping mechanisms and constructive ways of helping our loved ones maintain dignity and receive respect. She believes that even though these diseases are traumatic for everyone involved, there is a "continuing potential for mutually rich relationships." Strauss's compassionate caring is evident throughout the entire book. Her resources section lists books for adults, books for adolescents and books for young children who are trying to cope with Alzheimer's disease in a loved one. It lists Web sites as well.

See Resources for more information.

Medicare, Medicaid and Other Insurance Options

What Is Medicare?

Medicare is a federal insurance program which pays medical bills for insured persons with money from the Social Security Trust Fund. Medicare is for almost everybody who is age 65 or older, whether or not they are rich or poor. It also helps some disabled persons who are under age 65 and certain other persons with kidney failure. Medicare pays for nursing home services only under very limited circumstances. A Medicare card is usually good for a lifetime after you become insured.

Right now, Medicare is the country's only national health insurance program. Individuals entitled to Social Security retirement insurance who are 65 years of age or older and individuals entitled to Social Security disability benefits for no less than 24 months are eligible to participate in Medicare. Persons entitled to Railroad Retirement benefits or Railroad Disability benefits and individuals suffering from end-stage renal disease are also entitled to participate. Furthermore, anyone not otherwise eligible for the program, but who is over age 65, may purchase coverage by paying a monthly premium.

Since the 1980s, most federal employees may count their government work toward eligibility for the Medicare hospital insurance program (Medicare Part A).

Passed in 1965, as Title 18 of the Social Security Act, and part of President Lyndon Johnson's Great Society, Medicare was intended to pay some of the cost of some health care services in order to ensure access to a basic level of health care for the aged. Medicare was always intended as a health insurance program. It was, and continues to be, based upon a private health insurance model. Medicare requires deductibles and co-payments by the insured, and it pays only a portion of the cost of certain services for certain patients. Claims must be submitted to an insurance company or other entity for approval prior to payment and payments are usually made directly to the health care provider.

The Medicare Act allows for coverage when the services received are medically "reasonable and necessary for the diagnosis or treatment of illness or injury or to improve the functioning of a malformed body member." Medicare coverage is excluded, by statute, for custodial care, except in the case of hospice services. To clarify in plain language, Medicare rarely if ever pays for long-term nursing home care. The requirements of the law, that the care be medically reasonable and necessary for treatment or diagnosis, and that the care be "skilled" are interpreted very strictly by those who administer the Medicare program. These strictly interpreted requirements create the most frequent obstacles to coverage under this program.

Under Medicare Part A, a beneficiary is entitled to 90 days of Medicare coverage for hospital care during each benefit period or "spell of illness" after the beneficiary meets the deductible ($840 in 2003.) In addition, the beneficiary is entitled to 60 days of hospital care as a "lifetime reserve." Once exhausted, lifetime reserve days may not be replenished.

Major benefits under Medicare Part B include payment for physician's services, durable medical equipment, outpatient therapy, diagnostic x-rays and laboratory tests. Part B is optional. Since 1973, individuals entitled to Medicare Part A are automatically enrolled in Part B unless they decline coverage.

This brief clarification should give you some basics useful for comparison when you hear about new plans or proposals for Medicare. This information occasionally seems boring, but it is not boring when you are the person arguing with Medicare over the payment of a medical bill.

See the Resources section of this chapter for more information on Medicare.

Medicare Covers Preventive Care

Medicare is paying for more preventive benefits these days. It will pay for annual mammograms for female beneficiaries age

40 and over. The Part B annual deductible is waived for these services. Also, Medicare pays for one pelvic exam (including a clinical breast exam) and Pap test every two years. Women at high risk for cervical cancer can have these tests covered on an annual basis. Medicare will provide coverage for home blood glucose monitors and testing strips for all diabetic beneficiaries without regard to a person's use of insulin.

Medicare pays for an annual prostate cancer screening test for men over age 50. Medicare also pays for glaucoma screening for people at risk of glaucoma (those with a family history of glaucoma or with diabetes) and for medical nutrition therapy services for patients with diabetes or kidney disease. Nutrition therapy payments are for a registered dietician or nutrition professional. Deductible and co-insurance rules apply to this service.

What Is Medicaid?

The Medicaid program was established in 1965 as a federal-state partnership to help needy individuals obtain medical care. Like Medicare, it was one of President Johnson's Great Society programs and part of the antipoverty program enacted during those years. The program encouraged all states, even poor ones, to offer basic medical assistance through the new program. The intent was to make coverage available to a greater number of individuals.

Medicaid started out as a welfare program linked to other federal cash assistance programs. In 1996, changes in the welfare laws separated Medicaid from cash assistance welfare programs for families with children. The Supplemental Security Income Program (SSI), which provides cash assistance for the elderly and disabled, is still connected to the Medicaid program in most states. Eligibility for Medicaid is still largely based on federal law, although as state budgets get tighter, more and more states are proposing and adopting tighter restrictions for eligibility.

Medicaid is the only program that can, under some circumstances, provide coverage for benefits not covered under Medicare, the non-needs-based federal health program. Medicaid includes benefits such as prescription drugs, optometry, podiatry, and long-term care, if the individual's ailment or disability warrants such services. Medicaid is sometimes called Title 19 (it was established under Title XIX of the 1995 Social Security Act). In California, it is called Medi-Cal.

Medicaid is both a federal and state program. Each state has its own Medicaid laws and regulations, which are usually part of the state welfare code, and the programs vary considerably from state to state. Be aware that the rules are very complicated, and often change. The Centers for Medicare and Medicaid Services (CMS) maintains a Web site containing state laws, regulations, the state Medicaid manuals and other resources.

Maryland Medicaid Eligibility Requirements

The Maryland State Medicaid Manual fills two very thick three-ring binders, and the rules and interpretations are constantly changing. But, generally, if you are a U.S. citizen, and at least 65 years of age or if you are disabled, eligibility for Medicaid is based on two criteria: Financial (Income, Resources, and Asset Transfers), and Medical.

Income eligibility requires that the Medicaid applicant's available income (after allowable deductions) must be less than the cost of care at the nursing home. The rule for nursing home residents regarding income is that they must pay all of their income, minus certain deductions, to the nursing home once they have qualified for Medicaid. The deductions include a personal needs allowance, a deduction for medical insurance premiums (such as Medicare), and if the applicant is married, an allowance for the spouse living at home if he or she needs income support. A deduction may also be allowed if there are certain dependent family members living at home.

Resource eligibility requires, generally, that the applicant may have no more than the state's resource allowance for an individual ($2,500 in 2004) as of the date of application. If the nursing home resident is married, the countable assets of both the community spouse (or the well spouse) and the institution-alized spouse are totaled as of the day the ill spouse enters the nursing home, as long as the stay is at least 30 days. It does not matter in which spouse's name the assets are titled as of this date. All of the assets could be titled in the name of the community spouse, but one-half of these assets are still attributed to the institutionalized spouse simply because the couple is married. Once the assets are divided, the institutionalized spouse's "one-half" is often considered the spend-down. The community spouse may keep up to one-half of the couple's total "countable" assets, but his or her one-half may not exceed the maximum community spouse resource allowance ($92,760 in 2004). The state also provides a minimum community spouse resource allowance ($18,552 in 2004), meaning that if the couple's assets do not exceed the minimum resource allowance, then the community spouse will be allowed to maintain those assets with no spend-down required.

Asset transfers are to be considered when determining financial eligibility because of the penalty assessed when assets are transferred or given away for less than their fair market value. Because the government does not want you to give all your money away and then apply for Medicaid, Congress has imposed a penalty for transferring assets without receiving fair market value in return. This penalty is not a monetary penalty, but a period of time during which the person transferring the assets will be ineligible to receive Medicaid. Transfers made during the 36-month period preceding the application for Medicaid (or 60 months if the transfer is made to certain types of trusts) may be subject to penalty. This 36-month period is often called the "look-back" period, and all assets that were held during this period of time must be disclosed during the Medicaid application process so that the case worker can determine eligibility. It is important to keep in mind that if any substantial transfers of assets are made within the 36-month period prior to the Medicaid application, Medicaid eligibility could be delayed.

And, last but not least, *medical eligibility* requires that the Medicaid applicant must need, at a minimum, health-related services above the level of room and board that can be made available only through institutional facilities. These "medically needy" criteria are being reviewed ever more closely by the state as they deal with tight budgets. The Delmarva Foundation, through a contract with the State of Maryland, reviews the information submitted by the provider to make a level of care determination for Medical Assistance applicants. Delmarva reviews the type of care needed and provided, and makes a decision about the level of care actually required. Simply, if Delmarva determines that the applicant needs less than "skilled nursing facility care, under the supervision of a licensed medical professional" then Medicaid will be denied.

Income of the Community Spouse—State of Maryland

The Medicaid law provides special protections for the spouse of a nursing home resident to make sure that spouse has the minimum support needed to continue to live in the community. One way that the law does this is by not considering the spouse's income as a factor for Medicaid eligibility.

That's right! If you are the Medicaid applicant and you are married, the income of your spouse (i.e., community spouse) is *not* counted when determining your eligibility to receive Medicaid benefits. Only your income is counted in determining Medicaid eligibility.

This means that even if the community spouse is earning $6,000 a month, not one penny of his or her income has to be contributed to the cost of caring for the spouse in the nursing home as long as that institutionalized spouse has qualified, and remains eligible to receive Medicaid.

Unfortunately, it is often the case that most of the couple's income is in the name of the institutionalized spouse, leaving the community spouse with a limited income that is not enough to support his or her needs.   In this case, federal law provides the spouse of the applicant a Monthly Maintenance Needs Allowance (MMNA) in order for that spouse to live in the community.   The amount of this allowance is based on the community spouse's sole income and the amount in living expenses the community spouse must pay (i.e., mortgage, heat, electricity, water, sewage, etc.).

Medicaid and Your Home in Maryland

If you need Medicaid to pay for nursing home care, probably the main question keeping you awake at night is "Will the nursing home or the state take my house?"   If you are the Medicaid applicant, your home is considered exempt, whatever its value, if your spouse or certain dependent or disabled relatives live there with you.   Your home may also be exempt for six months, no matter who lives there, if you check the box on your Medicaid application that says you intend to return to it—even if it is unlikely that you will return.

For some people, owning a house presents a Medicaid eligibility challenge. Some may have to sell the house in order to pay for nursing home care, others may have to transfer title to a family member, but in no case does the state "take" the house.

In fact, the most the state will do is put a lien on the house. The state may impose liens against real property of institutionalized Medicaid recipients during their lifetime, but only under certain conditions. First of all, the state has the burden of proving, after notice and a hearing, that the institutionalized individual cannot reasonably be expected to return home from the institution. If your home was excluded as a countable resource because you said you intended to return home, Medicaid may place a lien on it, unless you can prove it is medically reasonable that you will return home.

When the property is sold or if you die, the state will usually attempt to collect on its lien. The amount collected will not exceed (1) the net proceeds from the sale of the property or (2) the amount paid by the state toward your long-term care (whichever is less).

The state may not place a lien on your home if it is lived in by certain individuals, for example your spouse, your unmarried child who is under 21, or your blind or disabled child of any age.

Medicaid Myths Debunked (with thanks to Charlie Sabatino, ABA commission on law and the elderly)

Myth One: "Medicaid planning is the fraudulent sheltering of assets done to help people become eligible for Medicaid." In reality, Medicaid planning is legal and accepted under federal law. It is not fraudulent or illegal. The term "Medicaid planning" describes legal changes in one's estate plan, one goal of which may be to obtain or preserve Medicaid coverage. Transferring assets to other family members may be one aspect of planning, but not the most common. According to a 1993 General Accounting Office (GAO) study, a more common planning step is to fix up or improve assets, such as one's home, that are already exempt under Medicaid law.

The GAO study of practices in Massachusetts (a state with a reputation for a high level of Medicaid planning) revealed that about 90 percent of Medicaid planning involved merely the conversion of countable assets into exempt assets—most typically setting aside money for burial arrangements, making home repairs or purchasing an automobile. These asset conversions trigger no penalty period whatsoever.

Where countable assets are transferred under certain circumstances, federal law imposes a penalty in the form of a period of disqualification under Medicaid. Penalties are imposed under federal law in other contexts, too. For example, you are penalized under federal tax law for early withdrawals of money from Individual Retirement Accounts (IRAs) or 401k plans. The existence of a penalty does not make the transaction illegal.

In the right hands, Medicaid planning should be part of a larger process that examines the full range of long-term care options, issues and costs relevant to the client's circumstances. It includes pursuing the goals of preserving and promoting the individual's dignity, self-determination and quality of life as they age, and it respects the individual's fundamental values and preferences as self-defined.

Myth Two: "Gaming the system to get Medicaid coverage of nursing home care is widespread." The reality is that the only really widespread activity is informal unpaid family caregiving of individuals needing long-term care. Families are the bedrock of the long-term care system. Of the people with long-term care needs, 83 percent live at home and 75 percent receive care solely from unpaid caregivers like family and friends. The number rises to 93 percent when you include those who receive both paid and unpaid caregiving in the community. Most families seek Medicaid eligibility only after they have become worn out from informal caregiving. And even after Medicaid is helping to pay costs, spouses and adult children continue to provide unpaid care. Additionally, fewer than 4.2 percent of seniors receive care in nursing homes at any one time, and seniors overwhelmingly prefer to be in home- and community-based settings, not in nursing homes.

NAELA (National Academy of Elder Law Attorneys) conducted a poll of members during 2003. Seventy-seven percent of respondents reported that transfers of assets that could result in a penalty period were used in half or fewer of their cases. The GAO study in 1993 found that only about 10 percent of the total cases they reviewed involved asset transfers, typically to family members, and these transfers averaged $46,000 with one in every three transfers less than $10,000. Whether the purpose is giving a legacy to family members, or helping loved ones meet expenses for housing, school or other needs, these are reasonable family transactions affecting modest middle-class families.

Myth Three: "Elder law attorneys help rich people get Medicaid." The rich have no need to rely on Medicaid, nor would they want to. Medicaid is a valuable program, but there are many disadvantages to relying on Medicaid—such as limitations in access to health care providers, limitations in coverage, exposure to recovery against one's estate after death and state-by-state variations in eligibility and coverage. Elder law attorneys help individuals understand the pros and cons of all the legal options available to them.

No one yearns to be on a program like Medicaid. Seniors engage in Medicaid planning mainly because they find themselves in a lose-lose corner. First they lose their health, and then they learn that they will have to lose virtually their entire estate to pay for their care.

Seniors are willing to pay their fair share, as they already do under Medicare. However, paying 100 percent out-of-pocket until they reach Medicaid's definition of impoverishment is not a fair share. Congress created a partial remedy to this harsh result by allowing people to protect part of their estate if they are willing to pay the penalty of non-eligibility for a period of time.

Myth Four: "Asset transfers result in huge additional costs to the Medicaid program." The reality is that it is very difficult to quantify the extent of asset transfers made in connection with Medicaid. However, a few studies provide informative insight. A 1995 study estimated that if every elder with a significant incentive to divest assets in order to become eligible for Medicaid actually did divest every penny, the amount transferred would equal about 4 percent of Medicaid nursing home expenditures.

As a practical matter, this estimate overstates the scope of disqualifying transfers because, as the 1993 GAO study of practices in Massachusetts showed, about 90 percent of Medicaid planning involves only the conversion of countable assets into exempt assets. Most typically, applicants are setting aside money for burial arrangements, making home repairs or purchasing an automobile. Asset conversions such as these trigger no penalty period and comprise the bulk of transfers.

Another fact essential to understanding the big picture is that the cost of administrative errors and fraud by providers far outweighs the dollars involved in Medicaid planning. While no reliable national estimates exist showing the extent of total improper payments, a 2001 GAO report identified three states that measured error rates of 24 percent (Kansas), 7.2 percent (Texas) and 41.7 percent (Illinois).

Myth Five: "Long-term care insurance will solve this entire problem." About four million Americans had private long-term care insurance (LCI) in the year 2000. LCI provides fixed daily payments toward the cost of care in a nursing home and, under most policies currently sold, also in-home care and assisted living facilities. A recent in-depth analysis of LCI by the Kaiser Family Foundation concluded that the private LCI market has emerged mainly in response to the demands of a small, relatively affluent market, and that most policies are not affordable for most people. In addition, many policies are not very well designed to meet the real needs of people who can afford only modest coverage.

Stand-alone LCI products are a feasible investment for only a small minority of active workers. And few retirees are able to afford comprehensive long-term care protection, especially since the cost of policies rises dramatically with age. Many people would not qualify, even if they could afford the cost, because of stringent underwriting requirements. For example, the Kaiser Family Foundation booklet *Private Long-Term Care Insurance: Who Should Buy It and What Should They Buy?* says that more than one out of five people age 60 to 64 would fail to pass current underwriting screens. LCI products do provide an important planning option for some seniors, and the estate planning advice provided by elder law attorneys includes evaluation of that option.

Myth Six: "Making penalties for transfer of assets more severe will prevent cheaters from taking advantage of Medicaid." The reality is that making asset transfer penalties more punitive will mainly hurt seniors who act in good faith yet fall innocently into the crosshairs of state budget-cutting measures. One proposal to make penalties harsher calls for changing the start of the penalty period from the date of the transfer to the date one applies for Medicaid. A few of the likely victims of such measures are the grandparents who take care of a grandchild and who provide savings to help pay for the grandchild's education (529 plans are an eligible resource for the Medicaid applicant), the devoted church supporter who donates personal assets to his or her church, the widow who lacks records of her deceased husband's spending or the caring sister who uses savings to help a more needy sister remain in her home. Under state proposals to close transfer of asset "loopholes," each of these individuals will be cut off Medicaid if they subsequently get sick and need long-term care.

These proposals will also force many well spouses to choose between poverty and divorce. Indeed, most Medicaid planning enables marriages to continue and ensures that healthy spouses have sufficient assets and income to maintain their independence.

Planning to pay for long-term care—including Medicaid planning—is the rational process engaged in by families faced with the prospect of paying $50,000 to $70,000 a year for nursing home care. It is important to educate yourself in order to understand the crucial differences between myth and reality in the Medicaid arena.

Quick Reference: Medicare vs. Medicaid

Unlike Medicaid, neither Medicare eligibility nor program payment is predicated upon the income or assets of the beneficiary. Medicaid is a shared state-federal program, paid in part by both entities, and administered by state agencies with federal oversight. Medicare, on the other hand, is entirely a federal program and benefits are paid from entirely federal sources. Both programs are now overseen by the Centers for Medicare and Medicaid Services (CMS), formerly the Health Care Financing Administration (HCFA.) CMS is under the U.S. Department of Health and Human Services (HHS).

What Is Long-term Care?

Long-term care refers to the day-in-day-out assistance you need if you are incapacitated due to accident, illness or aging and need assistance for more than 90 days. Long-term care includes a wide range of services delivered in your own home, or in adult day-care centers, assisted living facilities, continuing care communities and nursing homes.

The level of care is most frequently at a custodial or personal level of care. About 95 percent of the people who reside in nursing homes are receiving custodial care. The need for custodial care may be the result of an injury, illness, chronic condition or the frailty of aging.

Why Do You Need Long-term Care Insurance?

Sixty percent of people will require long-term care at some point in their lives, according to the *Washington Post*. The older you are, the greater the probability that some degree of long-term care will be required. Of those entering nursing homes, half will stay less than three months, many requiring care as part of a convalescing process. The average stay for the other half entering nursing homes will be a little over two and a half years and can cost more than $60,000 per year.

If you need long-term care, do you know how you are going to pay for it? What will happen if you become disabled during your lifetime? In fact, what will happen if your parents become disabled during their lifetimes?

For the wealthy or the very poor, the answer is not difficult. Those who are wealthy will pay for their own care; those who are poor will be eligible for government assistance. Who is left? "Financing long-term care is a uniquely middle-class problem," states the *White Paper on Reforming the Delivery, Accessibility and Financing of Long-Term Care in the United States*, published by the National Academy of Elder Law Attorneys (NAELA).

For those in the middle-income range, long-term care insurance (LCI) may be the best option to ensure that an unexpected or prolonged disability will not deplete financial resources. An individual's future need for long-term care is uncertain. Having LCI makes the cost of long-term care definable and funded. Even for people of means, this is very desirable. Couples purchase coverage for reasons that include not wanting to become "an albatross around the other's neck" or a "burden to their children." Single people may be very motivated to purchase it because there is no one available to provide care if it is needed.

If a business pays the premiums on behalf of an employee, premiums are deductible by the entity. The amount depends on the type of business entity, but closely follows the rules for the deductibility of health insurance premiums.

In 2004, if an individual has unreimbursed medical expenses that are in excess of 7.5 percent of adjusted gross income, the LCI premiums (tied to a schedule by age) can be deductible. There can also be a deduction or tax credit at the state level varying by state. Consult your tax advisor for specifics and note that deductibility is for tax-qualified LCI policies as defined by the 1996 Health Insurance Portability and Accountability Act (HIPAA).

With an appropriately planned and priced LCI policy, the purchaser prepays for one year of long-term care in today's dollars. Then if the insured ever needs care, he or she has a large pool of money upon which to draw.

Another way to view the relative value of these policies is to realize that if an insured collects benefits for just one year during their lifetime, the benefits in that year will be more than all of the premiums expected to be paid into a policy over one's life expectancy.

Long-term care policies are very important and provide a significant improvement over using government benefits, like Medicaid, for the cost of long-term care. Even if you think it is not for you, I urge you to consider the possibility of this type of insurance.

The Nuts and Bolts of Long-term Care Insurance

Provisions that affect the annual cost of LCI premiums include the actual benefit period, the daily benefit amount, whether home health care is elected, inflation protection and the deductible or waiting period. As long as the premium is paid on time, with a "guaranteed renewable" policy, the insurance company must renew the policy annually, even if the client's health has deteriorated. Premiums will generally remain at the level stated in your policy for the life of the policy and can change only if the state insurance commissioner approves the change for everyone who has the policy in your state.

Over the past several years, LCI policies have improved and many now offer coverage for community-based services and home care. Policies are more highly individualized to meet a person's goals, needs and budget. Also, people are buying LCIs as they realize such insurance can be a good alternative to Medicaid. But policy provisions and options can cause a lot of confusion. What is actually paid for and what is not?

LCI policy benefits are usually triggered by the satisfaction of two sets of requirements. The first is the insured's inability to perform a specified number of "activities of daily living" (ADLs). There are six ADLs:

- Bathing
- Dressing
- Eating
- Transferring
- Toileting
- Continence

To trigger policy benefits, a patient must usually be unable to perform at least two. Look for a policy that requires the loss of the fewest number of ADLs. More subtly, look to be sure the policy does not leave out some of the six. Doctors say that bathing and transferring (e.g., moving from bed to chair) are often the first ADLs to be lost by an individual. The policy should definitely list those two; otherwise it is essentially requiring the loss of more than two ADLs.

The second requirement is generally a cognitive impairment or a medical condition requiring long-term care. A cognitive impairment can range from simply forgetting what day it is to not remembering how to get home after taking a short walk. Study the policy carefully to determine exactly how these terms are defined and what kind of doctor or professional must certify that such a condition exists.

Look carefully for loopholes that may allow a company to refuse benefits and for overly broad language that only seems to make it easy to qualify for coverage. Examine the policy for pre-existing conditions that are not covered and such things as geographical limitations. What if you move to another state to be closer to relatives? Is your policy still effective? If not, can it be transferred?

Although policies may restrict where benefits are paid, most policies will pay benefits in a variety of settings including at home, in an assisted living facility, in a nursing home, in an adult day care center or in a hospice facility.

Long-term care benefits are paid in two ways—a situation that can be confusing. They are paid either in indemnity benefits or in cost-incurred benefits. An indemnity benefit is paid to the insured regardless of the actual costs of care incurred. The stated daily benefit amount is paid in full in some LCI policies even if Medicare payments are being received for the same care. A cost-incurred benefit reimburses for actual costs up to the state daily benefit amount.

LCI policies generally have an elimination period. This is similar to a deductible in other types of insurance. It is a waiting period during which the insured pays for his or her own long-term care costs until the policy benefits kick in. I have heard of this period being as short as 20 days or as long as a year. Choosing a longer term for this period may reduce your premium amount.

What to Consider When Comparing Long-term Care Insurance Plans

Here are some points to ponder as you consider the purchase of LCI.

1. *Deductible.* First of all, be aware that the long-term care insurance industry never refers to this particular item as a "deductible." However, I often do because deductible is a familiar term to all of us and it helps us to understand what the provision does. This refers to conditions that must be met before the insurance company is obligated to begin benefit payments. It is not cash, as in many other types of insurance, but a waiting period before the insurance payments begin. Medicare and other types of insurance often pay at the beginning of a nursing home stay, especially if you are receiving therapy that is benefiting you, so you can choose a waiting period roughly equivalent to when those types of payments end. If you are reviewing several policies, avoid those that call for the waiting period to be reset when you move from one type of care to another, such as from home to assisted living or nursing home.

2. *Physical condition.* In addition to a waiting period, for the majority of policies you must need help for at least 90 days with at least two "activities of daily living" such as bathing and dressing. You may also be eligible if you are diagnosed as having a severe cognitive impairment, such as Alzheimer's disease.

3. *Maximum daily benefit.* This refers to the amount per day that an insurer will reimburse you once your policy is in effect. If you are single, have a generous pension and considerable assets, you may wish to choose a low daily benefit, because you have enough funds to self-insure and pay for some of the cost. You can lower your premiums by choosing a lower maximum daily benefit. On the other hand, if you have assets barely sufficient to meet your needs, you probably want to choose a higher daily benefit. Daily benefits usually range from $30 to $500 per day. Some policies use a monthly maximum rather than a daily one. This may offer you more flexibility in meeting expenses. Also, consider where you will be living.

As you know, prices tend to be higher on the East and West coasts, and lower in mid-America and the South.

4. *Maximum lifetime benefit.* This refers to the maximum, or total, dollar amount the insurance company will pay out under your policy. You can lower your premium by choosing less than lifetime benefits, and most experts recommend that people buy at least three years of coverage. A recent flyer from *Kiplinger's Retirement Report* explains the maximum lifetime benefit in this way: If you buy three years of coverage with a daily benefit of $100, your lifetime benefit is 365 x $100 x 3 = $109,500. If you spend $50 a day for home care, your coverage would last six years.

5. *Inflation adjustment.* All the policies offer an inflation rider. Most experts agree this is a must-have. The burden of future increases in the cost of long-term care rests on the receiver of the care. So be sure to make some provision in your long-term care policy for those cost increases.

6. *The insurance company.* Be sure to check the financial ratings of any company trying to sell you a policy. The insurance will only be as good as the company that sells it. Standard & Poor's, A.M. Best and Duff & Phelps are three of the insurance company rating systems. You can review the ratings at your local library.

Last, Jerry Hyman, an elder law attorney in Wilmington, Delaware, writing in *The Elder Law Report* in September of 2000, advised consideration of the "New York" factor. Hyman said, "It is generally acknowledged in the insurance industry that New York has the most stringent requirements for sales of insurance policies. If the policy you're considering has been approved for sale in the state of New York; that adds an extra layer of comfort."

What Will Medicaid and Medicare Pay for Long-term Care?

Despite all the printed material, the sales solicitations, and the federal government's current actions, many people remain uninformed about the actual costs of long-term care and who pays those costs. That fact is not surprising according to Elinor Ginzler, manager of long-term care issues for AARP, who says that the complications surrounding the whole long-term care system in America are "a recipe for confusion."

In 2004, the national average for monthly care in a nursing home is approaching $5,000—almost $60,000 per year. An AARP survey found that most people believe that Medicare pays long-term care costs. Not so. Medicare does not cover long-term care in a nursing home, which is defined as more than three months of regular care for a chronic condition. This type of care is often referred to as "custodial" care and neither Medicare nor most private insurance will pay for it over the long haul.

Judith Stein, executive director and attorney for the Centers for Medicare Advocacy, has written about this issue. While Medicare coverage of long-term care services is not comprehensive, Stein writes that it can be an important source of coverage for beneficiaries who need skilled care. The SNF (Skilled Nursing Facility) benefit is available for a short time at best—up to 100 days during each benefit period. A benefit period ends after someone has been out of the hospital and/or SNF for 60 consecutive days. However, it is important to know that most people receive much less than 100 days of coverage.

The eligibility requirements for Medicare coverage of SNF care are as follows:

- A physician must certify that you need SNF care.
- You must generally be admitted to the SNF within 30 days of a three-day qualifying hospital stay.

- You must require daily skilled nursing or rehabilitation.
- The care you require must, as a practical matter, only be available in a SNF on an inpatient basis, and the SNF must be a Medicare-certified provider.

If those requirements are met, you are entitled to full coverage of the first 20 days of SNF care.

From day 21 through day 100, Medicare pays for all covered services except for a daily co-insurance amount, which for 2003 was $105 per day. This co-insurance may be covered by supplemental insurance. After day 100, even if you have Medicare insurance, you are personally responsible for all costs associated with your care in an SNF.

Unfortunately, Medicare coverage is sometimes denied to individuals who qualify under the law. In particular, beneficiaries are often denied coverage because they have certain chronic conditions such as Alzheimer's disease, Parkinson's disease and multiple sclerosis, or because they need nursing or therapy to maintain rather than improve their condition.

This is a heartbreaking and frustrating situation, and these conditions in themselves are not legitimate reasons for Medicare denial of SNF care. Stein writes that the question to ask is "Do you need skilled nursing and/or therapy on a daily basis?" Not, do you have a particular disease, or will you recover?

If the nursing home tells you that Medicare coverage is not available, and you think you satisfy the requirements, ask the nursing home to submit a claim for a formal Medicare coverage determination. Often the nursing home staff feels they know what Medicare will do, so they do not submit a claim. However, they must submit a claim if the nursing home resident or his or her representative makes that request. Then you are not required to pay until a formal determination has been received from

Medicare. Your doctor is your most important ally when it comes to Medicare coverage. Ask your doctor to help you show that you meet the eligibility requirements for coverage.

People who do not think Medicare pays for long-term care seem to think that Medicaid does. It is true that Medicaid might pay—after nursing home residents spend down their assets to $2,500 (in Maryland) and agree to donate nearly all of their income to the cost of care. Exact amounts in these situations depend on which state you live in and whether or not you are married.

There are several Medicaid waiver programs, and the most recent one provides funds for at-home care and assisted living facilities in some cases. Providers must be licensed by the state and enrolled in the program. Availability and use of these programs varies by state.

Insurance industry experts say that less than 10 percent of us actually own a long-term care policy. It is important to remember that most conventional health insurance policies, including those now provided by the federal government, specifically exclude long-term care for chronic conditions.

Seven million Americans 65 and older will need long-term care this year, and by 2020 that number will nearly double, according to the Health Insurance Association of America. Only when people fully understand the magnitude of long-term care costs can they begin to do the necessary thinking and planning to prepare for the impact of long-term care on their own future.

Please pay attention here: Nearly every time someone asks for advice on long-term care insurance, it is too late to purchase it. Either the individual is already in a nursing home, soon will be or is too old or too ill to be eligible for the insurance at all.

The National Council on the Aging has information about long-term care options and insurance, as does the Health Insurance Association of America. Many states also offer free health insurance counseling for seniors where well-trained people help you identify the coverage you need and decide whether LCI is right for you.

See Resources for information related to LCI.

Resources

Researching a Doctor

America's Top Doctors: The Best in American Medicine (Castle Connolly: 2004)

American Board of Medical Specialties
Web site: www.abms.org
Phone: (866) 275-2267
Offers a searchable database of board-certified specialists.

Maryland Board of Physician Quality Assurance
Web site: www.docboard.org
Provides physician profile information, including
disciplinary actions.

Maryland's Health Claims Arbitration Office
Address: 6 Saint Paul Street, Suite 1501, Baltimore, MD 21202
Provides information on doctors in its Defendant's Index for
matters filed and arbitrated through that office.

General Health

Ageless Lifestyles Institute
Web site: www.drbrickey.com
Discusses the role attitude plays in aging.

American College of Rheumatology
Web site: www.rheumatology.org/patient/jra.htm

American Geriatrics Society Foundation for Health in Aging
Web site: www.healthinaging.org
Provides information about aging and research related to
aging issues.

American Heart Association
Web site: www.americanheart.org
Provides a information on cardiovascular health.

Arthritis Foundation
Web site: www.arthritis.org
Phone (national): (800) 933-0032
Phone (Maryland chapter): (410) 544-5433
Offers a variety of arthritis resources, events and programs.

*The Arthritis Helpbook: A Tested Self-Management Program for
Coping with Arthritis and Fibromyalgia* by Kate Lorig, R.N. and
James Fries, M.D. (Perseus Publishing: 2000)

The Arthritis Sourcebook by Earl Brewer Jr., M.D. and Kathy
Angel (McGraw-Hill: 2000)

Association for Applied and Therapeutic Humor
Web site: www.aath.org
Provides links to related resources and information about its
annual humor conference.

Choose to Move
Web site: www.choosetomove.org
Phone: (888) 694-3278
Offers a free fitness program for women from the American
Heart Association.

How to Keep From Breaking Your Heart: What Every Woman Needs to Know about Cardiovascular Disease by Barbara H. Roberts, M.D. (Jones & Bartlett: 2003)

Humor Matters
Web site: www.humormatters.com
Dr. Steven M. Sultanoff's humor site.

Institute for Healthcare Advancement
Web site: www.iha4health.org
Phone: (800) 434-4633
Offers *What to do for Senior Health*, an easy to understand self-help medical book for seniors.

It Takes More Than Love: A Practical Guide to Taking Care of an Aging Adult by Anita G. Beckerman and Ruth M. Tappen (Health Professions Press: 1999)

Jest Health
Web site: www.jesthealth.com
Patty Wooten's humor site.

Join the Active People Over 60
Phone: (800) 243-3425, extension 1273
The Maryland Department of Aging offers this fitness and exercise guide.

The Maryland Pharmacy Assistance Program
Phone: (800)-226-2142
Address: PO Box 386, Baltimore, MD 21203-0386

Medication Reminders: Pill Vial Alarm
Web site: www.epill.com
Phone: (800) 545-0095
Offers medication reminders and practical patient compliance systems.

National Association for Continence (NAFC)
Web site: www.nafc.org
Phone: (800) 252-3337
Address: NAFC, P.O. Box 8310, Spartanburg, SC 29305
Provides support and information about the causes, prevention, diagnosis and treatment for incontinence.

National Coalition for Women with Heart Disease
Web site: www.womenheart.org
Phone: (202) 728-7199
Address: Women Heart, 818 18th Street NW, Suite 730, Washington, D.C. 20006
Works to decrease death and disability among women resulting from heart disease; membership is free.

National Heart, Lung and Blood Institute (NHLBI)
Web site: www.nhlbi.nih.gov
Phone: (301) 592-8573
Address: NHLBI Health Information Center, PO Box 30105, Bethesda, MD 20824-0105
Offers information about hypertension and the booklet *Facts About Lowering Blood Pressure* (write and ask for publication number 00-3281).

NHLBI's DASH Eating Plan
Web site: www.nhlbi.nih.gov/health/public/heart/hbp/dash/
Offers a diet to reduce blood pressure.

National Institute on Aging
Phone: (800) 222-4225
Address: NIA Information Center, PO Box 8057, Gaithersburg, MD 20898-8057
Offers informational brochure, *AgePage*.

National Institute of Health's Senior Health
Web site: www.nihseniorhealth.gov
A senior-friendly site with health information for elders.

Memory and Dementia

Alzheimer's Association
Web site: www.alz.org
Phone: (800) 272-3900
Address: 225 North Michigan Avenue, 17th Floor,
Chicago, IL 60601-7633
E-mail: info@alz.org

Alzheimer's Disease International
Web site: www.alz.co.uk/alz/almain.htm
An umbrella organization for Alzheimer's associations all
around the world.

Association for Frontotemporal Dementia
Web site: www.ftd-picks.org
Address: PO Box 7191, St. David's, PA 19087
Offers information about this type of dementia for patients
and caregivers.

Joyce Simard
Web site: www.joycesimard.com
Provides information on Mild Cognitive Impairment; Simard is
a nationally recognized geriatric consultant.

Medical Care Corporation
Web site: www.mccare.com
Offers a screening test for Alzheimer's disease and other
services and information.

Memory: Remembering and Forgetting in Everyday Life by Dr.
Barry Gordon (MasterMedia Publishing: 1995)

National Institute on Aging's Alzheimer's Disease Education
and Referral Center
Web site: www.alzheimers.org
Phone: (800) 438-4380
Address: PO Box 8250, Silver Spring, MD 20907
Conducts and supports studies of Alzheimer's disease.

Talking to Alzheimer's by Claudia J. Strauss (New Harbinger: 2002)

What If It's Not Alzheimer's? A Caregiver's Guide to Dementia,
edited by Lisa and Gary Radin (Prometheus Books: 2003)

Medicare, Medicaid and Long-term Care Insurance

Adventist Health Care
Web site: www.adventisthealthcare.com
Phone: (800) 542-5096
Conducts free classes across the country on how to select long-
term care insurance.

Center for Medicare Advocacy
Web site: www.medicareadvocacy.org
Helps individuals to secure proper access to Medicare services.

Centers for Medicare and Medicaid Services (CMS)
Web site: www.cms.gov
Contains laws, regulations, the state Medicaid manuals and
other resources.

Center for Medicare Education
Web site: www.medicareed.org
Phone: (202) 508-1210
A resources for public and private agencies that provide
consumer information about Medicare.

Health Insurance Association of America
Web site: www.hiaa.org
Phone: (877) 582-4872
Provides information on long-term care options.

Kaiser Family Foundation's Medicare Prescription
Drug Costs Calculator
Web site: www.kaisernetword.org/static/kncalc.cfm
Calculates if, and how much, the new Medicare prescription
drug coverage will save you.

Maryland Department of Aging
Web site: www.mdoa.state.md.us
Phone: (800) 243-3425
Provides information about state programs for seniors.

Maryland State Health Insurance and Assistance Program (SHIP)
http://www.mdoa.state.md.us/Services/ship.html
Phone (Anne Arundel County): (410) 222-4464
Phone (Prince George's County): (301) 699-2893
Provides information about the SHIP program.

Medicare
Web site: www.medicare.gov
Phone: (800) 633-4227
Medicare's official Web site.

Medicare Rights Center
Web site: www.medicarerights.org
Clearly and simply answers questions about Medicare coverage.

Mr. Long-term Care
Web site: www.mr-longtermcare.com
Provides a thorough long-term care decision-making guide.

National Council on the Aging
Web site: www.unitedseniorshealth.org
Phone: (800) 637-2604
Offers the informational booklet *Long-term Care Planning: A
Dollar and Sense Guide*. Visit its Web site for information about
long-term care options.

4
Housing for Seniors

The Significance of Good Housing

Appropriate housing is vital for the well-being and productivity of any senior. Money, of course, is the bottom-line issue, but it can only solve problems in those situations where the word housing means nothing more than shelter. If housing means anything more, money is often not enough to meet the goal.

Lawrence A. Frolik, a renowned elder law attorney and professor at the University of Pittsburgh Law School, writing in the journal of the National Academy of Elder Law Attorneys, suggests that housing, in the larger sense, embodies several concepts. These include security, a sense of place, a sense of community, recreation and a sense of self.

Security, Frolik contends, is not limited to the idea of actual safety. Security includes a sense of knowing the risks and safety of the community. People may feel secure when they understand the relative risks of their environment, but may feel insecure in a perfectly safe but unknown environment. Security is knowing whether it is safe to walk down this or that street after dark or knowing who to turn to for aid and assistance if you should become sick and need a ride to the doctor's office. Those are the types of things that elders know when they have lived for years in the same house and community.

Another concept important to the idea of appropriate housing is a sense of place. Many seniors have lived in their homes since the sixties and early seventies. They have feelings that arise from a sense of the past, with its inevitable traditions, memories and rituals. That sense of belonging where you are is a very important component of an individual's well-being, no matter their age.

The community itself is important when considering the idea of appropriate and supportive housing. Not only friends, says Frolik, but the community's "fabric of daily life provided by acquaintances, business and service persons." There are longtime neighbors, church friends, grocery store checkers, doctor's staff—it goes on and on. If you move away, who is going to help you like these people do?

Where seniors live depends on many factors—health, available money, safety, family, community support services and personal preferences. Because this country has more seniors than ever before, there are now more housing choices than ever before.

The Home

Staying at Home

The first option is staying at home. Frolik writes, "[T]he phrase aging in place is not just an idiosyncratic choice, not just an ideal that must give way to practical realities. For staying in place is for most elderly not a luxury, not a mere preference, but a silent cry to be recognized as a person. For too many elderly, to be asked or to be forced to move is not just an inconvenience or an unfortunate event—it is the first large step towards oblivion. A move to a nursing home is the loss of those little freedoms such as when and what to eat...conversely, to stay at home means that life continues no matter how diminished or reduced in scope."

It takes imagination, creativity, stamina and sometimes strength and brute force for family helpers and caregivers to succeed in helping their loved one remain at home. Yet it is very often worth all the frustration. If you have a loved one who wishes and hopes to stay home rather than move, take another, broader, look at the situation. What kind of support is available from the community, from various clubs, religious organizations and volunteers? What services are available from the area Agency on Aging or other government entities? This is often difficult, but not necessarily impossible. See the Resources section for organizations that will help you accomplish this goal.

Community Support Helps Seniors Stay Home

The Heritage Harbour Community in Annapolis, Maryland is a wonderful and innovative community initiative to help senior residents stay longer in their own homes without assisted living facility or a nursing home. It is an idea that could work in almost any location.

In 1990, some 100 residents of the Heritage Harbour Community got together and founded the Heritage Harbour Health Group (HHHG). Their intention was to cooperate to provide home health nursing care, as well as case management, so that residents could age at home. The main idea was to provide services right there in the community that would help people remain in their homes if they became frail or ill.

Today, the group includes 1,400 members and has succeeded beyond the wildest dreams of its founders. The group searched in other states for a community-based home health program formed by and for seniors. They could not locate any, so they designed their own. Members of the HHHG pay annual dues for which they receive assistance at home from pre-screened home health aides. Services are both medical and non-medical. For instance, the HHHG office has a notary public and staff members to help with insurance and Medicare and Medicaid forms. There is an information library, and bereavement and dementia support groups.

On the medical side, members can have their blood pressure taken three times per week, flu vaccinations, consultations with a registered nurse and drug testing. Case management for private-duty home health aides or live-in companions is implemented and supervised by the HHHG professional nurse.

According to an article in the *Washington Post*, the list of services offered is fairly ordinary, but "the program is novel because it is funded, packaged and governed entirely by its members—all residents of the Heritage Harbour seniors community."

A very important part of the whole picture is the Volunteers Caring Network. These community volunteers work in cooperation with the HHHG and provide transportation to and from medical appointments for members, temporary loans of medical equipment and aids and a safety line. They provide daily check-in phone calls and host monthly meetings with programs of interest to senior residents of the Heritage Harbour Community.

The Heritage Harbour Community is composed of townhouses, single family homes and high-rise condominiums, and it houses a large concentration of seniors. Sharp realtors

> **Branson, Missouri is a Popular Retirement Spot**
>
> *Branson, Missouri is a hot place for senior retirees these days. This music resort town is gaining a reputation as a place where people can "settle in without having to actually settle down." Seniors there can be found selling tickets in the box offices, ushering, greeting guests and selling knickknacks in the many gift shops.*
>
> *City Planning Administrator Christopher Coulter said, "Seniors who visit are overwhelmed by the friendliness and caring of the community. They see people their own age working in the theaters and other businesses, and I think that contributes to the town's growth as a retirement destination. Elderly people are not always given a functional use in society, but that's not the case in Branson."*
>
> *Modern Maturity, the AARP magazine, lists Branson among the best places to live in the United States. Studies by AARP show that golf courses, sun and senior centers are no longer at the top of the list as priorities for retirees. More important are neighborliness, work availability (part-time or otherwise) and good restaurants. Worthy of note: The average home price in the Branson area is approximately $107,000.*
>
> ■ ■ ■

have learned to use the HHHG as a selling point when community homes come on the market.

Retirement Communities

Continuing Care Retirement Communities

The first type of housing specifically available to seniors is called "retirement communities." These vary significantly in costs and benefits offered and are not subject to any particular regulation by any governing body. Basically, these communities provide age-segregated, independent living units. They tend to offer personal care services, social activities and limited nursing supervision for generally active adults.

A popular type of retirement community is called a continuing care retirement community (CCRC). These communities offer a broad level of care. These offer eligible individuals the option to receive guaranteed care in a skilled-nursing facility as part of the price of admission. In other words, the typical agreement is that this facility will "take care of you until you die." Living options range from independent-living apartments to assisted-living to skilled-nursing home care. Most require a substantial entrance fee as well as monthly fees. A few may allow you to buy an ownership interest in your living unit with a personal and health services package included. These ownership arrangements are very complex, and have special advantages and definite risks.

If you are considering this retirement option, legal advice is a must because CCRC contracts are complex and, of course, strongly favor the facility. You should investigate whether the facility is accredited, how stable its finances are and what type of consumer protections it has in place. See the Resources section for CCRC information.

Questions to Ask Any Residence Facility

The most helpful thing you can do, when considering any type of senior housing, is to visit various facilities at length and ask lots of questions. Answers to the questions below will help you compare and evaluate the housing situations you are investigating. The more places you visit, the more information you seek, the better able you will be to make an informed decision.

Do not rely on advertisements. Talk to staff members as well as residents. Ask for a copy of the facility's standard contract. Read it carefully and have it reviewed by an attorney you trust. Check with your state's Department on Aging to find out whether the facility is regulated and whether there have been any reported problems with it.

What is the provider's background and experience? The provider is the person or entity legally and financially responsible for providing the housing. Some facilities advertise that they are connected with nonprofit groups or churches that, in reality, have no legal control or financial responsibility for the housing.

Is the provider financially sound? Ask a professional to review the facility's financial, actuarial and operating statements.

Are all levels of care providers licensed or certified by the state? If you cannot get a satisfactory answer to this question, check with the Department on Aging.

How does the facility ensure the quality of its care and services? It should be accredited by a recognized private accrediting organization. Verify the information you are given with the organization.

If there is an entrance fee, how much is it? Can I get a refund of all or part of it? The facility should provide a formula for at least a pro rata refund, based on the resident's length of stay, regardless of whether the facility or the resident initiates the termination. Many newer facilities offer fully refundable entrance fees.

What is the monthly fee? How often and how much can it be increased? What happens if I am already a resident, but I cannot afford higher fees? Some facilities provide financial help to residents if they become unable to pay the higher fees.

What services are included in the regular fees? For example, are meal services included? If so, is the schedule for meals reasonable and flexible? What is the policy on eating in your room? What about special diets? Are utilities included in the monthly fee? Is cable television available? If so, who pays the monthly fees? Who is responsible for unit repairs? Is there an extra fee for laundry? Is housekeeping included in the fee?

How much say do I have in choosing where I live? How large is the living unit? Can you change or redecorate it? Can you bring your own furnishings—an important component of feeling at home.

What security systems and policies are in place? Safety is important. What is the fire emergency plan? You should check this very carefully.

What about recreational and cultural activities? What is available on-site? Is transportation provided to off-site activities? When? Where? Is there a limit on the number of trips included in the fee?

Does the facility provide religious services? Are these available on-site or are residents provided with transportation to their desired place and time of worship?

How and when can services for residents be changed? To what extent does the facility have the right to cut back, change or eliminate services? Can the facility ask you to move if you become too ill or impaired to be cared for by that facility? Who decides that you need more care, and on what grounds? What are the criteria and procedures for determining when a resident needs to be transferred from independent living to assisted living, or to a nursing care unit, or to an entirely different facility? Who is involved in these decisions?

What about the staff members? What are their professional qualifications? What is the ratio of staff members to residents (that is, does the facility have enough staff)? What types of emergencies are staff members expected to handle, and how are they trained for them? Are the general operating rules of the facility reasonable? What happens if a resident breaks a rule? Is there an appeals process? What if a resident wants an exception to a policy or to routine scheduling? Is there a resident council? How are complaints and disputes handled?

Are the general operating rules of the facility reasonable? What happens if a resident breaks a rule? Is there an appeals process? What if a resident wants an exception to a policy or to a routine scheduling? Is there a resident council? How are complaints and disputes handled?

Housing decisions are not small ones, and they are seldom inexpensive. An excellent facility will welcome your questions and be pleased to explain more about their benefits. You should never feel awkward about asking questions, and you should definitely beware of administrators who try to evade them. There are many good facilities out there. I hope these questions will help you locate them.

Assisted Living

Supportive Housing

The next type of housing is typically called supportive housing by the American Bar Association and varies from single-family homes that offer board and care to larger institutional complexes. Their common characteristic is that each provides some combination of housing and supportive services. Residents usually have their own furnishings in their apartment and come together to share meals or participate in field trips, book clubs, classes or exercise programs. In small facilities, residents often live like members of a family and even share some chores and responsibilities.

Staff provides help with activities of daily living (ADLs), such as eating, dressing, transferring, using a toilet and bathing. They also provide help with instrumental activities of daily living (IADLs), such as preparing meals, taking medications, walking outside, using the telephone, managing money, shopping and housekeeping. Finally, each has protective oversight by monitoring, reminding or otherwise supervising the resident.

> ### Look for Assisted Living Guidance on the Web
>
> *Assisted Living INFO is an online guide for selecting an assisted living facility, retirement community or other personal care facility anywhere in the United States. Several helpful tools are offered on this site, including one that allows the user to pinpoint a destination close to family and friends. An educational component to the site offers information as to what, for instance, "assisted living" actually is. See Resources for a link.*
>
> ■ ■ ■

Public housing is obtainable through the federal department of Housing and Urban Authority or the county housing authority. Homes and apartments are available where landlords agree to accept prearranged, reduced rent. Waiting lists are very long for this type of housing.

Assisted Living Facilities

Assisted living housing has more than tripled in the last decade. Assisted living facilities (ALFs) have many forms, and this term can actually have different meanings in different parts of the country. ALFs are generally more residential than medical. Although some of the residents may be frail, they generally do not need continuous skilled nursing care.

Residents in ALFs generally have less complicated medical problems and, on the whole, are still mobile and active. These facilities offer living quarters, meals, help with medication management, access to transportation and health care, social and recreational activities and, depending on the level of care required, help with dressing, bathing or eating. In ALFs, residents have their own bedrooms and social opportunities are afforded by common areas and shared meals. Regular monitoring of needs provides 24-hour staffing and personal care support. ALFs appeal to elders who can no longer live at home, yet do not need professional nursing care.

Their size ranges from very small—in many communities residential homes have been converted to assisted living facilities which house six to eight residents—to large, expensive-looking, professionally decorated places.

ALFs are licensed to correspond with the level of care they are authorized to provide. Maryland ALFs must be licensed by the Maryland Department of Health and Mental Hygiene before they can operate. You should be aware that they are not as highly government-regulated as nursing homes. Families and family advisors who are considering assisted living should do good research and conduct a thorough examination of the facility prior to signing a contract or making any commitment. See Resources at the end of this chapter for related information.

The Cost of Assisted Living Facilities

Costs for this type of housing depend on the level of care required. As a general rule, assisted living facilities are private pay, and many do not accept any type of government-assisted payment. Some government subsidies of around $500 per month are available for these residences.

An Exemplary Assisted Living Facility

Episcopal Senior Ministries (ESM) is a nonprofit organization, started in 1924 to serve seniors. It provides several services and sponsors Henderson House, a new, family-style assisted living residence in Pointer Ridge, Bowie, Maryland.

Henderson House is the second such area facility sponsored by ESM. The first is Our Place, located in Silver Spring, Maryland. Henderson House is a converted ranch style home. There are eight living spaces available at the house. Because of the substantial help from local congregations and ESM, Henderson House is able to charge below-market rates for resident spaces and can serve area residents in low- and moderate-income categories.

Henderson House has spacious living and dining areas with an eat-in kitchen. The eight private bedrooms are all on one floor. Admission is open to people 62 years of age or older who need assistance with one or more activities of daily living, or with instrumental activities such as food preparation, taking medications, shopping and cleaning. Included in the monthly fee are all meals and snacks, laundry services, medication management, housekeeping, medical service coordination and 24-hour staff supervision. Volunteers from partner congregations and the community provide extra activities and attention for the residents.

Henderson House is not a locked facility; therefore it cannot accommodate people whose Alzheimer's symptoms include wandering. The residence can accommodate people with Mild Cognitive Impairment (MCI) or who are in the earlier stages of dementia.

Volunteer opportunities are always available at Henderson House, and the church partnerships provide a great volunteer base. Families have discovered that volunteering at the assisted living facilities is a great way to get the entire family working together at something worthwhile. Volunteer opportunities tend to center around holidays, birthdays and other special occasions—although other assistance, such as transportation, is always needed. Ruth Shea, interim director of the home, told me that when she attempts to thank family volunteers for their assistance, they nearly always reply that "We should be thanking you!"

> ## Publications Offer Guidance
>
> *The Elder Law Section of the Maryland State Bar Association has published an assisted living guide,* Assisted Living in Maryland: What You Need to Know. *The handbook offers information on everything from site selection, services, staffing, contracts and facility documents to legal rights. It covers long-term care insurance, medical assistance, residential agreements, liability fees and payment schedules. Additionally, there is a comprehensive list of resources organized by county. See Resources for information on obtaining a copy.*
>
> ■ ■ ■

ESM runs another very successful program for seniors in the District of Columbia: Age in Place. This mostly volunteer program organizes 700 volunteers who are currently serving 150 seniors. Volunteers do yard work, housecleaning and odd jobs needed by older people who cannot do these things for themselves. ESM also provides an information and assistance line for seniors and family members who are searching for solutions to senior problems including, among other things, housing, health care, home care or finances.

See Resources for information about Henderson House and the subsidy program.

Nursing Homes

Planning Ahead for a Nursing Home

Various statistics float around about how many of us will actually spend time in a nursing home before we die. The Maryland attorney general says that one in every five Marylanders over the age of 60 will spend time in a nursing facility and that the average stay is almost three years. Even if we ourselves never reside in a nursing home, the chances are extremely good that someone we love will do so. Planning ahead can avert a crisis when the need arises.

Nursing homes are very expensive and becoming more so. Much of the financial planning to absorb the cost needs to be done well in advance of actual need. The following are some basic guidelines to assist you in thinking about this important issue.

1. *Consider your future realistically.* When you plan your retirement, you probably look forward to spending more time with your family and friends, taking it easy or perhaps traveling. Nobody wants to think about illness or institutions. But it is a fact. It is likely that we or someone close to us will need care in a nursing home, and we must be realistic in thinking about that —and how such care will be paid for.

2. *Prevent a crisis.* Most people are forced to learn about nursing homes when they or loved ones become ill. Time is short, money is needed quickly and family members are upset. To prevent a crisis, find out ahead of time how nursing homes work. Learn about the laws that protect nursing home residents and their families. With this information, you can make better decisions when the time comes.

3. *Talk to your family.* If you become seriously ill or have an accident or stroke, who will take care of you? You may be surprised to learn how much care—or how little—your family

would be able to provide for you at your home or their home.
Let them know your feelings and what your wishes are. Avoid
pushing your family members into making promises they might
be unable to keep. Sometimes, no matter how much your
family loves you, they may not be able to provide the personal
care you might want or require. Consider this possibility and
make provisions accordingly.

4. *Take a hard look at your finances.* Nursing homes are
expensive, and Medicare and traditional health insurance plans
seldom cover the cost. How will you manage to pay the bills?
You may need to consult an attorney or accountant who
specializes in medical assistance eligibility and nursing home
law. An expert can help you plan wisely for the future.
Additionally, give some serious thought to purchasing long-
term care insurance. You may think that premiums are
expensive (depending on your age) but they are nowhere near
as expensive as the costs of a nursing home itself.

5. *Learn what is available.* Every Maryland county has
resource people who can help you select a nursing home facility
or obtain nursing care in your own home.

Selecting a Nursing Home

Nursing homes provide care for chronically-ill people. They
also offer rehabilitation services that allow some older people to
return home. Nursing homes provide 24-hour attention, activity
and care. There are many wonderful nursing homes and, unfortunately, many not so wonderful that would best be avoided. If
time allows, do plenty of research and visit several of them in
order to make an informed choice.

Congress sets standards of care for nursing facilities, including
measures designed to prevent abuse through training, funding and
certification requirements. The federal government monitors

nursing home certification and sets minimum requirements for institutions that receive Medicaid and Medicare reimbursements. See Resources for information on nursing homes.

There are so many nursing homes and so much misinformation and confusion regarding them that it is almost impossible

---

Things to Think About at a Nursing Home

- *Is the facility free of offensive odors?*

- *Is it a noisy facility or is there a relatively quiet residential hum of voices?*

- *Are common areas and floors free from dirt and spills?*

- *Is the staff wearing clean uniforms, and are they treating the residents with respect?*

- *Is the lighting in the common rooms, living areas and hallways appropriate for the residents?*

- *Are the residents well groomed and appropriately dressed?*

- *Do they appear comfortable throughout the facility?*

- *Are the appropriate security measures in place to prevent residents from wandering?*

- *What about safety issues (fire alarms, smoke detectors and sprinkler systems)?*

- *Is the physical building itself old or new?*

- *If it is old, have safety features been upgraded?*

- *Are the hallways and rooms clear for residents to move around safely?*

- *A residents assisted when needed?*

■ ■ ■

to know how to begin to select the best one for your family or loved one.

If you are seriously considering a certain facility, you should visit it more than once and at different times. Check to see how the staffing is on weekends or in the evenings at times when visitors are less likely. Check to see if the services that are being offered seem to match the requirements of the prospective resident. Be sure to request a written description of all costs and fees—not just a daily or monthly rate list. There will probably be additional charges for rehab services or a private room, for instance. On these visits, make sure the facility is doing a good job in providing for the most basic of services. While you are there, trust your instincts and observations. Look around and make mental notes. Do the residents themselves appear appropriately happy? Take the opportunity to talk with visiting families of other residents and see what their experience has been.

The choice of a long-term care facility can be frustrating and difficult. However, as the American Bar Association says, "There is no search that is more important to the individual and to the family of the individual who requires care."

The Web site www.MyZiva.com includes basic information about every licensed nursing home in the United States and has been designed to simplify the process of choosing the most suitable nursing home. The site is user-friendly and allows you to evaluate and compare nursing homes, understand the services that a nursing home provides and be informed of how one pays for nursing home care. You can also compare different nursing homes side-by-side. Of course you will still want to visit the facility, but having this comparison available gives you more information to use in choosing which facilities to visit.

Remember, accreditation is not the same thing as Medicare or Medicaid certification. The Centers for Medicare and Medicaid Services (CMS) do not recognize nursing home accreditation. Accreditation represents a certification by a private sector organization that a nursing home meets certain standards it has established. Accreditation is voluntary for nursing homes and does not affect the home's eligibility to act as a Medicare or Medicaid care provider.

Before you sign a nursing home contract, you should obtain a copy of the contract and review it ahead of time in the privacy of your own home. If the facility refuses to give you a copy, ask why not. If you still want to consider entering that facility, you can obtain a copy of its contract from your state's Licensing and Certification office. You may also get a copy of the state's model nursing home admission contract, written in plain English, to see how it compares.

Ask the nursing facility about any part of the contract that you find confusing or unfair. If you make changes in the contract, be sure that both you and institution's representative initial the changes in the margin. If the nursing home is not cooperative, you may want to take an advocate with you to negotiate the changes. Make sure there are no blank spaces, and that the contract is fully completed and correct at the time you sign it. You should get a photocopy of the original contract after it has been filled in and signed by both you and the nursing home's representative (whose name you need to record on the document).

See the Resources section for information on selecting a nursing home.

Your Rights in a Nursing Home

In 1986, the National Academy of Sciences published a report calling nursing homes basically "warehouses" for the elderly. The report criticized existing nursing home law, saying that it focused on the capacity of each facility to provide services rather than on the quality of the services received by the residents. That is, the focus was on mechanical aspects of nursing homes—square footage, staffing numbers, kinds of equipment and payments.

Congress responded with the federal Nursing Home Reform Act of 1987 (NHRA). The act was intended to focus on the needs of individual residents—ensuring that residents are treated as persons rather than as "units of reimbursement." The stated purpose of the NHRA is to ensure that nursing home residents are treated with dignity and respect and that certain minimum standards are in place to assure quality of life and quality care.

Additionally, the Centers for Medicare and Medicaid Services (CMS) issues guidelines to the regulations that are found in the appendix of the CMS State Operations Manual. Finally, every state has a separate body of law that applies to every licensed nursing facility in the state and that occasionally provides residents with more protection than the federal law.

One of the most important sections of the NHRA is the Residents' Bill of Rights. One of the first rights is freedom of choice. Did you know each nursing home resident has the right to choose his or her own personal attending physician? Unfortunately, this right is one of those rights that is probably real in theory only, for most physicians will not make house calls—even to nursing homes. In reality, most facilities arrange for one or more physicians to make rounds regularly. However, if a resident is able to prevail upon his or her physician to visit the facility, or if the resident is physically able to visit his or her physician, the right can be meaningful.

Under the broad topic of freedom of choice, residents have a right to be fully informed, in advance, concerning care and treatment, and they have the right to participate in planning care and treatment. Of course, sometimes the condition of the resident makes this right impossible to actually achieve. However, if the resident is able to participate and the family aggressively pursues and asserts this right, it can be achieved.

Nursing home residents have the right to be free from both physical and mental abuse, and from physical and chemical restraints. Residents have a right to privacy with respect to accommodations, medical treatment, communications and visits. This, I have observed, is a right that is frequently violated. Staff often fails to maintain adequate privacy in bathing residents, administering treatment and/or discussing a resident's care.

Even incompetent residents have rights under the NHRA. These rights may be exercised by a person appointed under state law to act on the resident's behalf. This could be a person who has been appointed guardian or a person acting as agent under a validly executed power of attorney.

Nursing home residents have a right to be informed about their rights. At the time of admission, each facility must give the resident a written statement of the Resident's Bill of Rights and a statement that a resident may file complaints with a state survey and certification agency.

A nursing home resident has a right to confidentiality of personal and clinical records. They have a right to voice griev-ances with respect to treatment or care, and facilities have an obligation to resolve grievances promptly. Residents have a right to organize and participate in resident groups, and residents' families have a right to meet in the facility with families of other residents.

Commonly Believed Falsehoods Related to Nursing Home Care

The Nursing Home Reform Act has been very helpful, although there is still much room for improvement. In spite of the NHRA, families are often misled by nursing home personnel. Family members are usually distraught, stressed and feeling guilty when admitting a family member to a nursing home. Unfortunately, during that admission procedure, and at other times during your family member's stay, it is possible to make mistakes and errors that may haunt you for a long time.

Also, family members need to be prepared for the transition from caregivers to care advocates. Without an effective advocate for the nursing home resident, the likelihood of problems caused by the lack of good care will greatly increase. It is the old squeaky wheel gets the grease story.

By far the majority of nursing homes today are run honestly. Nevertheless, here are some falsehoods frequently told to nursing home residents and their families by the facility staff and management.

This is a favorite: *"We cannot continue to give your mom therapy, because she is not making progress."* Medicare reimbursement is not necessarily dependent on the resident making progress. Although the resident must need "skilled nursing services" or "skilled rehabilitation services" to be eligible for Medicare payment, the availability of Medicare should not affect the care provided. Additionally, the facility must try to maintain a resident's condition: "A facility must ensure [a] resident's ability in activities of daily living do not diminish unless circumstances of the individual's clinical condition demonstrate that diminution was unavoidable."

"We cannot give your mom therapy services because her Medicare has expired, and Medicaid does not pay for therapy." Therapy should be provided regardless of the form of payment. First, services should be provided if they are required "to attain or maintain the highest practicable physical, mental and psychosocial well-being." Second, a nursing facility "must establish and maintain identical policies and practices regarding transfer, discharge, and the provision of services required under the state [Medicaid] plan for all individuals regardless of source of payment." Therapy services must be provided as part of the facility's per diem rate, even if they are not specifically enumerated in the state plan.

"Your mom needs a feeding tube because she is not finishing her meals at mealtime." A nursing facility must assist a resident in maintaining the resident's ability to eat. This includes prompting the resident to eat, providing therapy to improve swallowing skills and actually feeding the resident. Tube feeding should be done only if absolutely necessary, and not because the facility is understaffed.

"We are going to be forced to discharge your mom. She must leave because she is difficult." Being difficult is not a justification for eviction. Nursing facilities exist in order to care for people who have physical and mental problems. Under the Nursing Home Reform Act, there are six legitimate reasons for eviction from a nursing facility:

1. The resident has failed to pay.
2. The resident no longer needs nursing facility care.
3. The facility is going out of business.

4. The resident's needs cannot be met in a nursing facility.
5. The resident's presence in the facility endangers others' safety.
6. The resident's presence in the facility endangers others' health.

"Your mom's Medicare-paid days are ending [date]. She cannot receive any more Medicare reimbursement because we have determined that she needs only custodial care." Medicare pays for up to 100 days if the resident was hospitalized for at least three nights prior to admission to the facility and if he/she needs skilled nursing services or skilled rehabilitation services. There is a daily co-payment for days 21–100. Although the nursing facility can make an initial determination of whether or not to submit a bill to Medicare, the resident may disagree with the facility's assessment and has the right to force the facility to submit a bill to Medicare. This is called a "demand bill." When this bill is submitted and there is an actual written refusal from Medicare, the resident may appeal a negative Medicare decision. The resident will not be responsible for any amount Medicare subsequently pays.

"We can't admit your loved one unless you accept full financial responsibility." The NHRA specifically prohibits nursing homes from requiring a third-party guarantee of payment. Some nursing homes have developed a subtle system to evade this prohibition. They have the family member or friend sign the nursing home agreement as a responsible party. The person signing understandably believes that the responsible party is the contact person in case of emergency. However, the contract contains a paragraph defining responsible party as a person who understands he cannot be required to assume financial responsibility for the nursing home invoices, but who nevertheless voluntarily

assumes such responsibility. That definition is illegal and unenforceable. You can sign to pay the bills from the resident's resources, and you can voluntarily sign to assume personal responsibility for the bill. Just make sure you do not do any of it by accident. Read the contract carefully.

"Medicare won't pay any longer because you do not need skilled care." It is true that Medicare will not pay unless skilled care is required, but the statement is misleading because the nursing facility itself makes the initial determination whether to bill Medicare, but that decision is not final. The nursing home is

---

An Excellent Nursing Home Resource

The National Citizens' Coalition for Nursing Home Reform (NCCNHR) has more information available on senior residence issues than you can absorb in one or two visits to their Web site. If you must place a family member in a nursing home, or are considering the possibility, I urge you to look at the materials from this group.

One of their publications is Nursing Home Staffing: A Guide for Residents, Families, Friends, and Caregivers. NCCNHR's *guide reviews nursing home staffing—the greatest single indicator of quality care in a nursing home. This guide will help you determine whether there is good—or even adequate—staffing in your loved one's facility and provide you with step-by-step instructions on advocating for higher staffing and better care. Another NCCNHR publication,* A Consumer Guide to Choosing a Nursing Home, *helps prospective residents and their friends and family members navigate consumer information resources, understand the information and make an informed choice. See Resources for more information.*

■ ■ ■

required to give the resident written notice of the decision, as well as written notice of the resident's right to force the facility to submit the bill to Medicare. When the bill is ultimately submitted to Medicare, the facility cannot charge the resident for anything that Medicare might possibly pay until Medicare actually denies the claim.

Understaffing Is an Issue in Nursing Homes

Substandard care in nursing homes is epidemic—and the stories I hear often bring tears to my eyes. Are today's nursing homes full of tyrants who have no concern for seniors? Not generally, although there are a few bad apples. Almost every sad story boils down to the same formula—not nearly enough staff, and the available staff, which is both overworked and underpaid, is constantly turning over.

Web Site Offers Long-term Care Jobs Listings

The Department of Labor is attempting to help address the long-term care staffing shortage by use of a Caregiver Jobs Clearinghouse. This is an online job listing for long-term care positions. The free service links job seekers to long-term care employers. Potential applicants can search local job listings and post their resumes for positions available anywhere in the country. In addition, employers can post job listings and review resumes online. The American Health Care Association and the American Association of Homes and Services for the Aging worked with the Department of Labor to develop the site. With the growth of the senior population, the government estimates that 800,000 new caregivers will be needed over the next seven years. See Resources for a link.

■ ■ ■

A Department of Health and Human Services (DHHS) study said that patients in homes with substandard care were more likely to experience bedsores, malnutrition, weight loss, dehydration, pneumonia and serious blood-borne infections.

Families and visitors to nursing homes always complain about the smell. Typically, it is the first negative thing they notice. Not too long ago I spoke with a wonderful and caring friend who is a veteran of years of nursing home employment. She is a very experienced and degreed nurse and administrator and currently works as an infection control specialist at a suburban facility. She said that a bad smell in the nursing home is the first indication there is probably not enough staff, or that the staff is not being managed well. If diapers and linens were changed in a timely fashion, when needed, she said, there would be no lingering smell. Too often, the smell is not only from lack of attention to obvious need, but also results from too many residents being labeled "incontinent" when the truth is, there is just not enough staff to help them transfer from the bed to the toilet.

Nursing home residents often have malnutrition and dehydration because there is not enough staff to feed them or to help them eat when meals are delivered. Some residents have Alzheimer's or a related dementia and do not even realize they need to eat. Some, because of stroke or other condition, are simply unable to feed themselves without assistance. But most nursing homes simply do not have enough staff to dedicate people to help with feeding.

Families are not without guilt in this story. Many nursing home residents never have a visit from a family member, much less one who will pitch in and help out. I have observed over and over again that the residents who get the best care are the ones who have family on the scene often. That being said, given the rates that are charged by the facilities, it is even more frustrating to realize the bottom line here: If you want your family member to have even adequate care, family members must be present almost 24/7 and/or private help has to be paid by the family to pick up the slack left in their loved one's care.

The shocking item in the DHHS study is that this situation does not exist in just a few nursing homes, but in so very many of them. The report said that, in 2000, over 91 percent of nursing homes had nurse aide staffing levels that fell below the thresholds identified as minimally necessary to provide needed care. Where can we find the remaining 8 percent in order to place loved ones needing care in those facilities?

Survey Ranks Nursing Homes

The Centers for Medicare and Medicaid Services (CMS) has rated the quality of nursing home care in six pilot states. On Medicare's nursing home Web site (see Resources) you will find a thorough and very easy to navigate site with detailed information about the nursing homes you select, including the number of beds, type of ownership, ratio of staff to patients and other fascinating tidbits.

Tom Scully, former CMS chief, said the information was not really a rating of nursing homes, but a comparison of how they perform on nine quality measures: residents who need more help doing daily activities, residents with infections, residents with pain, residents with pressure sores, residents in physical restraints, residents who lost too much weight, short-stay residents with delirium, short-stay residents with pain and residents who improved in walking.

It will be interesting to see what nursing home administrators and owners have to say about the site as time passes. A story in the *Washington Post* quoted Sheila McLean, administrator of the ManorCare Chevy Chase nursing home. She emphasized that consumers should not evaluate a facility based only on the numbers from the site. She explained that there are several reasons you cannot just take the ratings as black and white. For example, a particular nursing home may actually specialize in the care of patients with pressure sores, it would have many more such patients than the average facility.

McLean advised consumers to review the information and visit the facilities that interest them. She commented that the ratings, and their resulting publicity, would assist facilities in developing benchmarks to measure their own improvement. I think this rating system will end up as a wonderful resource for residents and their families, but it may have a net effect of ultimately raising costs as facilities attempt to improve their ratings.

The "Eden Alternative" Makes Nursing Homes More Livable

In my elder law practice I often have occasion to visit area nursing homes, and I frequently talk to families who have a loved one in these homes. Although some families are pleased with basic and needed services, I have yet to meet anyone who does not think that admission to a nursing home is absolutely the last resort for any caregiving problem.

A 2002 poll by the PBS *News Hour*, the Kaiser Family Foundation and the Harvard School of Public Health found that almost half of all Americans think people are worse off after going into nursing homes than before they went in. And more than four in 10 would find it "totally unacceptable" to move into a nursing home themselves.

Not enough staff, high turnover of overworked and underpaid employees, frequent turnover of administrators and the hygiene, staffing and caregiving problems that result from these situations are astounding and pitiful. As Dr. William H. Thomas says in his book, *Life Worth Living: How Someone You Love Can Still Enjoy Life in a Nursing Home*, "It's like a hospital and a poor house got together and had a baby, and the baby was a nursing home...At its deepest heart, it's an institution, and that is just not any way to live a life."

When a much-loved member of my family was in a nursing home for rehab after surgery, I actually had to hire a health aide to stay with her in order for her to even get her pain medicine in a timely fashion. Forget about staff help with bathing, dressing and eating. Not every family can afford, even with budget stretching, to pay an aide to make sure their loved one gets proper care. And, far too often, their loved one does not.

This problem has no easy answers. The facilities themselves have a ready response to constant criticism. Mostly their problems can be boiled down to finances. Tight budgets do not allow them to pay salaries to hire excellent (or even adequate) staff. When residents are on government programs, the very low rates paid to the homes do not allow them to provide the services they should.

Dr. Thomas writes, "Patients understand the enormous difference between simply receiving treatment, and being well cared for." And that is the situation he has set about to change. He envisions "high-value nursing home care that can be delivered at a reasonable cost and can strengthen the connection among generations." He calls this approach the "Eden Alternative." Hopefully, Eden Alternative is an idea whose time has come.

In February 2002, Dr. Thomas was interviewed by Susan Dentzer on PBS for a program titled A *Nursing Home Alternative*. The program highlighted standard features of an "edenized" nursing home that includes houseplants, on-site daycare centers for children of nursing home workers and various animals scurrying about. Residents see and interact with children from the daycare center who, along with the plants and animals, make the environment seem more energetic and alive.

Of course, not all residents like plants or pets—or children, for that matter. So the real issue, says Dr. Charles Roadman, CEO of the American Health Care Association, is choice. Nursing home residents are provided with many of the same choices they have on the "outside," and therefore they perceive some control over their own existence.

St. Luke's Home in Utica, New York is one of more than 200 nursing homes that have adopted the Eden approach. Bread is baked every day before mealtimes, so the aroma of baking bread wafts through into the halls, stimulating the appetite of residents. Meals are served family-style in dining rooms with soup placed in a crock-pot for residents to help themselves. While this approach is obviously more labor intensive than plastic trays delivered quickly to a resident alone in her room, the result is a group of happier, more sociable and generally healthier residents.

Another aspect of the Eden Alternative is cross-trained staff. A team of workers will focus on a resident and perform a variety of needed functions. Aides get to know a patient's needs by consistently caring for the same person. Additionally, residents are encouraged to take an active role in the nursing home's operations. This is designed to stave off what Dr. Thomas says can be "a devastating slide into passivity and helplessness."

Advocating for Loved Ones in a Nursing Home

"My mother is in a nursing home. I'm frustrated by the lack of care she receives. Even this sub-standard care is expensive. What can I do?"

By law, there are services that all nursing homes are required to provide. The Baltimore County Department of Aging suggests several steps for dealing with this question. First, identify the issue. If possible, determine exactly who is responsible for causing the problem. Second, if it is a single occurrence, speak directly to the staff person who is responsible. If that person is not responsive, go to the person's supervisor. If the problem is recurring or is of a more serious nature, immediately go to the employee's supervisor. If you do not receive satisfaction, continue to move up the chain of command. Ultimately, the administrator is responsible for investigating any complaints made against the facility within 30 days.

Every nursing home is required by law to have a formal grievance policy. Ask for a copy of the grievance procedure and feel free to use it, regardless of the nature of the complaint. Additionally, under the Older American's Act there is an ombudsman program available to assist you and your family with these types of problems (see Resources).

Resources

AARP Home Design Page
Web site: www.aarp.org/universalhome/home.html
Checklists to help make your aging relative's living
environment safe.

Assisted Living INFO
Web site: www.assistedlivinginfo.com
An online guide for selecting a residence facility.

Assisted Living in Maryland: What You Need to Know by the
Elder Law Section of the Maryland State Bar Association
Phone: (410) 706-3378
E-mail: cmarshal@law.umaryland.edu

Caregiver Jobs Clearinghouse
Web site: www.carecareers.net
Nationwide listing of jobs in the long-term care field.

*The Continuing Care Retirement Community: A Guidebook for
Consumers* by the American Association of Housing Services
for the Aging (AAHSA)
Phone: (800) 508-9442

Consumer Protection Division of the Maryland Attorney
General's Office
Web site: www.oag.state.md.us/
Provides useful information about nursing home care.

Episcopal Senior Ministries (ESM)
Web site: www.esm.org
Phone: (202) 414-6311
E-mail: volunteer@esm.org
Offers services or volunteer information.

Henderson House Assisted Living Facility
Phone: (301) 218-6972
Address: 16404 Pointer Ridge Drive, Bowie, MD 20716
A small, high-quality Assisted Living Facility

Life Worth Living: How Someone You Love Can Still Enjoy Life in a Nursing Home by Dr. William H. Thomas (VanderWyk & Burnham: 1996)

Maryland Department of Health and Mental Hygiene
Web site: www.dhmh.state.md.us
Phone: (877) 463-3464
Address: 201 West Preston Street, Baltimore, MD 21201
Licenses senior residence facilities and makes copies of facilities' residence contracts available.

Maryland's Long-term Care Ombudsman, Maryland Department of Aging
Web site: www.mdoa.state.md.us/Services/Ombudsman.html
Phone: (410) 767-1100
Address: 201 West Preston Street, Room 1007,
Baltimore, MD 21201
Program to mediate concerns and problems with nursing homes.

Medicare's Nursing Home Overview
Web site: www.medicare.gov/Nursing/Overview.asp
Compares nursing homes in "Nursing Home Compare" section.

National Citizens' Coalition for Nursing Home Reform
Web site: www.nccnhr.org
Phone: (202) 332-2276
Address: 1424 16th Street, NW, Suite 202,
Washington, D.C. 20036
An information and advocacy group that offers two useful publications, *A Consumer Guide to Choosing a Nursing Home* and *Nursing Home Staffing: A Guide for Residents, Families, Friends, and Caregivers*.

National Resource Center on Supportive Housing and
Home Modification
Web site: www.homemods.org
Safety checklists and a guide to home modifications for
senior safety.

*Nursing Home Staffing: A Guide for Residents, Families, Friends,
and Caregivers* (National Citizens' Coalition for Nursing Home
Reform: 2002)

Nursing Homes: What You Need to Know by the Consumer
Protection Division, the Maryland State Bar Association, the
University of Maryland School of Law's Law and Health Care
Program and the Maryland Office on Aging and Legal Aid
Phone: (410) 576-6500

Solving Nursing Home Problems: A Guide for Families
Address: AARP Fulfillment, EE01522, 601 E Street NW,
Washingto, D.C. 20049
Offers an informational booklet; be sure to include the title, stock
number (D17065) and your mailing address in your request.

Subsidy for Prince George's County, Maryland Assisted
Living Facilities
Phone: (301) 699-2731
Address: Prince George's County Department of Aging,
5012 Rhode Island Avenue, Hyattsville, MD 20781

5
Other Challenges
Facing Seniors

Seniors Raising Grandchildren

Legal Issues When Raising Grandchildren

In the past 25 years, the number of children living in households headed by grandparents has increased by more than 50
percent. Across the country, more than six million children—
approximately one in 12—are living in households headed by
grandparents or other relatives. According to the 2000 Census,
Maryland has more than 129,000 children living in households
headed by grandparents or other relatives. Approximately one
third of these children have no parent present in the grandparent-headed household.

Grandparent-headed households are found in every ethnic
and socioeconomic group. In many of these households, grandparents and other relatives are the primary caregivers ("kinship
caregivers") for children whose parents cannot or will not care
for them because of substance abuse, illness and death, abuse and
neglect, economic hardship, incarceration, divorce, domestic
violence and other family and community crises.

A lot of the problems experienced by grandparents raising grandchildren arise from the lack of legal authority to make decisions for the child. It is possible to gain legal authority to make personal, medical, educational and various other decisions for the child through written consent from one of the child's parents. Although this option exists, according to Robert Fleming, a Fellow of the National Academy of Elder Law Attorneys and author of *Elder Law Answer Book*, parents rarely give written consent. Additionally, it would be cumbersome to frequently provide written consent on a day-to-day basis. Legal avenues for grandparents that involve more permanent legal authority to make decisions for a grandchild include obtaining legal custody, guardianship and adoption.

Let us take a quick overview of the first option: custody. A grandparent who has legal custody of a grandchild may determine the child's upbringing, and has a legal obligation to make appropriate decisions regarding the child's education and health care. Maryland courts require a showing that granting the grandparent custody is in the best interests of the child. One potential negative of legal custody is that a parent may return (perhaps years later) and request that the court return the child to the custody of the parent. This could severely interfere with the child's need for stability.

The second option is guardianship. In general, a guardian is one who legally has the care and management of a person. Guardians must be named by the court, and they are supervised by the court, which requires regular inventories and accountings. A grandparent seeking guardianship has to accept that the court is essentially a participant in parenting the child. Any interested party may intervene and may contest the grandparent's actions regarding the child. Guardianship may be challenged by the natural parents even after it has been established. Grandparent guardians are required to seek court approval for certain actions, such as moving to another state or changing the child's legal name.

Adoption grants the grandparent the most complete legal right, acting to sever any parental rights of the child's natural parents. Legal adoption requires that the natural parent sign a form consenting to the adoption and terminating parental rights. Following court-ordered adoption, parents no longer have rights, responsibilities or duties toward the child. The grandparent becomes legally responsible for the child, just as they were for their natural-born children.

There are ways in which a grandparent may be eligible to receive tax refunds or credits. Maryland has a state Earned Income Tax Credit (EITC) that provides a refund to families who do not have to pay federal income tax. In order to qualify, the grandparents must be employed and meet an income requirement. Additionally, a grandparent may also be eligible for the Child and Dependent Care Credit, which is designed to help families who must pay for childcare work or look for a job. Check with your tax adviser.

Generations United is an organization that, among other things, sponsors the National Center on Grandparents and Other Relatives Raising Children. They have books, pamphlets and other resources to share with families in this situation.

See Resources for contact information.

The Difficult Subject of Senior Driving

Senior Driving Statistics

"Should I allow my elder loved one to continue to drive?" is a difficult question. This dilemma can only grow more difficult with time. Estimates are that by 2030 more than 32 million drivers over the age of 75 will be on the road—that is double the number there are today.

Family members are perplexed and troubled. They truly want to protect the elderly driver—and others—from the driver's potential recklessness, and yet they want to preserve their loved one's self-esteem and independence. These conflicting desires make families reluctant to take any action, other than to knock on wood, pray hard and hope for the best.

It seems to be fairly well known that people over 65 almost always wear seat belts, seldom speed and rarely drink and drive. In addition to being among the most responsible and experienced drivers on the road, they are less likely to hit pedestrians and have fewer accidents than any other age group. However, this group also drives fewer miles. Masonicare's Web site says that when you adjust figures for crashes per mile, drivers over 75 are second only to teenagers, the group at highest risk. In addition, the Institute for Highway Safety reports that a 65-year-old is more than three times as likely to die in a serious two-car collision than a teen.

State lawmakers are nearly as confused as families. Some states that require additional testing after a certain age are being sued for age discrimination. Also, the legislators know that many 30-year-olds are terribly unsafe drivers, and many people over 80 are very safe drivers.

How to Talk About Poor Driving Habits

Some years ago, when my son got his learner's permit to drive, he was out practice driving with my husband in our family car when an elderly man driving in a large car hit our family vehicle. As the man approached my husband he pleaded, "I will pay for this. I will pay for this. Just, please, don't tell my son!"

One of the most difficult issues facing the children of aging parents is the necessity of taking the car keys away from the person who taught them how to drive. It is incredibly sad for everyone involved.

A friend told me that she was discussing this issue with her elderly mother who responded in no uncertain terms, "You need to pay attention to your own problems instead of sticking your nose into my driving!"

The ability to drive represents independence. That is why it is so important to teenagers. They want the freedom to visit friends, go to the movies and shop without having to rely on a parent to drive them. It is exactly the same for seniors. They want the freedom to choose when to go to church, visit friends, go to the doctor or go grocery shopping at their convenience. They do not want to wait until it is convenient for someone else to take them.

Additionally, they are facing certain types of losses with each new day, each one representing a blow to their independence. The loss of the ability to drive often forces the issue of facing up to other unpleasant realities. When seniors can no longer drive, they have even fewer social contacts and become increasingly dependent on others for basic human interactions.

Unfortunately, the issue is most often resolved when the senior finally has an accident—often injuring him or herself or others. Dr. Mary Pipher suggests senior driving be discussed frequently and years before a decision must be made. This way, the idea is not as threatening. You can simply say something like, "You know, we are concerned with Grandpa's ability to drive. I realize that one of these days you may face the same dilemma with me. This is how I would like you to handle it."

When we say, "This is how I would like you to handle it," we are making (in our own minds) a sort of commitment that we will realize the time has come to give up the keys, and we will respond appropriately. There probably will be plenty of "slips between the cup and the lip" on this idea, but at least it is better than no conversation at all about this difficult topic, which is typical of most families.

The Complete Eldercare Planner by Joy Loverde provides instructive insight for caregivers. She writes that our first instinct when a loved one is doing something that we know is potentially harmful is to tell him or her what should be done. Unfortunately, adult relationships become strained or even severed this way. For the best results, Loverde says, resist the urge to command an elder to stop driving and instead negotiate him or her off the road by asking questions. This approach will, of course, take longer, but will most likely encourage the senior to self-evaluate driving skills. Some questions suggested to get the ball rolling include:

1. Sometimes when I drive at night; it is hard to see. Do you notice that too?
2. Do other drivers make you nervous?
3. Do you get jumpy when everybody seems to be going too fast?
4. Isn't parking getting more difficult and expensive these days?
5. Have you read anything on the Driver Safety program offered by AARP?

The issue will not be resolved quickly or easily. Give your beloved elder enough time to think between conversations and to do some mental adjusting. Remember that psychologists say keeping the conversation in the form of questions creates a more trusting communication environment and gives better results. While you are working on this problem, it is important to research transportation alternatives and let your elder know what is available and encourage him or her to try a few of the options. Also, try to prevent social isolation. One of the best ways is to get your loved one involved in a local senior center.

How to Tell When Driving Is Unsafe

Safe driving demands the complex coordination of a host of skills. CaregiverZone.com lists some physical and mental changes accompanying aging that diminish the ability to drive. None of these changes alone automatically means that seniors should not drive. But caregivers need to regularly evaluate a senior's ability and assess whether the person needs to alter driving habits or stop driving altogether.

- Slowdown in response time
- Loss of clarity in vision and hearing
- Loss of muscle strength and flexibility
- Drowsiness caused by increased use of medications
- Reduction in the ability to focus or concentrate
- Lower tolerance for alcohol

Age is not necessarily a good indicator of how safely anyone drives. State legislators are notoriously, and correctly, wary of picking a specific age at which someone must relinquish their driver's license.

"You can't just as a matter of course say, 'Once you reach 85, you can't drive anymore,'" said Susan Ferguson, senior vice president of research at the Insurance Institute for Highway Safety, which is funded by auto insurers. "It would take driver's licenses away from people who are perfectly fine to drive." Nevertheless, stories of seniors in car accidents must give us pause.

Geriatric medicine specialist Dr. Robert Wang says a senior can identify his or her own driving problems in a self-examination by asking these questions:

- Do I have trouble turning the steering wheel or trouble looking over my shoulder when backing up?
- Do I avoid driving at night?
- Do other drivers honk at me?
- Do other drivers drive too fast or do other cars appear out of nowhere?
- Do I have trouble seeing signs in time to respond?

Any of these questions answered with a "yes" may be warning signs. But Wang says to keep in mind that normal driving may disguise problems that will not surface until an emergency arises. Wang said the American Medical Association is planning to issue guidelines that will help physicians know when their older patients have become risky drivers, not to persuade them to get off the road, but to get them help and training so they can continue to drive as safely as possible.

Cognitive Impairment and Driving

According to Jack Paul Gesino, of Masonicare, a Connecticut health care and retirement living provider, "It is hard enough to explain to people who have a physical problem that they should no longer drive, but at least you can have a dialogue about it. Cognitive impairment is far more difficult because these people simply are not capable of recognizing that there is a problem. In addition to often not realizing their own declining abilities, those with diseases that impair brain function frequently do not appreciate the inherent risks of driving."

There is a pamphlet prepared by the Maryland Department of Motor Vehicle Administration (MVA) and the Alzheimer's Association, dealing with the ticklish subject of when seniors should give up driving. "Is It Time to Stop Driving?" is a sensitive guide for caregivers of people with Alzheimer's and related disorders. It is available at any MVA office.

Alzheimer's can cause a number of problems for the driver, including memory loss, an inability to perform routine tasks, impaired judgment, disorientation related to time or place, impaired visual and spatial perception, slowed reaction time, diminished attention span and an inability to recognize cues— such as stop signs, traffic lights and the police.

The MVA pamphlet says that if a person with Alzheimer's, or any related disorder, experiences one or more of the following problems, it may be time to limit or stop driving:

- Gets lost while driving in a familiar location
- Takes longer than usual when driving alone to and from familiar places, and then denies being lost
- Drives at inappropriate speeds
- Fails to observe traffic signs and signals
- Becomes angry, frustrated or confused when driving
- Gets involved in or causes accidents, including fender benders and "close calls"

The Alzheimer's Association suggests that you talk with the doctor about your concerns for your senior's ability to drive safely. Most people say they will listen to their doctor. You can often get the doctor to advise your senior to reduce his or her driving, go for a driving evaluation or new test or stop driving altogether. If the doctor wants to encourage the senior to voluntarily stop driving, ask him to prescribe it, in writing, on a prescription pad.

Realizing that your senior has had many years of independent driving, you should plan in advance what you want to say to the driver and perhaps seek the support of others—such as family members or physicians and health care providers. When you are all prepared, encourage the person to stop driving voluntarily. Prepare in advance how to meet the person's passion to continue driving with assurances that a ride will be available when wanted.

If you plan to simply take the keys away, you should avoid long explanations about why you are doing so and why driving is no longer an option. Focus, instead, on other activities the senior may still be able to enjoy. Try to get his or her mind off this development, and do not be drawn into long arguments over the issue.

Before looking at the MVA pamphlet, I was not aware that you can contact the Maryland MVA's Medical Advisory Board for a reexamination of the driver, regardless of age. Your report is strictly confidential. The MVA board will ask you to include a short description of the driving problems and any incidents that have been observed that are of concern. This will start a request for more information on the medical condition from the doctor, driver and family. Additional screening tests may be conducted to determine the person's fitness to drive, including a behind-the-wheel assessment.

Senior Driving and the Law

According to Maryland law, any person who has been treated by a physician or hospital for one of a number of physical or mental disorders is required to notify the Medical Advisory Board (MAB) of the Maryland MVA of their condition. Conditions that must be reported include diabetes, cerebral palsy, epilepsy, multiple sclerosis, muscular dystrophy, heart condition, stroke, brain injury, alcoholism or alcohol abuse, drug addiction, loss of limb or limbs and any other illness in which there was a lapse of consciousness, blackout or seizure.

It is each individual's responsibility to notify the MAB either by phone or in writing about their injury or illness. The MAB will then give instructions as to the proper procedure to follow before resuming driving.

The MAB may require those with such problems to have a physician complete a form indicating diagnosis, prognosis, medicine and therapy. The MAB then decides if the condition affects the ability to drive. Potential drivers may be asked to appear before a panel of doctors for an interview, whereby they would have the opportunity to present additional information regarding their condition. Finally, they may be required to take the written exam or the actual driving exam, or both.

Programs That Offer Help to Senior Drivers

Sinai Hospital on West Belvedere Avenue in Baltimore offers a driver evaluation and training program that can re-certify seniors to drive and/or simply reassure their families that they are safe behind the wheel. The evaluation is a two-part process, each part taking an hour and a half to two hours. The first section is a pre-driving screening, and the testing is done by a licensed occupational therapist. The therapist administers tests to assess the would-be driver's vision, perception, cognition, functional ability and reaction time.

The vision section includes visual acuity, peripheral vision, color blindness and sign recognition. The perception part tests for visual discrimination, spatial relationships and depth perception. Cognition refers to memory, attention and problem-solving skills. Functional ability tests strength, coordination, range of motion and sensation.

As a general rule, the hospital will not schedule the two tests on the same day because if someone fails the pre-driving screening he or she is not allowed to continue to the-behind-the-wheel evaluation. At the end of the first period of testing, the therapist will go over the driver's results with the driver and any interested family member who is present. If the applicant passed the pre-screening, an appointment is made to return to Baltimore for the-behind-the-wheel section of the test.

This section takes place in a Sinai-owned and insured vehicle that has a variety of adaptive controls for individuals with disabilities. The occupational therapist assesses the applicant's needs for special equipment, if necessary. The applicant is asked to drive a specific route, with directions provided by the therapist sitting in the passenger seat.

Most health insurance plans do not cover the cost of any portion of this re-certification, which may also include driver training sessions. Both evaluations are charged by the hour, and the applicant must pay on the day of the test. If necessary or desired, the therapist will submit recommendations to the MAB.

A pilot program in Maryland also intends to address the problem of driving and age. The program, sponsored by the American Association of Motor Vehicle Administrators in conjunction with Virginia, Maryland and the District of Columbia, encourages older drivers and their caretakers to be aware of how aging can affect driving ability and to take steps to address driving issues as they appear.

The Maryland program will develop screening instruments for drivers. These tests will analyze vision, physical capability, memory, cognition and perception. Maryland Delegate Adrienne Mandel says that such tests have not yet been determined to be accurate risk indicators, and she recommends the GrandDriver program.

GrandDriver volunteers speak to Rotary Clubs, physicians' groups, clergy meetings and senior centers. It provides information on where people can sign up for driver-refresher courses and where to get information regarding alternative transportation. Volunteers also tell seniors where to find more information about how aging can affect their driving ability.

Driving is one of those things like a person's finances—it is often very difficult to bring up for conversation between an elderly loved one and their family. Importantly, the GrandDriver volunteers encourage people to talk—before the situation reaches crisis level. They encourage older people to talk to each other and to their doctors about age and safe driving. "The program encourages people to discuss their experiences and to listen to the experiences of others," said Delegate Mandel.

AARP offers programs for older drivers; so does the Association for Driver Rehabilitation. See the Resources section at the end of this chapter for information on these and other resources.

National Academy of Elder Law Attorneys member Robert Fleming of Tucson, Arizona suggests that families draft a document titled something like "Agreement with My Family About Driving." The wording in such an agreement could be along these lines:

"I have discussed with my family my desire to drive as long as it is safe for me to do so. When it is not reasonable for me to drive, I would like **name** or **name** to tell me that I should no longer drive. I wish for **name** to assist by consulting with my physician or a driving rehabilitation specialist about my ability to drive safely. If I am unwilling or unable to surrender my driver's license after a professional concurs that I am unable to drive safely, I agree that the following steps may be initiated by **name**:

1. he/she may contact my physician so that he/she may alert the state department of motor vehicles, or he/she may do so directly;
2. he/she may take possession of my car keys;
3. he/she may take possession of my car; and
4. he/she may sell my car and use the proceeds to pay for alternative transportation.

Alternatives to Senior Driving

Stopping driving should not mean sacrificing quality of life. The families and friends of seniors should get together and talk to the senior to determine where the senior wants to go and what he or she wants to do. Alternative transportation solutions can surely be worked out. We know there is already home delivery of groceries, prescription medicines and meals. Perhaps hairdressers could make home visits.

Supplemental Transportation Programs for Seniors (STP) are essentially volunteer, grassroots-type programs to provide seniors with alternative forms of transportation. There are about 300 of them in the United States, the vast majority of which are not affiliated with any government or municipal transportation organization. Most are staffed by volunteers.

STP literature explains that "Strapped-for-cash municipalities don't have funds available to cater to the specific challenges posed by our aging population. While seniors continue to drive at ever older ages, more and more 'senior seniors'—those aged 85 and

**Help for Senior Drivers on
the Internet**

*The AAA Foundation for Traffic Safety sponsors Senior Drivers,
a Web site to "help senior drivers stay safely behind the wheel as
many years as possible." A wonderful menu of flexibility and
range of motion exercises is on the site, with detailed instructions
for each available on video clips or in text. This site is directed to
seniors themselves, not caregivers. There are preparation suggestions, an area for clicking on driving situations that may be
causing you trouble (such as four-way stops) and tips for long-
distance traveling, all hosted by a senior couple. Additionally,
self-testing is available on the site. You can test your knowledge
about sleep and driving and take a self-assessment test. See the
Resources section for more information.*

■ ■ ■

higher—have no true transportation alternatives. Their special
needs require the services of a niche provider, such as those who
sponsor, organize, maintain and administer STPs." Sponsored by
the AAA Foundation for Traffic Safety and the Beverly
Foundation, their Web site is a resource for those who wish to
start a STP. For more information, see the Resources section.

Adult children sometimes feel that their parents are too
proud to use public transportation. However, the Beverly
Foundation points out many reasons that seniors cannot use
public transportation, and none of them have to do with pride:

1. Many public transportation vehicles are designed in such
   a way that access to them is very difficult for seniors.
2. Sometimes the transit stops are too far away—a senior
   needs transportation to the bus stop.
3. Seniors are often unable to wait or travel for long

periods of time: many of them are in need of assistance from escorts, some are fearful of getting lost and many are fearful of falling.

4. Some seniors do not have available funds to pay the cost of public transportation.

5. Seniors are concerned about safety (such as muggings) on public transportation or to and from the stops.

6. Many seniors remain unaware of existing transportation options.

Senior Benefits

Older Americans Act Helps States Provide a Variety of Services

Did you know there is an Older Americans Act? In 1965, the same year Medicare was enacted, Congress passed the federal Older Americans Act (OAA). The act has been tweaked from time to time, such as adding a national nutrition program for the elderly in 1972, but it is still the primary vehicle for organizing and delivering social and nutritional services to seniors in this country. The OAA was enacted during President Lyndon Johnson's Great Society legislation, and it requires that funds be targeted at those seniors in greatest social and economic need.

In-home services include homemaker and home health aides, visiting and telephone reassurance, chore maintenance and supportive services for families of people with Alzheimer's disease.

The *Legal Services Program* provides legal advice and representation to assist seniors with economic or social needs. Priority is given to issues involving health care, nutrition, income maintenance or disability benefits, protective services (abuse, institutionalization, guardianship) and housing and utilities aid.

Staff will assist in defending a senior in a lawsuit where there is a substantial risk to the client's person, property or civil rights.

Another service supported by funding under the OAA is the "Long-term Care Ombudsman and Elder Abuse Prevention Program." This program serves to protect and enhance the health, safety and rights of residents of long-term care residential facilities by investigating possible violations or abuses that may adversely affect the quality of life or care. There is a lot to be done in preventing this type of criminal conduct, which is especially heinous when it is done by those being trusted to provide a loved one with warm and tender care.

The "Senior Health Insurance Assistance Program" (SHIP) offers face-to-face or telephone assistance and counseling about problems seniors encounter regarding health insurance. It helps Medicare beneficiaries understand their health insurance benefits, bills and rights. The SHIP office provides trained staff and volunteer counselors who offer assistance in the following general areas:

- Medicare
- Medigap Plans
- HMOs
- Assistance for disabled Medicare beneficiaries under age 65
- Medicare Plus Choice
- Long-term care insurance
- Medical assistance programs, including Medicaid
- Pharmacy assistance benefits
- Billing problems
- Assistance with denials, appeals and grievances
- Free community presentations and more

The OAA also includes the *public guardianship programs*. Under OAA, Maryland law permits the director of the state or local Department of Aging to be appointed by the court as the guardian of the person for adults age 65 or older for whom no other suitable guardian is available. Public Guardianship Review Boards in each jurisdiction evaluate these guardianships regularly.

In Maryland, OAA services are provided by the Maryland Department of Aging and local area agencies on aging. It is important to know about the types of services that might be available to you and those for whom you care. Supportive services help older adults avoid declines in physical, psychological and social well-being. Nutritional services, through congregate meals and in-home delivery, help to assure that older adults are receiving at least one meal a day that provides at least one-third of the daily recommended dietary allowance.

Senior centers are funded under the OAA. These centers are a focal point for service delivery, and in Maryland they provide nutrition programs, information and assistance, health insurance counseling, continuing education, travel, volunteer opportunities, education and health screenings, physical and recreational activities, transportation, leadership and mandated services.

Senior Care is a Maryland state-funded program, available to seniors who meet income eligibility guidelines. Program staff members provide a comprehensive assessment of the client's needs and a case manager to coordinate community-based in-home services for seniors with disabilities who are at risk of institutionalization. There are three senior employment services in Maryland to help provide part-time employment for unemployed low-income adults who are 55 years of age or older.

If you call the Office of Senior Information and Assistance, you may be able to have a case worker come to your home and assess your needs, or those of your spouse or another loved one for whom you care, and recommend services for which you may be eligible under the Older Americans Act. See Resources at the end of the chapter for contact information.

Are You Getting Your Benefits?

Among the myriad of statistics that cross my desk, this one caught my eye: More than five million older Americans are currently missing out on benefits programs that can provide help with health care, transportation, income support, legal services, housing, energy assistance, meals and other important services. They are missing out because they do not know that the programs are available.

James Firman, president of the National Council on the Aging (NCOA), a nonprofit advocacy group for older Americans, and America Online, Inc.

All Veterans Are Entitled to Benefits

There are approximately 25 million veterans in the United States and less than 10 percent of them receive VA service-connected disability compensation (paid for disabilities incurred or aggravated during their military service). Because of a widespread belief that veterans must have been injured during military service in order to qualify for VA benefits, many elderly and disabled veterans and their survivors are not aware that they may qualify for certain VA benefits. Information concerning VA benefits and services, including a VA pamphlet, Federal Benefits for Veterans and Dependents, *may be found on the VA Web site (see Resources). Claims for compensation and pensions may also be filed over the Internet. In order to qualify for VA benefits, veterans must generally have a "good" discharge—a discharge under conditions other than dishonorable.*

■ ■ ■

recently announced a partnership to try and remedy that situation. They have launched a new online service that identifies all federal and state assistance programs available to older Americans.

The program, called BenefitsCheckUp, is a free public service that will help individuals quickly and easily determine what benefits they qualify for and how to get them.

Here is how it works: You take a few minutes to enter information about your financial situation into an online questionnaire. The program then explains what benefit programs you may be eligible for and how to apply for them. This is completely confidential. It does not require your name, address, phone number, Social Security number or any other information that could be used to identify you. You enter simple information, such as your age, income and zip code. I have tried this out myself, and ended up with a lovely seven-page report identifying public benefits programs for an older relative to consider. The report included details such as program descriptions, local contact information where questions can be answered or applications can be completed and a listing of necessary documentation to aid in the application process. There is a simple disclaimer that points out that final program eligibility determination can only be made by the agencies administering the program(s). See the Resources section for how to use BenefitsCheckUp.

How to Avoid Scams and Fraud

Telemarketing and Scams Target Seniors

Financial exploitation is the improper use of a vulnerable adult's funds or property. A vulnerable adult is someone who lacks the physical or mental capacity to provide for all of his or her daily needs. People over 60 years of age are the most rapidly growing segment of our population. Old people may be very vulnerable to abuse, and unscrupulous people increasingly target them as victims. The media and average citizens tend to focus on the most visible tragedy: physical abuse of older adults. But, according to statistics, a more frequent form of abuse is financial exploitation. Adult Protective Service agencies throughout the country find that over 20 percent of their substantiated cases of mistreatment involve financial exploitation. There are an increasing number of con artists targeting elders. Many cases go unreported or are not discovered until the victim has been stripped of all assets.

What You Can Do to Prevent Fraud

The Department of Aging for Baltimore County suggests the following ways to avoid being a victim. It is a useful list of "Nevers" for you to keep in mind.

Never do business with someone who refuses to send you written information on their product, offer or charity. Never respond to pressure to act today. Legitimate businesses allow you time to make an informed decision. Never judge a person's integrity by how they sound. If they say something like "I've spoken with your husband" (or another trusted person), check out that matter with the person before believing it.

Never provide credit card information to a person who calls you. Only give your credit card number if you placed the call yourself to a legitimate business. Never provide bank account information to a person who calls you. Your bank already knows your account number.

Never pay taxes, duty or shipping charges on a prize you are told you have won. Legitimate businesses will arrange for you to receive your prize without a delivery charge. With a cash prize, the promoter will withhold the taxes or report the amount of your winnings to the IRS. Never buy something in order to win a prize. This practice is illegal, and reputable businesses do not require a purchase in order to enter a contest.

Never invest your money without thoroughly investigating the company or business you are considering. Never make an investment with an organization that refuses to send you information in writing.

Never purchase a trip, a time share or vacation without checking the company's record and the satisfaction of previous travelers.

Never contribute to a charity if the person soliciting you offers to send a messenger to collect your contribution. Never contribute to a charity that says you pledged money when you know you did not (or even if you think you did not).

Never contribute to a charity until you have seen the annual report and know how much money goes to fund-raising and how much to administration. Legitimate charities may spend as much as 10 percent on overhead, but more than that may indicate that intended clients are not benefiting from the funds raised.

Never contribute to a charity just because you think the name sounds familiar. There are plenty of unscrupulous charities that have chosen names very similar to legitimate organizations. Ask for a financial report.

Never invest in out-of-state or foreign lotteries. The only legal lotteries are those operated by a state government within the boundaries of that state.

Never enter 90#, 90* or #00 on your telephone if someone tells you they are checking the lines or for any other reason. If you do, you will find yourself billed for long distance phone charges you did not make. Telephone service technicians never ask customers for help in checking the lines. Never return a call to an area code with which you are unfamiliar. To identify area code locations, look in your phone book.

Lastly, never, ever be embarrassed or afraid to report telemarketing fraud or abuse. You may be helping your relatives, neighbors and many other people.

How to Reduce Junk Mail and Telemarketing Calls

It is possible to at least reduce the number of telemarketing calls and junk mail you receive.

The Federal Trade Commission manages a National Do Not Call Registry. This government service gives you a choice about whether to receive telemarketing calls at home. Most telemarketers should not call your number once it has been on the registry for three months. If they do, you can file a complaint with the FTC. You may register up to three telephone numbers at one time on the Web site. Your registration is effective for five years.

You can register your phone at the Web Site www.donotcall.gov. An informative list of frequently asked questions about the registry is also at this site. You can verify that your phone has been registered by calling the registry's toll free number (1-888-382-1222).

If you give a company your written permission to call you, they may do so even if you have placed your number on the National Do Not Call Registry. If you do not want to be on the National registry, but want to limit telemarketing calls, you can ask the individual vendors to put you on their company's do not call list.

Further, you can get a lot of companies to stop calling you by registering with the Telephone Preference Service. This is an umbrella do-not-call list that company members of the Direct Marketing Association (DMA) are required to honor. You will be kept on this list for five years. Registration with the DMA will help reduce the number of telemarketing calls you receive, but it will not stop all such calls. Telemarketers who are not members of the DMA are not required to use the list.

There is always the possibility of getting an unlisted number. This is frustrating for friends who are trying to get in touch, and you could lose a phone call that might be important to you. Also, it does not prevent calls from telemarketers that dial numbers in sequential order by computer.

Whenever you give a business your number, ask that they not share it with other companies.

If all else fails, you can avoid having to talk with telemarketers by using an answering machine or a caller ID to screen your calls before you decide to pick up. Many telemarketers hang up if they reach a machine. Also, learn to recognize the sounds of an auto-dialer—you answer your phone and there is a pause. If you do not want to be connected to a sales person, just hang up.

More than one client has mentioned to me that the amount of junk mail he or she receives, especially from credit card companies, amounts to harassment. You can reduce your junk mail by, again, registering with the DMA's Mail Preference Service.

The attorney general's Web site says that those credit card offers that come in the mail are from companies who get your name and address from one of the credit reporting agencies. You can tell all three of the major credit reporting agencies—Equifax, Experian and TransUnion—to remove your name from their mailing lists. Your request will be honored for two years.

Notify magazines and charities that you do not want them to share your name and address with other businesses or charities. Request the same from mail order companies, and cancel catalogs you do not use.

Think twice before entering sweepstakes and drawings. The main purpose of many contests is to compile mailing lists. If you enter one contest, you are likely to receive mailings from other contests.

It was a surprise to me to read that most warranty and product registration cards are used to compile information on consumers that is sold to companies for marketing purposes. The Consumer Protection Agency says that most of the time your purchase receipt will ensure that you are covered by the product warranty if an item turns out to be defective. If you decide to fill out the card anyhow, do not provide the "lifestyle" information requested, such as your income or hobbies.

Junk mail that arrives in envelopes stamped "Address Correction Request" or "Return Postage Guaranteed" can be returned unopened by writing "Refused—return to sender" on the envelope. This may encourage the company that mailed it to you to remove you from its mailing list.

Junkbusters Corporation is a privacy advocacy firm that helps people get rid of junk messages of all kinds: spam, telemarketing calls, junk mail, junk faxes and more. Their Web site is fascinating and chock full of information regarding how to rid yourself of all kinds of stuff that clutters up your life and adds to stress.

You can read more about your rights under the Telephone Customer Protection Act at the Federal Communications

Commission Web site, and the Federal Trade Commission Web site has a lot of information about avoiding telemarketing fraud as well.

See Resources for more information.

Protect Personal Information and Prevent Identity Theft

In addition to being a victim of theft, those who have had their identity stolen face years of explanations, letter writing and frustration as they attempt to straighten out a problem for which they are not at all responsible. According to the Secretary of the Treasury, 12 million Americans have already been victims of identity theft. Thieves target the most vulnerable members of society, including families of the recently deceased, hospital patients, military personnel serving overseas and, of course, the elderly. Here are some ideas to help us avoid identity theft.

To guard your mail and trash from theft, deposit outgoing mail in post office collection boxes or at your local post office rather than in an unsecured mailbox. Promptly remove mail from your mailbox. If you are planning to be away from home and cannot pick up your mail, call the U.S. Postal Service to request a vacation hold. The Postal Service will hold your mail at your local post office until you can pick it up or are at home to receive it.

To thwart an identity thief who may pick through your trash or recycling bins to capture your personal information, tear or shred your charge receipts, copies of credit applications, insurance forms, physician statements, checks, bank statements, expired charge cards and credit offers.

Before revealing any personally identifying information (for example, on an application), find out how the information will be used and secured and whether it will be shared with others. Ask if you have a choice about the use of your information. Can you choose to have it kept confidential? If it will be shared with others, who are they?

Do not carry your Social Security card with you. Leave it in a secure place. Give out your Social Security number only when absolutely necessary. Ask to use other types of identifiers when possible. Maryland does not use Social Security numbers on driver's licenses, but people who live in a state that does should ask that a different number be used, if possible.

Carry only the identification information and the credit and debit cards that you will actually need on each specific errand or shopping trip. Pay attention to your billing cycles. Follow up with creditors if your bills do not arrive on time. A missing credit card bill could mean an identity thief has taken over your account and changed your billing address to cover his tracks.

Be wary of promotional scams. Identity thieves may use phony offers to get you to give them your personal information. Naturally, you want to keep your purse or wallet in a safe place at work and at home.

If you have been a victim of identity theft, call the Identity Theft Hotline of the Federal Trade Commission (FTC). Counselors will take your complaint and advise you on how to deal with the credit-related problems that could result. In addition, the FTC, in conjunction with banks, credit grantors and consumer advocates, has developed the ID Theft Affidavit to help victims of ID theft restore their good names. The ID Theft Affidavit, a form that can be used to report information to many organizations, simplifies the process of disputing charges with companies where a new account was opened in your name.

Your employer and financial institution will likely need your Social Security number (SSN) for wage and tax reporting purposes. Other businesses may ask you for your SSN to do a credit check when you apply for a loan, rent an apartment or sign up for utilities. Sometimes, however, they simply want your SSN for general recordkeeping. You do not have to give a business your SSN just because they ask for it. If someone asks for your SSN, ask the following questions:

- Why do you need my SSN?
- How will my SSN be used?
- What law requires me to give you my SSN?
- What will happen if I do not give you my SSN?

Nowadays most businesses are aware of identity theft and they have instituted different means for identification. But sometimes a business may not provide you with the service or benefit you are seeking if you do not provide your SSN. Getting answers to these questions will help you decide whether you want to share your SSN with the business. Remember, the decision is yours.

One of the best ways to keep an eye out for identity theft is to review your credit report regularly. Each of the three major credit reporting companies, Experian, Equifax and TransUnion acts independently and provides different sorts of information, so it is important to check all three reports to get the entire picture of your credit history.

When you receive the reports, what do you do then? Well, they are not the easiest documents in the world to read. Be sure to read the instructions for understanding the report and for learning the meaning of each entry. The reports contain personal information, payment status of open accounts and public information such as lawsuits, bankruptcies, liens and court judgments.

The report also tells you who has asked for your credit history within the past year. For instance, if you bought a new car in the past year and received a loan to pay for it, you should see the automobile company's request for your credit information.

It is useful to have a highlighter in your hand when studying these reports. That way you can mark certain information that is bothersome to you. Is the entry outdated? An example of that might be a lien that you know has been satisfied but is still appearing on your credit history report. Highlight that. Is an entry just flat-out wrong? An example of that might be when you have paid a bill and can prove it, but the store's records were not updated correctly so they have reported you to the credit reporting agency. Highlight entries that are in error.

You should mark entries that look bad but can be explained. For example, if you moved but your mail was not forwarded to the new address. The Fair Credit Reporting Act allows you to write an explanation describing the reason for the negative entry.

When you have finished highlighting all the bothersome items, contact the reporting agency. Sometimes it is easier to write a separate letter for each complaint. That way nothing gets lost in the shuffle and each bothersome item can be tracked separately. Whenever you send something in the writing to the credit reporting agency, you should send it via certified mail, so it can be tracked if there is no response.

According to Mr. John Nardini, writing in *American Profile*, it is a very good idea to check your credit report at least six weeks before applying for a car loan, lease, mortgage or job. That should allow you time to dispute and correct any inaccuracies in the report.

See Resources for more information.

Tips for personal scam protection, gathered from the VOTE Web site, the National Consumer Law Center and the National Consumers League:

1. Never give anyone your personal information, especially if you do not know who they are. That includes even confirming your address, bank account, credit card numbers, phone numbers or date of birth. The scam technique of confirming information is very clever. If what you are asked to confirm is correct, you will tend to say yes right away. If the information is wrong, your natural tendency will be to provide the correct information.

2. Do not write account numbers on the outside of payment envelopes, even if asked to.

3. Do not keep PIN numbers in your purse or wallet.

4. Do not enter contests. That is a sure-fire way to be added to direct mail lists.

5. Check with police, the Better Business Bureau or the Postmaster's Office to see whether there are any complaints pending against a company.

6. If telemarketers will not identify themselves, hang up.

7. Guard your Social Security number. You are not required to provide this information except for legal matters.

8. Destroy canceled checks, receipts, deposit slips, etc. before throwing them away. Tear them into tiny pieces and put them in trash bags containing coffee grounds, vegetable peelings, etc. Few people want to pour through garbage. You could also invest in an inexpensive shredder.

9. Indicate little or no income if you fill out a survey form. That way, you will not be attractive to marketers.

10. Pay with cash when you can. No personal information is gathered in cash transactions.

11. Do not allow yourself to be pressured into anything.

(cont'd)

12. *Be wary of strangers who try to ingratiate themselves with you too quickly. Strangers are not friends.*

13. *Remember, if something sounds too good to be true it probably is.*

14. *Never give all the money up front. Pay for services when they are finished, not before they begin. If a deposit is required, 10 percent is usually sufficient. Some contractors want a third on signing a contract for major work, another third halfway and the final third on completion. If more up-front money is required, you should think twice, or even forget it.*

15. *When possible, deal with local, established businesspeople that can provide local references and must keep a good reputation within the community. Local Chambers of Commerce are good resources to provide such names.*

16. *Take all the time you need to decide. Do not fall for the old ploy of a better discount or option if you accept the offer right now. You will hear words such as "This is a very special price just for you right now upon signing" and "I'm afraid this offer won't last much longer." Actually, the offer next week may be a whole lot better.*

■ ■ ■

Organizations That Help Prevent Senior Scams

Remember, few people readily admit that they have been the victims of a telemarketing scam. It is embarrassing no matter what your age. If the victims are elderly, they may fear that their judgment will be questioned or that their children or someone else will want to take over their finances. It is important to remember that everyone is vulnerable to a scam artist. Also remember that telemarketing scammers are professional thieves; they make a living stealing from people, and many of them are excellent at their profession.

In Maryland, an initiative called Project SAFE (Stop Adult Financial Exploitation) started by Attorney General Joe Curran, combines public/private partnerships in a collaborative effort to combat financial exploitation of seniors. Through Project SAFE, employees of financial institutions can be trained to identify and report financial exploitation without breaching customer confidentiality. In addition, employees are given information regarding practical help that might assist a vulnerable customer in avoiding targeting by scam artists. Such resources might include transportation to the bank, homemaker services, grocery deliveries and help with financial management. These and many other services make the senior less vulnerable to exploitation or abuse by those with bad intentions.

The Department of Human Resources in each state administers and monitors a system of Adult Protective Services. The primary focus of Adult Protective Service agencies is on ending or alleviating the vulnerable adult's threatening situation through providing a variety of services and interventions. Core services that can be provided are intervention and counseling, coordination of services, advocacy and court petitions. Other services that may be provided or arranged for include assistance with finances, medical services and therapies and home health services.

A senior advocacy group called Voice of the Elderly (VOTE), which works to educate seniors about scams and fraud, was profiled in the *Washington Post* and Leonard Burchman, the group's president and founder, urged seniors to hang up when telemarketers call. Burchman said it is important to repeat stories of scams and frauds often so that elderly people can remember them and recognize when the same thing happens to them. Burchman said, "As we get older, it is important to hear things over and over again because we start to lose some of the things we had stored in our memories."

The good news on this topic is that many states have enacted laws that allow residents to put their names on a list that telemarketers cannot call without risking a government fine. Also, recent sessions in Congress have passed the Senior Fraud Prevention Act, designed to educate senior citizens and raise awareness about the dangers of fraud, including telemarketing and sweepstakes fraud. The act authorizes $5 million over five years for TRIAD, a network of local programs that promotes collaboration between senior volunteers and law enforcement agencies.

Contact information for the organizations mentioned here can be found in the Resources section at the end of this chapter.

Help for Seniors Coping with Increasing Prescription Costs

Facing the Cost of Prescription Drugs

The cost of prescription drugs remains one of the biggest problems facing today's seniors and others on fixed incomes. Pharmacy assistance programs help eligible residents pay for medically necessary prescriptions. Many states have a pharmacy assistance program and a drug discount program. For purposes of clarity, I will use my home state of Maryland as an example in this section.

The Maryland Pharmacy Assistance Program is for people with monthly incomes at or below $869 for one person and $1,010 for a couple in 2004. Total assets must be below $4,000 for one person and below $6,000 for a couple. Under this program, participants pay $5.00 for each prescription and each refill, and the state pays the rest. Proof of income and assets is required. Eligibility is established for a 12-month period.

The Maryland Pharmacy Discount Program (MPDP) guarantees Medicare beneficiaries, with incomes below a certain level, the ability to purchase prescriptions at 65 percent of the Medicaid price for each prescription and each refill. There is also a $1.00 processing fee. The state pays the remaining cost of the prescription. This program is for people who receive Medicare and have monthly incomes below $1,310 for one person and below $1,768 for a couple in 2004. There is no asset test for this benefit. There is no monthly premium to enroll in either program.

You may apply for both programs (Maryland Pharmacy Assistance Program and Maryland Pharmacy Discount Program). Your income and asset level will determine the program for which you are eligible.

Another discount drug program called Medbank helps low-income, chronically ill, uninsured and underinsured individuals get prescription medications at low or no cost. This is done by accessing patient assistance programs maintained by pharmaceutical companies. Not all companies have programs and not all pharmaceuticals are available from patient assistance programs. Brand-name medications for chronic illnesses are often available, but not all brand- name medications are available.

The Maryland Medbank Program serves eligible individuals in Maryland who meet certain financial criteria. The program cannot help individuals with prescription coverage or those who qualify for Medicaid or the Maryland Pharmacy Assistance Program. An individual with a prescription discount card may still qualify for assistance from Medbank.

Patients above the poverty line for Maryland must also be below certain income guidelines determined by the drug companies. Most drug companies list this as 200 percent above poverty. Exceptions do apply. Some companies also consider assets. Thus, someone who appears to qualify from an income guideline may be denied based on assets. On the other hand, some companies also consider out-of-pocket expenses, such as other prescription costs and lab fees. This may allow someone over the income guidelines to qualify.

Most programs provide a 90-day supply of medication that will be sent to the physician's office. Each company and program is different. Some programs give a one-year supply while other programs may give a one-month supply. Most of the prescriptions are free. Some require a co-pay of $5 or $10 per prescription.

It can take two to six weeks from the time your applications reach the pharmaceutical company before you receive your medications the first time. This service is for chronic illnesses. The long wait comes from obtaining all the required information and signatures and the time it takes the pharmaceutical companies to process the applications.

Under the new Medicare Drug Benefit, states that have the authority to act as an authorized representative of a beneficiary (as defined by state law) will be permitted to enroll low-income beneficiaries in drug cards automatically. See Resources for contact information.

The Medicare Drug Discount Card

The Medicare Act of 2003 created a prescription drug discount card program as a temporary way to assist Medicare beneficiaries with their prescription costs until other new Medicare drug benefits actually go into effect in 2006. The temporary drug discount card program is to be in effect from June 2004 through December 31, 2005. Even though it begins in June

2004, enrollees must pay the full yearly fee for 2004. Yearly fees cannot exceed $30.

The program provides eligible Medicare beneficiaries with access to discount prices negotiated by a drug card sponsor that has received an endorsement from Medicare. The discount prices are available for prescriptions that are included in the card's formulary. (A formulary is a book listing medicinal substances along with their formulas, uses and methods of preparation.)

> **How much will the Medicare Act of 2003 actually save me?**
>
> *The Kaiser Family Foundation has released an updated drug benefit calculator that can help you gauge how much the new legislation will assist you in paying for prescription drugs. Some people may actually pay more. Kaiser's online calculator allows you to enter your own prescription drug costs to see what you may pay under the law. See Resources for a link.*
>
> ■ ■ ■

If you are a Medicare beneficiary and you do not receive prescription drug coverage through Medicaid, you may enroll by filling out an application with the card sponsor. What is a card sponsor? A discount card may be offered by a pharmaceutical benefit management company (PBM), a wholesale or retail pharmacy, an insurance company or a Medicare managed care plan. If any of these entities decide to offer a drug discount plan under the new law and the entity has received an endorsement from Medicare to offer the cards, they are referred to as sponsors of the card. Discount cards that are approved by Medicare will display a Medicare-approved mark on the card.

By filing the application, the individual authorizes the Social Security Administration and the state Medicaid agency to provide verification of the individual's eligibility for the program. You can enroll in only one discount prescription drug card endorsed by Medicare. Also, once you have selected a discount card and enrolled, you will not be able to change the card until the next year's open season unless exceptional circumstances exist, such as moving outside the card's service area.

The prescriptions that are covered by the card and the price of each covered prescription are subject to change and will vary, depending on the card. Each discount card sponsor may change its formulary at any time. A sponsor may also change the price of a prescription medication on the formulary at any time except for the beginning of the open season. There are rules and regulations regarding how a sponsor may increase prices, but they are complicated.

Consumers need to consider several factors when choosing a card. Of course, the discount on your current prescriptions will be a big factor, but as prices are subject to change at any time, price alone should not dictate your decision. You should also consider the convenience of the pharmacies that participate in the card as well as enrollment fees and other services such as discounts on over-the-counter drugs.

This program is completely voluntary, and Medicare beneficiaries are not required to participate. Certain enrollees in a low-income category may also qualify for as much as $600 to help them pay for prescription drugs. Eligibility for this assistance will be based on a beneficiary's income and whether he or she already has any other prescription drug coverage. You can easily figure out whether you are eligible for the extra $600 by visiting the Medicare Web site.

I strongly suggest that those considering these discount cards consult with their State Health Insurance and Assistance Program (SHIP) for additional information in making the right decisions. The SHIP program can help with gathering information and making the calculations that go into deciding whether to enroll in a discount drug card and which card to choose. The SHIP counselor can also provide you with information about state programs to help pay for prescription drugs.

See the Resources section at the end of this chapter for contact information.

Other Drug Discount Programs

We have known for a long time that almost all pharmaceutical companies have programs to provide prescriptions at low cost to people meeting certain criteria. However, very often only physicians know about these programs, and the paperwork is too voluminous and time-consuming for doctors and their staff to help patients who need the assistance. It is probably safe to say that most patients are unaware such programs exist.

The Maryland Medbank Program, which is funded through the Department of Health and Mental Hygiene, assists health care providers and patients in completing the paperwork required to enroll patients in Pharmaceutical Company Patient Assistance Programs.

Persons eligible for help under this program are those who are not eligible for entitlement programs like Medicaid or the Maryland Pharmacy Assistance Program. Additionally, applicants must meet the financial guidelines set by the pharmaceutical companies, and must have no other prescriptions drug coverage. Medbank Counselors provide in-person and telephone assistance in Medicare-related areas such as Medigap plans,

HMOs, disability, Medicare Plus Choice, long-term care insurance, billing problems, fraud and abuse and many more.

Eli Lilly is one of several drug manufacturers that issue a discount card for its products. The Lilly plan allows eligible Medicare beneficiaries to pay a flat fee for a 30-day supply of prescription drugs made by Eli Lilly. Beneficiaries qualify for the discount card if they have no other drug insurance coverage and their annual income is below a specified amount. Several other companies offer similar programs. Your physician may be able to provide brochures on the subject.

The Pharmaceutical Research and Manufacturers of America publishes a directory of Prescription Drugs Patient Assistance Programs. This directory lists some 50 programs that provide medications to people with low incomes or no insurance. See Resources for further information.

Financial Issues Affecting Seniors

Use Credit Cards with Caution

Since 1993, more than a million people aged 50 and older have filed for bankruptcy. One of the most important reasons seniors cite for filing bankruptcy is to escape the harassing debt collection tactics of common credit card issuers. Here are some useful tips for handling credit cards—tips to help seniors avoid having to declare bankruptcy for the overuse of the cards.

More than three billion credit card offers are mailed to consumers each year. These offers can be very enticing, promising wonderful things. However, information regarding the downside or the potential risks of a new credit card is never shared in the offer.

Experts at the National Consumer Law Center (NCLC) stress that we should, first of all, avoid accepting too many card offers. There is rarely a good reason to carry more than one or two credit cards. Seniors should be very selective about choosing which cards are best for them. Having too much credit can lead to bad decisions and unmanageable debts.

Lenders are looking for people who will run up big balances because those consumers pay the most interest. Credit companies may pursue you aggressively by mail and phone. Do not take that as an indication that you can afford more credit. The lender, says NCLC, may have a marketing profile based on your spending patterns, your credit record, your use of certain services such as home shopping, your magazine subscriptions or even your zip code, which may indicate that you are someone who is likely to carry a big credit card balance (and pay a good deal of interest). Do not listen to the solicitations.

You should always know the interest rate on your cards and should try to keep the rate as low as possible. However, says the NCLC, rarely is it a good idea to take out a new card solely because of a low rate. First of all, the rate only matters if you carry a balance from one month to the next. Second, a temporarily low rate may encourage you to spend more than you can afford. In addition, the rate can easily change with or without a reason. Even the best credit card interest rates are still relatively high-rate credit. Do not forget that other terms of the credit card may add to the cost, so that a credit card that appears cheaper is actually more expensive. Pay attention to annual fees, late charges, membership fees and the method by which balances accrue, all of which can add to the cost of credit.

An artificially low initial interest rate that lasts for only a limited time and may be for limited charges, such as transfers of balances from other cards, is called a "teaser" rate. Most of these rates are good for only six months or less. After that, the rate automatically goes up. Look at the permanent long-term rate on the card. That is much more important than the temporary rate.

Many credit card contracts, including those that advertise low permanent rates, have provisions in the small print to increase your rate of interest if you make even a single late payment. This may be on top of late charges or other penalties. Be sure to review your contract to see if such terms apply.

It is very important to understand how you will be billed. If interest will apply for the date of your purchase without a grace period, a low rate may actually be higher than it looks. If you intend to pay off the balance in full each month, terms of the grace period are important. You need to understand how the grace period works and remember that many lenders do not mail bills until late in the grace period. Your payment may be due quite soon after you receive the bill.

Avoid the special services, programs and goods that lenders offer to bill to their cards. Services and products offered in this way are almost always overpriced. Try to develop the habit of discarding such advertisements or read them with a high degree of skepticism and caution.

If you do take a credit card and discover terms you do not like, cancel it.

See Resources for more information on credit cards and money-saving services.

Who Is Responsible for Social Security Overpayments?

There is currently tremendous frustration with the Social Security Administration. I have several clients who received notices from the SSA informing them that they have been overpaid and must repay the government. One client "owes" $12,000. SSA letters tell recipients that their full monthly benefit will be taken until the overpayment is recovered. If some can show financial hardship, they can pay a smaller monthly amount taken from their benefit, or they can pay with a lump sum.

Politicians and the media continue to tell stories about the enormous amount of welfare fraud and about people who live by cheating and defrauding the government. I do not disbelieve those claims. Perhaps they are true. It is just that, as an elder law attorney, I have never met, talked to, or seen any of those people. The people I see are mostly honest, hardworking, older individuals, often on a fixed income. Few have extra money.

Treasure Hunt

The U. S. Treasury says that over 15,000 savings bonds and 2,000 interest payments are returned to the Treasury Department each year as undeliverable. In addition, eight billion dollars worth of savings bonds have stopped earning interest, but have not been cashed.

To help find the rightful owners of these bonds, the Treasury has developed online search capabilities for old savings bonds. You can search by name, Social Security number, city and state to see if the Treasury has any bonds in your name or in that of a family member. This service will be a great help to people who are trying to discover and account for assets and records of family members who are no longer able to manage, especially if the older person is unable to remember or communicate the location of these assets. See the Resources section for a link.

■ ■ ■

I am convinced the responsibility for overpaying hundreds of thousands of dollars lies with the agency, not the person who began receiving, say, an extra $80 a month without prior notice.

Most people deposit checks they receive, pay their bills and call the bank or check the computer for a periodic balance. Social Security benefits increase every year with a cost-of-living adjustment. Benefit recipients are mostly over 65 and just trying to cope with retirement, caregiving demands and health issues. How can they catch a benefit check change? If we do notice such things, we are likely to think Congress has made a change and not give it another thought.

Years of growing up in West Texas helped to make me fiscally conservative. I understand that our government cannot afford to right all wrongs, and that there are not sufficient resources to make sure every individual has everything to make life warm, fuzzy and perfect. But if I have seen so many overpayment notices, how many thousands must be out there? At least a portion of the overpayment should be considered the agency's fault. After all, the agency pays full-time employees to monitor such things and get them right to begin with. I simply cannot understand why Social Security beneficiaries on a fixed income must, alone, repay monies "overpaid" through no fault of their own. This is particularly unfair when repayment would result in financial hardship to the Social Security annuitant.

The Pros and Cons of Annuities

The main issue to consider with annuities for seniors is not whether they are a good investment or a bad investment. The issue is whether that particular annuity is suitable for that particular buyer. An annuity must help with the accomplishment of your goals and your needs. Your goals must be clearly understood by the annuity salesman, and a careful analysis must be made.

The National Association of Insurance Commissioners (NAIC) has issued a White Paper on the subject. NAIC is in the process of developing a Model Regulation. A small number of brokerage firms will not permit their representatives to sell annuities without a review by the home office on the issue of suitability.

In some cases, the sale of some annuities is literally financial exploitation of the elderly by people standing to profit by receiving exorbitant commission on the annuity sale. The issue is whose interest is being served. Is the sale of the annuity being made because it is in the salesman's best interest or the senior's best interest?

Elder Abuse

Stereotypes Harm Seniors

In 1975 Congressman Morris K. Udall addressed the National Council on the Aging. Reading the address today makes the 1976 presidential candidate sound like a prophet. Among other things, he spoke of age discrimination, of a failure to address the real health needs of the elderly by ascribing all their illnesses to old age, of older Americans being easy targets for scams, frauds and other crimes, and he suggested that the president appoint a White House advocate for aging Americans.

In the address, "Public Policy and the Future of Aging," Congressman Udall said that society has developed two basic stereotypes of the aged in order to justify our neglect—serenity and senility. On the one hand, he said, our images of old age are idealized. We can visualize Normal Rockwell paintings showing beloved and tranquil grandparents. We picture the serene and gracious white-haired matriarch dispensing her wisdom from the family kitchen, and the matching patriarch dispensing wisdom from the front porch rocker. Of several things not quite right with that picture, there is also the fact that no one is really listening to the wisdom being dispensed!

On the other hand, said Udall, the opposite image disparages the aged. Old age is viewed as irreversible decay, decrepitude and serious loss of mental powers. A Harris poll conducted around that time found that younger people regarded the aged as "inept, ineffectual, physically depleted and waiting for death." Older people, Udall said, are seen as "rigid, querulous and resistant to change; narrow and superficial in intellectual activity; and almost universally senile."

These images and ideas are self-perpetuating because, in truth, many elderly persons have, for instance, Alzheimer's disease, probably called senility in 1975. Many have become bitter because of the loss of their spouse, or because it is so hard to hear or because they can no longer read easily. These situations cut them off from society, and any self-esteem they once had is continually and continuously undermined. When I am with my mother who, while getting on in years, is still feisty, goal-oriented, determined and never willing to give up, it is striking how often people ask questions or make comments concerning her as though she is not in the room. It is no wonder that so many seniors lapse into what Udall called "patterns of despair."

Financial Abuse of the Elderly Is a Real Problem

In my practice and in my community discussions with seniors, I meet more and more people who have been financially abused in one way or another. Both family members and outsiders can abuse seniors financially. It is believed that only one in four or five cases is actually being reported because victims are so reluctant to admit the problem and seek help.

According to Lori A. Stiegel, of the American Bar Association's Commission on Legal Problems of the Elderly, financial abuse includes misuse of Durable Powers of Attorney and bank accounts and misuse or neglect of authority by a guardian or conservator. It also includes misappropriation of assets, failure to provide reasonable consideration for the transfer of real estate, failure to provide the goods or services for which one is paid, imposing excessive charges or unreasonable fees for services and using fraud or undue influence to gain control of or obtain money or property.

In 1996 the National Elder Abuse Incidence Study provided some general findings about financial abuse of the elderly. Persons ages 80 and older are abused and neglected at two to three times their proportion of the elderly population, female elders are abused at a higher rate than males and nearly half of those abused are not physically able to care for themselves. In almost nine out of 10 incidents of domestic elder abuse and neglect, the perpetrator is a family member. Adult children are responsible for nearly half of elder abuse and neglect.

Financial abuse of the elderly is something none of us wants to believe. We would like to think that if we do not admit the existence of something horrible, then it does not actually exist. I am afraid it is true—and we had better pay attention, for our own loved ones could be next.

A new Maryland state program developed by the attorney general's office offers training for bank employees, law enforcement officials and other providers of public services on how to recognize some indicators of financial exploitation. You should recognize them too. Indicators include:

- A lack of necessities or amenities when you know the older person can well afford them

- Missing property

- Recent new acquaintances, particularly those who take up residence with the older person

- Bringing strangers with them to meetings or while conducting financial transactions

- Exhibiting hoarding behavior such as carrying all papers in large bags all the time

- Changing patterns of making eye contact

- Being accompanied by a stranger, family member or other person who seems to coerce the senior into making decisions or transactions

- Giving implausible explanations about what the senior is doing with her money

These are only some of the signs that could prompt you to ask questions of an elderly acquaintance who would never disclose his or her situation voluntarily, but who will do so if asked. When you ask questions and demonstrate an awareness of the issue, you are letting elderly friends know they can turn to you in the future for discussion and help.

For those moms and dads who are still totally supporting adult children financially, Tough Love International is a wonderful way to start to understand that you might be enabling rather than helping. Tough Love International does not advocate or support throwing kids out, violence against children or parents or verbal abuse. Nor does it offer an instant fix. Most situations of this kind took a long time to develop and will take time to reverse. The organization works with teens and also with parents of abusive adult children. Contacting Tough Love does not indicate any type of commitment on your part and all calls are completely confidential.

I well remember when no one believed child abuse could actually exist, and when many people felt that reports of domestic violence were simply the exaggerations of a whiny spouse. Both of those crimes are today being recognized, treated and handled by mental health professionals, law enforcement personnel and civil prosecutors. In the future, I hope we will see widespread changes in our society's response to financial abuse of the elderly.

See the Resources section for contact information for Tough Love International.

Technology and Seniors

Technology Makes Senior Living Easier

Have you noticed that you need more light to read now than when you were younger? Older eyes need at least 50 percent more light than younger eyes to see the same detail. The physiological reason for this is that the size of the pupil becomes smaller with age and the lens becomes thicker. You need to add more light to your environment. Also, older eyes are more sensitive to glare, so it is important to have lampshades and not bare bulbs. Lastly, older eyes take longer to adapt to changes in brightness, so try to create a uniform level of light throughout your house.

The AARP Web site frequently contains computer hardware and software reviews. One product reviewed is computer keyboard called BigKeys. This is a keyboard with keys almost four times larger than normal ones. Although the key size makes the board look larger, it is actually a regular, full-size keyboard, with 60 oversized keys. Every key is a one inch square button with easy to read labels in large block print on bright white keys. The lettering itself is half an inch tall.

The keyboard is designed for adult computer users who require very large keys in order to locate and operate a keyboard. The AARP review says, "These are users who would have no interest in speed typing." It comes in two models, the Plus and the LX. The keyboard can be switched easily from the standard QWERTY arrangement to an ABC arrangement that may be easier for those who have never been trained to use a standard keyboard. Hunt-and-peck typists might enjoy an alphabetical approach. Letter keycaps can be removed and reconfigured to comply with both layouts. BigKeys is compatible with all major software packages and requires no special software. BigKeys allows credit card customers to try out the keyboard for up to ten days with no charges except shipping and handling. Cost is between $150 and $200.

Other types of technology are also available. ABLEDATA is an organization sponsored by the National Institute on Disability and Rehabilitation Research, an arm of the U.S. Department of Education. Its Web site provides a wealth of information regarding technology devices for anyone disabled by age or any other reason. The site has categorized and listed more than 19,000 assistive devices. The organization sells nothing but can refer you to sources for purchasing any item you like. The Web site includes consumer reviews of various products. The site is very easy to search and includes resource centers, so you can look up information on a particular topic, such as stroke or traumatic brain injury. The "Reading Room" includes classified ads, where

Fun and Helpful Web Sites for Wired Seniors

AARP's Web site, **www.aarp.org**, lists its 500 best Internet sites for people over the age of 50. From the front page, look under "Popular Choices" and click on "Internet Resources on Aging."

The site **www.coolgrandma.com** caters to senior interests. It is full of very useful information: a directory of "cool" Web sites, a learning center, online articles and discussion forums on almost any subject, from computer viruses to anti-lock brakes. No wonder they call this Grandma cool.

The site **www.learnthenet.com** teaches the basics of e-mail, Web surfing and downloading files. Click on "Master the Basics" to get started. The site includes tips for experienced users.

With its nice large type, easily read by those of us who need more light and bigger print, the site **www.ourservienioryears.com** offers a "computer tutor" with various technology features and sections on Medicare, Social Security, senior-related issues and travel.

The site **www.seniorsurvey.com** provides a forum for easily speaking your mind. It tracks opinions of seniors, regularly posts results from past and current surveys, provides information on upcoming surveys and requests opinions on a wide variety of senior-related issues. Survey results are given to providers of senior services and products.

The site **www.seniorwomen.com** has an energizing approach to attacking life as the female of the species. Lively sections on culture and arts, home and shopping, money and computing, relationships and going places and news and issues give you many options for spending hours at the computer—and learning.

At **www.slmseniors.com** you will find an online community for 50-plus adults, with portals in seven major areas: computers, *fun, home and family, money, health, travel and a library. It also offers links to a wide variety of other areas, including a PC support discussion board, a directory of Web sites for older adults, games, puzzles, craft projects, gardening tips, electronic greeting cards, family tree help, senior living choices, recipes, chronic and life-threatening medical conditions, health and wellness information and travel planning.*

*The site **www.wiredseniors.com** is a network of sites that serve as a Web portal aimed at adults aged 50 and older in Canada and the United States. The site includes a bulletin board, an e-mail club to meet other older adults, a discussion forum and more.*

■ ■ ■

users list used devices available for sale at a reduced rate. ABLEDATA also has an accessible showroom. See the Resources section for more information.

Seniors and Computers

Statistics demonstrate that older adults are using the computer at an ever-increasing rate. The 2001 census showed that one-quarter of the households with people 65 and over have computers and that 17 percent of those have Internet access. Among people 45 to 65, nearly 57 percent have computers and 46.7 percent have Internet access. Additionally, many libraries and senior centers have computers with Internet access. The saying about old dogs and new tricks is not applicable here. There are many Web sites that offer tutorials for computer newcomers or are designed for a senior audience.

Keeping Active Will Keep You Happy

Volunteering Helps Others and Self

Many seniors have more time on their hands than they used to have. If you are in that category, have you thought about becoming a volunteer for some needed service? Perhaps you have thought of volunteering, but do not know exactly where to start. Good news. There is a federal program called Retired and Senior Volunteer Program (RSVP). It assists retired or semi-retired individuals, age 55 and over, by connecting them to a variety of agencies, organizations and institutions designated as Volunteer Stations. RSVP volunteers serve without compensation, but may be reimbursed for such expenses as transportation. All you need to qualify for participation is proof of your age.

Along the same lines, you might like to look in the Service Corps of Retired Executives (SCORE). This is a nonprofit association run by the Small Business Administration. It is dedicated to entrepreneur education and the formation, growth and success of small businesses nationwide. Working and retired executives and business owners donate their time and expertise as volunteer business counselors and provide confidential counseling and mentoring free of charge. Volunteers generally work in their home communities or nearby and are reimbursed for out-of-pocket expenses.

Nearly everyone has heard of VISTA, Volunteers in Service to America. This volunteer program is not restricted to senior volunteers but does provide many opportunities for service.

See the Resource section for volunteering resources and contact information.

Being a Senior Companion Is Useful and Rewarding

An article in a local paper caught my eye regarding several retired people ages 68 and older who volunteered to help other seniors cope with later-life difficulties. It sounded like a wonderful program for both the volunteers and the seniors who receive the companionship and assistance.

The senior companions are a part of the Senior Service Corps, a national volunteer network organized by the federal government. For more than thirty years, the Senior Service Corps has been placing volunteer senior citizens in community service projects. The Corps serve three major areas:

1. The Foster Grandparent Program, which currently links senior volunteers to more than 2,200 young people with special needs
2. The Retired and Senior Volunteer Program, billed as "one-stop shopping" for seniors in search of volunteer opportunities
3. The Senior Companions Program, which is currently helping more than 300 other seniors live independently in their homes

According to the article, senior companions are typically 60 years of age and older and on a limited income. In fact, there are income requirements for volunteers. The volunteers give 20 hours of services, usually four hours for five days a week, and they can receive at least $200 per month in tax-free meal and travel reimbursement, some meals during service, an annual physical and accident and liability insurance while on the job.

Volunteers must complete 40 hours of orientation training before working with their first client and must attend an additional four hours of training per month. Maxine Brown, project coordinator for the Senior Companions Program in

Southern Maryland said that the real attraction for senior companions is neither training nor the small payment rate, but "the priceless feeling that, though nearing old age themselves, they are still able to make a difference in the lives of others."

Senior companions help their clients live independently in their own homes for what might be a longer period of time than would otherwise be possible. They assist with simple chores, buy groceries and provide transportation, companionship and friendship. They can also provide respite care, giving family members a much-needed break from the day-to-day challenge of dealing with Alzheimer's disease or other forms of dementia.

Susan J. Ellis of Energize, Inc. has some suggestions that might encourage more of us to volunteer. She says instead of considering volunteering as something you do for people who are not as fortunate as yourself, begin to think of it as an exchange.

"Consider that most people find themselves in need at some point in their lives. So today you may be the person with the ability to help, but tomorrow you may be the recipient of someone else's volunteer effort," says Ellis. Additionally, there is an element of self-help to volunteerism, as when we participate in our neighborhood Crime Watch, thus keeping our entire home neighborhood safer. There are many, many benefits to volunteering our help to others.

With the average annual cost of nursing homes pushing $70,000 annually, the annual federal cost of one senior companion serving 20 hours per week is approximately $3,850.00. It does not take much of a mathematician to figure a cost of $3,850 is pretty much preferable to a cost of $70,000 all the way around.

See the Resources section for information on how you can get involved in becoming a senior companion.

Senior Pageants

Senior America, Inc. is a nonprofit organization designed not only to enrich the lives of seniors, but also to tap their energy to enrich the lives of others. Their pageant mission is simple: "It is a search for the gracious lady who best exemplifies the dignity, maturity and inner beauty of all senior Americans. The Ms. Senior America philosophy is based upon the belief that seniors are the foundation of America, and our most valuable treasure. It is upon their knowledge, experience and resources that the younger generation has the opportunity to build a better society."

Created in 1971, Senior America, Inc. proposed to promote the positive aspects of aging in response to the very bleak media image of America's elderly at that time. The first pageant was held in 1972, and women over the age of 60 competed on the basis of their philosophies of life, community service, poise and talent.

There is also an auxiliary organization, Cameo Club, of which all contestants are members. Cameo Club members provide inspiration and encouragement by appearing in nursing homes, hospitals and children's facilities on a year-round basis, and they maintain a schedule of speaking appearances attempting to advance the dignity and value of senior Americans. The pageant is co-sponsored by the Jefferson County Office on Aging.

Similarly, the Ms. Senior Sweetheart Pageants of America Inc. is a nonprofit organization that started out as a Lions Club fundraiser in 1978. The intent of the founder and president, Len Kaplan, is to have lovely ladies over age 59 in a beautiful senior pageant, and to show the public that ladies over age 59 still have lots of pep in their step!

Kaplan described the pageant, held every October in Fall River, Massachusetts, as an "event to celebrate the intrinsic beauty of senior citizens, their wisdom, their experience, their contributions to our country and our families."

Contestants receive a 10-day vacation, meals, lodging and pageant expenses. Daily field trips are also planned to such notable sites as Foxwoods Casino and the Newport mansions, the New Bedford Zoo and the Lizzie Borden Museum, as well as dinners with such local dignitaries as the mayors of Fall River and New Bedford. The 10 days culminate in a pageant that includes an interview, talent competition, patriotic routines, dance numbers and evening gown presentations. For information about senior pageants see the Resources section.

Senior Stays Active by Volunteering Overseas

Age does not have to be a barrier to remaining an active, vital member of the community. One Maryland senior should be an inspiration to us all. Ruth Joy Gulley, a Crofton resident, retired in 1983 after 15 years as a full-time teacher. In a burst of incredible senior energy, Mrs. Gulley volunteered to go to Ukraine as a teacher.

When her husband died a few years ago, Mrs. Gulley went through those stages of grief common to most people who lose a spouse. Although she experienced health problems of her own, she attempted to fill the huge void in her life by returning to local schools as a substitute teacher. As she continued to look for something new to make her feel really useful and as though she was making an important contribution, she heard about New Hope Christian School, a school in Ukraine sponsored by the

Campus Crusade for Christ International (CCCI). The school, which includes kindergarten through 12th grade, enrolls about a hundred children of missionaries from Taiwan, Korea and the United States.

Mrs. Gulley consulted with her pastor, the Reverend David Price of Grace Baptist Church in Bowie, and found out that if she was accepted by CCCI, Grace Baptist would agree to be her sponsoring church. She applied, even though she was certain that CCCI would not consider her because of her age.

Elderhostel Energizes Seniors

Elderhostel is a nonprofit organization that plans travel and educational opportunities, trips and events at a reasonable cost for adults over 55. It offers more than 10,000 programs around the globe. Elderhostel also offers a variety of intergenerational activities where you and your grandchildren can participate together. See the Resources section for contact information.

■ ■ ■

Astounded and thrilled to be chosen, she began to work on the unique challenges surrounding such an endeavor. Because the CCCI missionary teachers are not given a salary, they must raise at least $15,000 to cover their living expenses during the school year. To help raise money, Mrs. Gulley spoke at local area churches, and she continues with speaking engagements each time she returns home.

For information about sponsoring the program, see the Resources section.

Taking Time to Play Makes for Healthy Aging

A Harvard study on aging has been going on for more than 60 years. Researchers continue to follow the lives of 824 men and women from adolescence to their senior years in order to learn what successful aging is and how it can be achieved. Interesting details of the study's results are in the book *Aging Well: Surprising Guideposts to a Happier Life* from the Landmark Harvard Study of Adult Development by George Vaillant, the current director of the study.

By the time a study participant reached his or her 70s, emphasis was on physical health. However, researchers spent an equal amount of attention on the subject's mental state and attitude. The study consistently found that elderly people could be divided into two categories: the "happy-well," who celebrate life and continue to love and learn from those around them, and the "sad-sick," who are ill and in a spiral of depression, self-pity and decay. According to Vaillant, the study repeatedly demonstrates that it is social aptitude (sometimes called emotional intelligence), not intellectual brilliance, wealth or parental social class that leads to a well-adapted old age.

Vaillant identifies four character qualities that provide healthy aging. First, the ability to anticipate and plan for the future; second, a capacity for gratitude and forgiveness; third, a capacity to love others; and fourth, the desire to connect with people and not harbor old resentments. When he writes about four basic ways to make retirement rewarding, one of them is to "rediscover how to play."

Playing is easier when there are grandchildren around, when the weather is lovely and the flowers are blooming. In warm weather it seems like the aches and pains of growing older are not as obvious. We actually feel more lighthearted. We feel more energetic when the days are longer, and night does not come so early. Maybe we even start to feel more like tackling some of those goals we postponed during the very long, snowy winter.

As the philosopher said, "Whether or not it is clear to you, no doubt the universe is unfolding as it should." When Jesus was teaching, he asked which of us, by worrying, can add one inch to our height? Worrying is generally considered to be a huge waste of time—most of the things we worry about never happen and often we worry about things that are not within our power to fix. So let us put ourselves in the crowd of the "happy-well" and get the giggles with our grandchildren.

Is a Home Business for You?

More and more seniors are finding reasons to work at home. Some are looking for more activity during retirement, some were forced to quit a commuting job because of caregiving responsibilities and many businesses are turning to telecommuting for at-home workers.

If you are already working from home, or are considering setting up a home office, you should get the book *The 60-Second Commute: A Guide to Your 24/7 Home Office Life* by Erica Orloff and Kathy Levinson.

According to the American Home Business Association, 8,000 people start a home business every day—that is one every 11 seconds, writes Orloff. Of course, not all are successful, and the book begins by whetting your appetite with brief stories of several very successful home entrepreneurs. For instance, while being a full-time homemaker raising children, Lillian Vernon started a gift and home furnishing business from her kitchen table in 1951. Today, Lillian Vernon's mail-order catalog empire grosses over $241 million annually. There are snippets about Michael Dell of Dell Computers, Jeff Bezos of Amazon.com, Bill Hewlett and David Packard of Hewlett Packard and others.

While these people represent amazing success, what is likely to happen if you try the same? Well, in the beginning of the book, there is a quiz to help you sort out whether working from home is right for you. The idea of the quiz, say the authors, is not that there is only a certain type of person who can be successful working from home. But that those who are the most successful at working from home seem to share common characteristics. If you do not possess those characteristics, you should not give up, but should "tune up some areas before you take the plunge." Identifying those areas that may be weak, however, is half the battle and this book is tailor-made to help you.

Traits the authors say a successful home office CEO needs include flexibility, the ability to multitask, judgment, tenacity, discipline and organization.

The book includes a very helpful and very specific chapter on setting up your home office. It points out items that cannot be skimped on and ones that can—and helps the reader to see and understand the difference. There are hints and techniques for getting the space and privacy you need, even in the most crowded home. There is a basic computer tutorial helping the reader decide questions such as how much memory will be needed, which Internet provider to choose and what configuration of equipment is most helpful.

The chapter on time management presents new and helpful ideas. A large portion of this chapter is devoted to procrastination and ideas for defeating this traditional obstacle to accomplishment. The chapter on being professional includes "nine ways to seem bigger than you really are." The chapter on organization provides multiple tips, including one suggesting that if you use a non-computer calendar, you write on it with different colored pencils, reserving red for business, blue for your child's soccer games and purple for your personal appointments. This system would allow you to check your calendar notations much more quickly, as you do not have to read every single entry in order to find one doctor's appointment. And, importantly, there is a chapter on your home business budget.

In addition to practical how-to tips, there are fascinating and vital chapters on insurance, taxes and legal issues for home business owners. Even very successful home businesses can trip up on these three issues, ruining a lot of great dreams and a lot of hard work.

There is a chapter on marketing, and a wonderful appendix that includes lists of government resources for small businesses, organizations and associations for in-home businesses, great Web sites and some places to get start-up assistance. This book is genuinely helpful for anyone wanting to start a home-based business, and seniors or their caregivers might be very interested in the book's advice.

Playing Piano Provides Therapeutic Benefits

In my visits to senior centers and various groups I am intrigued by the numbers of people who say (whether they really mean it or not) they wish they had learned to play the piano. Well, I recently met Bob Clark of Alabama, and he told me that "An 80-year-old has the same capacity to learn as a 12-year-old, plus better ability to stay on task, a more mature intellect and greater physical coordination. What great advantages!"

What he is teaching these 80-year-olds is piano. His program, Peer Power Piano Plus!, is set up so that students learn through a unique combination of group and individual training. He uses rhythm sticks to develop a good sense of rhythm and sight-reading ability. He uses computer disks to provide interesting and great-sounding backgrounds to even the simplest song, and Music Ace 2, an award-winning interactive program, for teaching music theory.

You say you cannot get out of your home? Well, Mr. Clark will bring his mobile studio to you. He has six keyboards plus a computer in his trailer. No parking space for his trailer?—he will bring smaller keyboards to your home. This requires a 5-by-6-foot area and an electrical outlet.

Beginner's courses are for 10 weeks. Those 10 weeks will likely improve your life. A Music Making and Wellness project at the University of Miami found that seniors who took keyboard lessons had decreased anxiety, were happier, suffered less depression and actually indicated that they were less lonely than the control group who did not take keyboard lessons.

The Web site of McLelland Piano says that for the past several years, pianos have been available at the annual American Psychiatric Conference. The pianos are not there for a performance by Ferrante and Teicher; they are for use by the therapists themselves. As Al Bumanis, communications director for the American Music Therapy Association, explains, "The idea is that the psychiatrist can stop by the booth to de-stress by playing piano." Psychiatrists using the piano to de-stress? Not a bad endorsement for the instrument's effectiveness in soothing the troubled spirit.

"Playing the piano has always added joy to people's lives, but we're just beginning to understand the full range of its benefits," says Brenda Dillon of the National Piano Foundation. "When I play the piano, I am able to get away from the daily challenges. It's like taking a mini vacation. By the time I walk away from the piano, I am truly relaxed."

That is no accident, says Alicia Ann Clair, Ph.D., music therapist, board-certified professor and director of music therapy at the University of Kansas, Lawrence. "When it comes to making music, the piano demands an attention and focus that does not allow interfering thoughts that might be distracting or distressful, and in that way it relieves the pressures and the stresses of the day," she says. "At the same time that we can use it as a way to provide relief, we have added bonuses. When you play and it's successful, it's extremely exciting and fulfilling. Relief, joy or fulfillment—all of those things add to well-being, which contributes to life quality which contributes to good health."

The piano is now being used around the world as an effective therapeutic tool. At New York's Nordoff-Robbins Center for Music Therapy, the piano is instrumental in helping children and adults overcome emotional and physical problems. Centers are also located in England, Australia, Japan, Scotland and South Africa. "In this approach, the therapist is usually at the piano," explains music therapist and the New York center's co-director Alan Turry. "The therapist and patient actually create music in a mutual fashion."

Therapists in the program, all of whom are trained extensively on the piano, work with autistic children, hospital patients, the developmentally disabled or emotionally disturbed, "as well as self-referred adults who want an alternative to verbal therapy," says Turry.

Bob Clark lists many advantages to learning piano, no matter your age. Playing instills a love and appreciation of music. It provides emotional release. Additionally, Clark says, it increases concentration span, instills self-discipline, develops coordination and instills self-confidence and poise.

The Role of Faith

Growing older is, of course, full of myriad events that don't seem, on the surface, to be "blessings," but I call it blessed because I am so very aware of those who are not allowed the gift of growing older. My dad, for instance, continually hovers around my memory—full of energy, fixer of all things, a safe, warm, and wise counselor, smiling that incredible grin just as when God took him all those years ago. He was three years younger than I am now. Amazingly, even children die, and parents and grandparents, stunned by life's most devastating blow, must figure out a way to go on—somehow. So, I insist that aging is a blessing.

Among clients, friends, and myself, I observe the many variations of aging. Mary Pipher writes of the "young-old" and the "old-old." A Harvard study contrasts the "happy-well" old with the "sick-sad" old.

I hope I have made you aware of options and choices to get you over to the "happy-well" side. However, I am forced to conclude that one could do all those things and still not be among the "young, happy-well" old.

Some of it is, of course, personality, inclination and disposition. I have an aunt who was "old" at 35 years of age and, today, at 90, is still very old. On the other hand, there are those like my mom who, even if she lives to be 110, will never be as "old" as her sister was at 35.

That said, how in the world can a person who has been reasonably happy for the majority of his or her life, been relatively successful by their own standards, healthy for the most part and optimistic—how can that person successfully cope with the challenges, daily losses and continual frustrations of getting older?

I know one thing. Even when you intellectually know that being happy is a choice, that you can choose to have a good day or a bad day, that you can choose to have a good attitude, the actual choosing itself is so much easier said than done. As Susanna Wesley once wrote, there are days when making that choice and acting on it is like "rowing against wind and tide."

Faith is key. Yes—it is. Study after study has shown that those individuals able to understand that the ultimate course of their lives is not in their hands, but in the control of the One who created DNA, have a formidable advantage allowing them to more successfully confront and navigate the demands of growing older. Strong faith extends our lives and contributes greatly to making those extra years healthier and happier.

Resources

Raising Grandchildren

AARP Grandparent Information Center
Web site: www.aarp.org/confacts/programs/gic.html
Phone: (202) 434-2296
Address: 601 E Street, NW, Washington, DC 20049
Provides legal and practical information about raising grand-children on the Web and through its free newsletter, *Parenting Grandchildren.*
E-mail: gic@aarp.org

Generations United
Web site: www.gu.org
Phone: (202) 289-3979
Address: 1333 H Street, NW, Suite 500 W,
Washington, DC 20005
Promotes intergenerational programs and policies.

GrandsPlace
Web site: www.grandsplace.com
Resources and advice for grandparents raising grandchildren.

The Internet Guide to Guardianship
Web site: http://guardianship.usalaw.com
Provides information about becoming a guardian and offers
articles to help you decide if you should take this step.

Something to Remember Me By Legacy Project
Web site: www.somethingtoremembermeby.org
Offers free online activity kits for schools, seniors, community
groups and families looking to become closer despite distance,
hectic schedules or divorce.

Senior Driving

AAA Foundation for Traffic Safety
Web site: www.aaafts.org
Phone: (202) 638-5944
Address: 1440 New York Avenue NW, Suite 201,
Washington, DC 20005
Sponsors the Senior Drivers Web site.

AARP
Web site: www.aarp.org/drive
Phone: (800) 424-3410
Safety tips and information about the AARP Driver
Safety Program.

Association for Driver Rehabilitation Specialists
Web site: www.driver-ed.org
Phone: (800) 290-2344
Refers people to a professional trained to help drivers with
disabilities, including those associated with aging.

GrandDriver
Web site: www.granddriver.info
Phone: (888) 472-6303
E-mail: granddriver@aamva.org

Maryland's Medical Advisory Board
Phone: (410) 768-7511
Offers instructions as to the proper procedure to follow before
resuming driving after injury or illness.

Senior Drivers, AAA Foundation for Traffic Safety
Web site: www.seniordrivers.org
Offers tutorials and tips to improve seniors' driving.

Sinai Hospital's Driver Evaluation and Training Program
Phone: (410) 601-5631

Supplemental Transportation Programs for Seniors, AAA
Foundation for Traffic Safety
Web site: www.seniordrivers.org/STPs
Provides information for those who want to set up
community transportation.

Senior Benefits and Services

Bowie, Maryland Senior Center
Phone: (301) 809-2300
Provides a variety of senior services and activities.

BenefitsCheckUp, National Council on the Aging
Web site: www.benefitscheckup.org
Quickly and easily identifies federal and state assistance
programs for older Americans.

OAA legal services / SHIP services / Office of Senior
Information Assistance
Phone (Anne Arundel County, Maryland): (410) 222-4464
Phone (Prince George's County, Maryland): (301) 699-2696
Offers counseling on a wide variety of senior issues.

U.S. Administration on Aging
Web site: www.aoa.gov
Phone: (800) 222-2225
Created by the OAA, it provides home- and community-based
care services for seniors.

Department of Veterans Affairs
Web site: www.va.gov
Provides information about veterans' benefits.

Telemarketing, Junk Mail and Fraud

1-800-5OPTOUT
Phone: (888) 567-8688
Eliminates credit card solicitations by telling the three major
credit reporting agencies to remove your name from their
mailing lists.

Consumer Data Industry Association
Web site: www.cdiaonline.org/consumers2.cfm
Provides consumer information about credit reports identity
theft and other issues.

Direct Marketing Association's Mail Preference Service
Address: DMA Mail Preference Service, PO Box 9008,
Farmingdale, NY 11735-9008
Write to this address to reduce junk mail. Be sure to include
your name and address.

Direct Marketing Association's Telephone Preference Service
Address: DMA Telephone Preference Service PO Box 9014,
Farmingdale, NY 11735-9014
Write to this address to be taken off telemarketing lists.
Be sure to include your name, address and telephone number
in the letter.

Equifax
Web site: www.equifax.com
Phone: (800) 685-1111
Call or write to get a copy of your credit report.

Experian
Web site: www.experian.com
Phone: (888) 397-3742
Call or write to get a copy of your credit report.

Federal Communications Commission's Consumer and
Governmental Affairs Bureau
Web site: www.fcc.gov/cgb/consumers.html
Provides information to consumers about communications
(including telephone) regulations.

Federal Trade Commission for the Consumer
Web site: www.ftc.gov/ftc/consumer.htm
Provides information about avoiding telemarketing fraud and
other consumer issues.

Federal Trade Commission's Identity Theft Hotline
Phone: (877) 438-4338
Call to report identity theft.

Federal Trade Commission's Identity Theft Web Site
Web site: www.consumer.gov/idtheft
Provides a comprehensive guide to preventing and dealing with
identity theft and copies of the ID Theft Affidavit.

Junkbusters Corporation
Web site: www.junkbusters.com
Provides advice on how to eliminate telemarketing calls and
junk mail.

National Consumer Law Center
Web site: www.consumerlaw.org
Phone: (617) 542-8010
Address: 77 Summer Street, 10th Floor, Boston, MA 02110
Provides expert advice on consumer law.

National Do Not Call Registry
Web site: www.donotcall.gov
Phone: (888) 382-1222
Call to have your phone number added to the national registry.

Privacy Rights Clearinghouse
Web site: www.privacyrights.org
A nonprofit consumer education and advocacy organization.

TransUnion
Web site: www.transunion.com
Phone: (800) 888-4213
Call or write to get a copy of your credit report.

TRIAD
Phone: (800) 424-7827
Address: NATI, 1450 Duke Street, Alexandria, VA 22314

U.S. Postal Service
Phone: (800) 275-8777
Call to have your mail held when you are away from home.

Voice of the Elderly (VOTE)
Web site: www.geocities.com/heartland/acres/8777/vote.html
Phone: (301) 598-6227
Provides advocacy for seniors who have been victims of fraud.

Prescription Drug Assistance

Eli Lilly's Discount Drug Card Program
Phone: (877) 795-4559
Offers discounts on drugs for qualifying seniors.

Kaiser Family Foundation
www.kff.org/medicare
Information on how new prescription drug program will
affect you.

National Conference of State Legislatures' Pharmaceutical
Assistance Programs
Web site: www.ncsl.org/programs/health/drugaid.htm
Information on state drug assistance programs for older people.

Needy Meds
Web site: www.needymeds.com
Gives tips on how to get free or discounted medications
directly from drug companies.

Pharmaceutical Research and Manufacturers of America
Web site: www.phrma.org
Phone: (800) 762-4636
Offers information on drug assistance programs.

Finances and Money-saving Resources

AOL
Web site: www.aol.com
Phone: (877) 523-4493
Offers up to a 10 percent discount to AARP members on
monthly Internet access rates.

Lower My Bills
Web site: www.lowermybills.com
Compares costs for things such as long distance, car insurance,
home refinancing and credit cards.

National Council of Senior Citizens (NCSC)
Phone: (888) 373-6467
Call to join and receive *Seniority*, a bimonthly magazine, and
Pension Plus, a monthly newsletter full of money-savings tips.

Smart Price
Web site: www.smartprice.com
Offers a free service that helps you save money on local, long
distance and wireless phone service.

Telecommunications Research and Action Center
Web site: www.trac.org
Offers price comparisons of long distance carriers and related
communications resources.

Ultimate Coupons
Web site: www.ultimatecoupons.com
Printable coupons to more than 100 major national retailers.

U.S. Treasury Department Treasure Hunt
Web site: www.publicdebt.treas.gov/sav/sbtdhunt.htm
Offers visitors the ability to search for lost Treasury bonds in
their name or the name of a loved one.

Elder Abuse

Tough Love International
Web site: www.toughlove.org
Phone: (215) 348-7090
Address: PO Box 1069, Doylestown, PA 18901
Counsels parents of financially abusive grown children.

Technology

300 Incredible Things for Seniors on the Internet by Joe West
(300Incredible.com: 2000)
Web site: www.300incredible.com

ABLEDATA
Web site: www.abledata.com
Phone: (800) 227-0216
Address: 8630 Fenton Street, Suite 930,

Silver Spring, MD 20910
Provides a wealth of information regarding technology devices for anyone disabled by age or any other reason.

Elder Store
Web site: www.elderstore.com
Offers useful products for seniors and the disabled.

Volunteering and Keeping Active

The 60-Second Commute: A Guide to Your 24/7 Home Office Life by Erica Orloff and Kathy Levinson (Prentice Hall: 2003)

Aging Well: Surprising Guideposts to a Happier Life from the Landmark Harvard Study of Adult Development by George Vaillant (Little, Brown: 2002)

CCCI
www.ccci.org
Provides information for financial support of overseas volunteers and explains how to volunteer.

Corporation for National and Community Service
Web site: www.seniorcorps.org
Offers a network of programs that tap the experience, skills and talents of older citizens; includes Senior Companions and RSVP programs.

Elderhostel
Web site: www.elderhostel.org
Phone: (877) 426-8056
Provides reasonably priced education and travel opportunities for seniors 55 and up.

Guide to Retirement Living
Web site: www.guidetoretirementliving.com
Phone: (800) 394-9990

Maryland Department of Aging RSVP
Phone: (410) 222-4464
Address: 2666 Riva Road, Annapolis, MD 21401
A volunteer program for seniors.

Maryland Governor's Office on Service and
Volunteerism (GOSV)
Web site: www.gosv.state.md.us
Phone: (800) 321-8657
Provides information about volunteering in Maryland.

Ms. Senior Sweetheart Pageants of America Inc.
Phone: (508) 675-0249
E-mail: information@msseniorsweetheart.com.

Prince George's County, Maryland RSVP
Phone: (301) 699-2797
Address: 5012 Rhode Island Avenue, Hyattsville, MD 20781
A volunteer program for seniors.

Senior America, Inc.
E-mail: maryland@senioramerica.org.

Service Corps of Retired Executives (SCORE)
Web site: www.score.org
Phone: (800) 634-0245
Address: 2525 Riva Road, Suite 110, Annapolis, MD 21401
Offers volunteer opportunities for seniors with
business experience.

Volunteers in Service To America (VISTA)
Web site: www.americorps.org/vista/index.html

6
Senior Moments—
Personally Speaking

The following personal vignettes have been written over a period of years for the newspaper column "Senior Moments" that was the inspiration for this book.

Highlighting Some Extraordinary People

My Extraordinary Mother

Mother's Day is yet another day of remembrance that has changed a lot since I was young. In our small town of Snyder, Texas, men, women and children wore flowers to church on Mother's Day. If your mother was living, you wore a red flower. If your mother had passed away, you wore a white flower. In my memory, the ladies in beautiful hats, white gloves, and organdy dresses set off by the Mother's Day flowers are just as clear as if I saw them yesterday. The memory makes me smile. I have been so fortunate and feel blessed to have been able to wear a red one all these years! And with that in mind, I would like to tell you about the woman whom so many people adore—my mother.

First off, you should know that my mom is adorable. She works hard to fight those wrinkles, but those that are left are joined by grace. She never includes herself among the "poor old people" we must help any way we can.

At a recent annual meeting in Chattanooga, Tennessee, the National Women's Auxiliary of the American Baptist Association honored my mom for 45 years of service. She received a beautiful plaque and a large memory scrapbook. Although the plaque cites "outstanding dedication and service, wisdom and vision," it doesn't tell the whole story. In 1958, my mother (married to a Baptist minister) was in large part responsible for the founding of the women's auxiliary of this organization. She got the West Texas church my father pastored to send a resolution to the ABA's annual meeting advocating the organization of a women's auxiliary. It passed, and the ladies held their first meeting in 1959.

After serving a term as president, my mom was elected publicity director, a service she performed with energy and enthusiasm until the summer of 2002, her eightieth year. As a part of her award, the 500 women attending the meeting unanimously voted to name her "Publicity Director Emeritus," a lifetime position entitling her to all "the rights and privileges of an officer of the National Women's Auxiliary" and giving her the right to address the ladies at any time during their annual meetings. (Oh, my goodness!)

The Memory Book is filled with notes, pictures, letters and poems from women all over the world. It's wonderful for an hour or two on a rainy day with a tissue in hand. I think not many of us get to look through a scrapbook and read notes people have written saying how wonderful we are and how we've influenced their lives. Most of that is done at the funeral when, unfortunately, the object of the remarks misses it.

When Robert Harling wrote *Steel Magnolias* in honor of his late sister, he didn't know it, but he was writing about my mom. I'm sure there are people everywhere who feel that way. It's a type of woman, I guess, more particularly a southern woman. My mom grew up in western Oklahoma, raised by an itinerate missionary who worked the oil fields during the week, then traveled all over the state on weekends as a circuit preacher. Her mother ran what today we'd call a day care center, and all of them tried to keep body and soul together during the Depression.

The "magnolia" part perfectly summarizes my mom's emphasis on politeness (it's rude to hang up the phone on somebody even if it's a telemarketer), on hospitality (more than one person showed up, unannounced, at her door with a suitcase and the words "They said if I came up to Washington, D.C., I could stay at Pastor Dean's house!"), and on appearance. My mom and dad were married on Thanksgiving Day in 1941. During the '40s and '50s, many rural preachers' wives often looked what can only be described as "dowdy." Mother, who to this day never leaves the house without looking perfect, was horrified at the idea that some young lady might not want to be a minister's wife because of the way they dressed and looked! My mom took personal responsibility for righting that wrong.

The "steel" part perfectly summarizes a formidable strength. When my dad died in 1979, I'm confident Mom grieved mightily in private. However, in public, she was the model of how someone with strong faith and enduring peacefulness would act. My mother worked full-time long before most women did—and pastor's wives in particular did not work full time outside the home. In fact, my mother worked full-time, downtown, as an administrative assistant to a California congressman and only retired, reluctantly, when he did. Both of them were 76 years old.

When I was a child, my mom told me: "Can't [pronounced caint] died in the cornfield in Arkansas." I was indoctrinated with the idea that I could do whatever I set my mind to do. (My mom may still think that if I decided to be a brain surgeon today, all I would have to do is start picking the right med school!) It is, I know, that internal mantra that made me think I could actually start law school when I was fifty years old, and made me think I could write a column that seniors might enjoy, and made me believe that my dreams could come true. Most have. I hope your mom is as wonderful. Thank you, Mom.

Grandchildren — Extraordinary[3]

During the time the "Senior Moments" column has appeared, there have been very few mentions of our perfect grandchildren. After all, those of you who have your own perfect grandchildren are likely to be bored—and those who have no grandchildren yet are likely to react as I once did in my pre-grandparent days (read on). I just haven't had a good enough excuse to go on and on in the column about these little angels.

When my first child got married—at a very young and tender age—I was in no mood to even think about being someone's grandmother. I felt too young, too energetic, too busy to even contemplate the thought! As the years passed, we acquired a "grand-dog," but no grandchildren. Frankly, during this period, my husband and I felt slightly superior and not a little smug when we took note of how "silly" our friends acted over each new grandchild. We seriously assured each other that we would never behave like that.

As time continued its swift passage, I started to feel friendlier toward the grandparenting idea. I began to think I might even be able to bear someone calling me "grandma"—not "now," of course, but "someday."

Then, one day, we were told we would in fact be grand-parents "next summer." We didn't even wait until the child was born to surrender completely to the silliness we had so often snubbed. We went Christmas shopping and told every frantically busy cashier who rang up our purchases that "we" were going to have a grandchild! Anticipation not unlike waiting for Christmas when you're a child took over our lives. Several weeks later, we received a call of the type that you believe to be important, and you go speedily. At our firstborn's house, we were shown sonogram pictures that showed not one, not two, but three beating hearts!

During the following months, we were like "Johnny One-Note." Our thoughts and conversations seemingly could be of nothing other than this incredible impending event—the birth of triplets! Along with the parents, the great-grandparents and our "co-grandparents" we prayed, read encouraging information, read discouraging information, heard so much about the high risks of multiple births, waited and prayed some more. We even went to "grandparent's class" at Anne Arundel Medical Center. The session was two hours long, and the single bit of teaching philosophy seemed to be "A lot has changed. You are not the parent. You are the grandparent. Keep your mouth shut."

Incredibly, the babies arrived safe and sound. The world was suddenly three times better! I was hypnotized, dreamily staring for long minutes into their little faces where I saw the past, the present and the future all at once—the past because their eyes, their mouths, their noses reminded me of loved ones now gone from us, the present because, amazingly, there they actually were in my arms—and the future because their potential was unlimited.

That was three summers ago. Last month, the three of them went to bed two years old, and woke up three years old! I just can't say enough—everything they do is wonderful, everything they say is precious. Somebody once wrote that a baby is God's opinion that the world should go on. Yes. I'm incredibly grateful for the babies that share my life.

A Loved One Taken by Alzheimer's— An Extraordinary Disease

The week that I wrote this remembrance I took my mother to Mississippi. When we arrived there we joined friends and family for a bittersweet reunion, and we buried my mother's sister.

I received the news of my aunt's death while I was in Connecticut, visiting my grandchildren, then age four—a situation ready-made for pondering the ironies of life. The four-year-olds of the world are (thank goodness) largely oblivious to the sad and sober tasks that life sometimes requires of us. They live in a world totally protected by those who love them, and their biggest worry is whether they can have a popsicle even though they didn't finish their vegetables.

Aunt Velma had Alzheimer's disease (AD) for several years. She did not want to leave her home after the death of her husband, and only did so when she was forced to after falling outside the back door and breaking her hip. She lay there without help for several hours. My mom and her sisters are possessed of formidable strength. Through determination, main strength and brute force they accomplish things that would lay the rest of us out in exhaustion.

During her last years, Aunt Velma did not recognize anyone. And sadly, when we sent flowers for her 92nd birthday, we were told she could not be made aware of their arrival. At 92, she could no longer overcome, nor force the events of the world into a mold meeting her strict standards.

Alzheimer's disease. Frightening words. The scourge of getting older. The Copper Ridge Institute, in connection with Johns Hopkins University, is devoted to Alzheimer's research. One of their programs is to train nurses, aides and health care providers how best to care for someone with this disease. This is a huge challenge, as apparently no one really knows how many cognitive functions remain at any one time, nor what an AD patient would desire in terms of care.

Upon reviewing some of the literature from the Institute I discovered this startling statistic. One of their doctors asked, "Do you want to live to be 85? Do you plan to live to be 85? If you are 85, the chances are 1 in 3 that you will get Alzheimer's disease." Wow.

My mother lived with Aunt Velma for a few months before I was born because my dad was away in the Merchant Marines during World War II. Velma lived in Ellisville, Mississippi. This explains the little-known fact that I was born in Laurel, Mississippi—a place I lived for only six weeks. The generosity demonstrated by the story of Aunt Velma making a home for my mom and me out of her home is telling. Members of my mom's family have that in common—an uncommon generosity, both of spirit and of material things. If you are their friend, what is theirs is yours and there is no holding back. I remember as a young bride admiring a brooch Aunt Velma was wearing, only to have her take it off her suit and give it to me!

There is a myth that Alzheimer's disease is not fatal. The Alzheimer's Association says the reality is that Alzheimer's is a fatal disease. Their Web site explains that AD begins with the destruction of cells in regions of the brain that are important for memory. However, the eventual loss of cells in other regions of the brain leads to the failure of other essential systems in the body.

Through the years Aunt Velma loved to tell me how they broke her heart when they took away "her baby" at only six weeks old. She referred, of course, to me. My dad had returned from service, and my mother and I moved home with him. Until I was a teen-ager, Aunt Velma faithfully sent me a dollar bill for every birthday, and only later did I comprehend how hard-won those dollars were for her.

To lose memory, as in Alzheimer's disease, is to lose everything. Memories teach us that life is precious, that it goes by in a blink and that we must find ways to cherish each second. When we left Connecticut my beautiful granddaughter gave me a polished rock she got from the science center. "I got ten of them," she explained. "To give to the people I love. Put it in your pocket, and remember me." This was said with the earnest expression and the distinctive "baby-talk" that only a four-year-old can pull off. Priceless.

Yes, Anna, I will hold on tight to your rock, and I will try hard to hold onto all the beautiful pieces of a life that began in Aunt Velma's house. Rest well, dear aunt, we will never forget you.

Ronald Reagan—Extraordinary President / Jack Dean—EXTRAordinary Father

My grandson, four years old, asks many questions. I recently read that the average four-year-old asks over 300 questions in a day. When he wants to learn what a word means, he asks in a very cute way. For instance, if you say lyrics, he says, "What's called lyrics?" If you say revolutions, he says, "what's called revolutions?"

Watching the newspaper coverage about the passing of Ronald Reagan, I find myself pondering my own questions, and using little Toby's words. What means true success? What means great communicating? What means comfortable in your own skin?

At Crofton Convalescent Center, where my mom has currently taken up temporary residence, I picked up a copy of their monthly newsletter. A quote at the top read: "People will forget what you do. People will forget what you say. But people will never forget how you made them feel."

In stumbling upon that quote, I believe I learned the answer to why we feel Ronald Reagan was successful, a great communicator and comfortable in his own skin. His obvious enjoyment of life, his unwavering belief that his core principles would hold true and his unfailing optimism no matter the circumstances made us feel safe and secure. He truly seemed strong enough for all of us.

Even more important, I think, was that those traits of his were usually communicated to us through such beautiful words. Many of the words were written by others, true, but seemingly by others familiar with the pulse and longings of Mr. Reagan's heart. Specific examples of the beautiful words have been played over and over again on weekend television, so I think I won't run through them again here.

Because our fortieth president was so widely adored and perhaps because Father's Day is coming very soon, I have been thinking of my own father, a gentleman also held in high esteem by many. December 2004 will be the twenty-fifth anniversary of his death. He died too young, too young, only 56 years old. When I think about the challenges of growing older, as I often do, I remember that is one challenge my dad never faced. Like Ted Kennedy said about John F. Kennedy Jr., my dad was given every gift except length of years.

Dad, too, was an optimistic person and comfortable in his own skin. As founding pastor of Grace Baptist Church in Bowie, Maryland, he over and over again surprised and confounded those with rigid prejudices and narrow-minded opinions about Baptist preachers from the South. Like Reagan, his belief in his own principles was bedrock. Like Reagan, that fact did not push people away, but drew them closer.

President Reagan died at age 93, but we actually lost him years before that. My dad died almost 40 years younger than the president, but we actually did not lose him until a couple of weeks before his death from a terminal condition diagnosed only one month before. My professional, working life is filled with thoughts of living wills, orders for Do Not Resuscitate, Medicaid eligibility work, pharmacy assistance, long-term care planning, senior housing and on and on. If everyone died at age 56, there would be very little work for attorneys who concentrate their practices in areas of elder law.

Really, we must all grow older. The alternative is to die young, as my dad did. But how can we do this aging with grace, dignity and optimism as President Reagan did? I wish I knew. Some of us are daffy because of dementia of some sort, so we can't get our minds straight to work out the grace, dignity and optimism thing. Some of us are so fearful of what may happen as we age that we are equally helpless. Some of us simply deny that we are even getting older and, in that way, we don't have to face the scary things associated with the process. (That tactic is very, very difficult for families, friends and caregivers.) If you know the secret, please share it with those you love.

I, myself, am searching for how to age with grace, dignity and optimism. I wish President Reagan had shared the secret with us. I wish my dad could have lived longer.

A Truly "Extraordinary" Caregiver

The "average" caregiver of an elderly loved one in this country is a 47-year-old woman with a full-time job and children in school. But I want to tell you about an extraordinary caregiver who is nowhere near "average."

I know this gentleman because in my law practice I spent many months trying to avoid guardianship procedures giving him control over the person and the business affairs of his wife's aunt, who has "medium" dementia and is confined to a nursing home at age 82. All we really needed to do was to get an area bank that was holding her cash assets to help us figure out how to pay the nursing home from her accounts there. Particularly one account, which has plenty of money to pay the cost for almost two years. However, the bank would not be moved; nor would they agree to any of my suggested "creative alternatives." At last, there was nothing to do but petition the court for guardianship, which was eventually awarded, so that the nursing home could be paid.

My caregiver hero had opened the family home to this aunt for a period of nine years before she entered the nursing home, and the caregiver's wife handled her aunt's business and personal affairs. In 1999, the wife was diagnosed with a brain tumor and began a lengthy series of chemotherapy and radiation treatments. Her husband, the star of this story, resigned a management position with the company where he had worked for thirty-two years, and took a staff position in order to have more time to devote to his wife's care. Subsequently, the wife lost her sight and much of her coherence. She is unable to manage her own affairs, much less the affairs of another. Although they have daytime aides, her husband is the major caregiver.

Additionally, this caregiver manages the personal and business affairs of his 88-year-old mother-in-law, who is in a nursing home across town from the aunt's nursing home. But that's not all. His father died last February, and his 87-year-old mother is now living with him.

As Elie Wiesel said when he accepted his Nobel Peace Prize, "Our lives no longer belong to us alone; they belong to all who need us desperately." The devotion with which this man, who will be 60 on his next birthday, watches over and cares for these four women is awesome. I'm struck dumb with admiration.

An Extraordinary Lady of Culture

> One of the things my life has taught me is how important it is to try to say "I love you" in ways that can be preserved, looked at, and read when you are alone or when there is adversity or when circumstances bring separation. (Nancy Reagan, preface to the paperback edition of *I Love You, Ronnie*, 2002)

An elderly long time friend of our family died recently. His wife and only child had passed away a few years before. So, sadly, there was no family near, and it became my responsibility to clear out the house. Even an empty house that you never lived in yourself can somehow be full of memories, shadows and the ghosts of past experiences. The task took longer than it should have because I stopped to read letters, look at pictures and shed a tear over heartfelt lines of poetry written half a century ago.

I want to share with you a letter I found, dated May 22, 1950. It is actually a recommendation for his wife when she was applying for a teaching job in a new city (names have been changed to protect the innocent):

> Dear Mr. Jamison. Mrs. Jones is one of the few substitute teachers that I have regularly marked

"Superior." She is a cultured lady, with such an unusual understanding and appreciation of children's problems that she has fine control of her room of happy children. Parents were glowingly appreciative of her work.

She brought her own Victrola and records, and did a great deal of work at her home in preparation for her class work. She knows the songs the children like, and was good in music and art.

The nicest thing about her, though, is the way children absorb her cultured behavior and fine manners. Any school would be fortunate to have her. Very sincerely yours, Mr. Brown.

I have read and reread this letter. Reading it, I can get lost in long, long thoughts. I realize that, as we get older, it's common to think of how things were nicer in the Olden Days, and I have truly tried to resist that type of thinking. After all, we didn't have computers then, did we? No. There were manual typewriters and Victrolas.

Nevertheless, look at the letter again. Mrs. Jones was referred to as "a cultured lady." Where are the cultured ladies of today? In fact, where is the "lady" at all? In the classic manner of having my cake and eating it, too, I'm very pleased to wear pantsuits and my Birkenstocks to work, but it's pleasant to think about the hats and gloves well-dressed women wore in my childhood. Proponents of school uniforms contend that children behave noticeably better if they are dressed nicely than if they are in their play clothes. Could that be true of adults, too?

Mrs. Jones had a schoolroom full of "happy children" who absorbed "her cultured behavior and fine manners." Makes you wonder what after-school hangouts would be like if children had absorbed cultured behavior and fine manners.

Whenever I get curmudgeonly like this, and sound like I long for the good old days, my long-suffering husband reminds me of the Socrates quote: "Children today are tyrants. They contradict their parents, gobble their food, and tyrannize their teachers." I guess it's true that every generation, once grown, is certain that the younger generation is going to you-know-where in a handbasket. All that being true, I still think it would be nice sometimes for somebody somewhere to demonstrate cultured behavior and fine manners.

As I continued to clean and clear out the empty house, I was able to get an intimate picture of the lives lived there because of letters. Letters that took me back in time. Letters to each other, letters to friends, to family. Nowadays we don't write many letters. We have e-mail, which I love, but not letters. We visit the card store and send a card or two, but no handwritten, personal letters. As Mrs. Reagan said in the prologue to a book of President Reagan's love letters to her, "In our throwaway era of quick phone calls, faxes and e-mail, it's all too easy never to find the time to write letters. That's a great pity—for historians and the rest of us. If only people could see Ronnie's letters, I thought, they'd realize so much, including how wonderful it can be to take the time to write what you feel to those you love."

If you have some time, and you'd like to try your hand at some "real" letter writing, there are, of course, Web sites with more helpful hints than you could ever dream of. One of my favorites is www.wendy.com/letterwriting. Also, take a look at the book *The Handcrafted Letter* by Diane Maurer-Mathison. Remember, as Mary Mitchell, also known as Ms. Demeanor, wrote on the iVillage Web site: "Not one modern communications marvel can replace a letter. It is more than a communication. It is a gift."

On Growing Older

Courage in the Face of Growing Old

Working in the field of elder law, I'm convinced that courage is the overarching characteristic that defines the quality of our lives as we inch closer to that "good night." *Webster's Dictionary* defines courage as "mental or moral strength to venture, persevere, and withstand danger, fear, or difficulty." I think God gives us so many opportunities to practice courage throughout our lives so that we have practiced enough to become good at it by the time we are senior citizens. Do you remember walking into your first-grade classroom? Courage is absolutely the quality most needed to face the frightening challenges confronting seniors every day.

Like you, I'm thinking of courage because of the hundreds of examples vividly demonstrated since September 11th. Ordinary individuals became extraordinary when they summoned the courage to confront awesome challenges, and we watched transfixed in admiration. Many of us ask ourselves whether we would have the courage to do a similar thing should it be required of us. Any answer is, of necessity, only hypothetical because the exact situation has not yet confronted us.

However, we all perform courageous acts on some smaller scale, such as managing not to lose our voice on opening night of our senior play, or running onto the football field when we really want to run away. That's the practice I spoke of earlier—the rehearsal for the continuing production of our senior years. Any individual who matriculates from "middle age" to "older age" is performing similar acts of courage every single day of their lives.

When tendonitis in your wrist that acted up about once a year since you were twenty is now acting up once a month, and is terribly painful, you just strap on the elastic wrist brace and go on about your work. Perhaps you realize you really need not one doctor's appointment, but about five or six more appointments, because it's time for your annual physical, you may have yet another urinary infection, the doctor said a cataract might be starting in your right eye and to come back in six months, your bunions are painful and the only thing that really helps is a visit to the foot doctor, your joints hurt, especially when it rains, and you feel exhausted just thinking about it! But you don't fall down on the bed and say "I'm sick." You do the best you can with all the indignities forced upon you, and you confront and meet your responsibilities.

Somehow you continue through this stage with a modicum of dignity, grace, and self-respect. If you are introspective enough to think about it, you try not to become irritable with others because of the various pains and inconveniences that seem to be taking over your life.

Almost before you know it, you've drifted into a scarier stage. It takes you longer to express a thought than it used to, and you notice that people (including doctors and other health care providers) are too rushed to listen. You wonder if maybe your hearing is deteriorating, but you don't want to accept that fact! Friends and family may begin talking as though you aren't even present! They can't seem to give you the time you need to focus your thoughts and join in the discussion. Then again, you may be driving home from a place you've been thousands of times, and all of a sudden you look around and can't recognize exactly where you are. You do get your bearings and make it home, but that odd little confusion continues to happen. Your car gets scratches on a predominant side because you keep lightly running into the curb, the garage door, and the bank drive-through. Maybe your distance judgment on one side is not as good as it once was? You're pondering all this in your mind when somebody says, "Look, you shouldn't be driving at your age. There are as many accidents caused by aging drivers as by drunk drivers. We're taking the car keys." You need courage to accept this new fact with grace.

Soon you may hear those same people say: "Mom/Dad, you really can't live alone any longer. What if something were to happen? Who would be there to help you?" And you must be courageous enough to leave your home of years and move. But to move where? To move in with a family we love, but they are already crowded, with moody teenagers or fussy toddlers? Nice places are expensive, and affordable places don't seem nice. Wherever it turns out to be, it's somehow not the home you want. You need courage to find pleasure in a different type of life.

These examples only skim the surface. When we feel frightened, alone, and misunderstood, it's difficult to call up courage. While watching David Letterman one evening, I noted that he mentioned his own personal experiences with needing courage. He said he has learned that "pretending to be courageous is as good, and yields the same results, as actually being courageous."

And so I salute, with much admiration, all seniors as they confront the myriad challenges of their ever-changing lives with the courage they have practiced.

Faith Can Improve Our Lives

"Senior Moments'" Senior Writer (smile) celebrates two personal, major life events each June, a very popular month for major life events. I'm celebrating mine by staring for hours across the Potomac River, peacefully watching little fish jump, blue herons fly in for a visit and ducks and geese "honking" as they hurry to their daily tasks. Clients, friends and my own age (next year, I'll enter my sixth decade) cause me more and more to contemplate the realities and the mystery and blessing of growing older.

Growing older is, of course, full of myriad events that don't seem, on the surface, to be "blessings." I call it blessed because I'm so very aware of those who are not allowed the gift of growing older. My dad, for instance, continually hovers around my memory—full of energy, fixer of all things, a "safe," warm, and wise counselor, smiling that incredible grin just as when God took him all those years ago. He was three years younger than I am now. Amazingly, even children die, and parents and grand-parents, stunned by life's most devastating blow, must figure out a way to go on—somehow.

So, I insist that aging is a blessing. Along with its many challenges, it occasionally allows us opportunities to observe the blue heron.

Among clients, friends (and myself), I observe the many variations of aging. Mary Pipher writes of the "young-old" and the "old-old." The Harvard study we discussed a few weeks ago contrasts the "happy-well" old with the "sick-sad" old. I wonder and wonder and wonder how I can assist those seniors within my sphere of influence to move into or to stay longer in the "young-old, happy-well" group.

(As I watch, the mother and daddy ducks swim by for the umpteenth time, left to right, right to left. I spend a minute wondering what motivation moves them. Ah, now they come back, left to right, with 38—yes, 38—babies in a straight line behind them, and another mom and dad bringing up the rear! But I digress)

In my columns, I've nudged readers in so many ways and directions. I've made you aware (I hope) of options and choices to get you over to the "happy-well" side. I've nagged you to get your important documents completed and executed so you needn't worry about that matter, shared literally hundreds of housing options available these days, insisted that you purchase long-term care insurance so that the possibility of losing your home because you have to go to a nursing home doesn't keep you awake nights. I could go on and on.

Sitting here, though, staring at an ant trying to crawl along the arm of my chair, I'm forced to conclude that one could do all the things on that list—every single one of them—and still not be among the "young, happy-well" old.

Some of it is, of course, personality, inclination and disposition. I have an aunt who was "old" at 35 years of age and, today, at 90, is still very old. On the other hand, there are those like my mom who, even if she lives to be 110, will never be as "old" as her sister was at 35! So, yes—personality and inclination are big.

That said, how in the world can a person who has been reasonably happy for the majority of his or her life, been relatively successful by their own standards, healthy for the most part, optimistic—how can that person successfully (or even by the skin of their teeth!) cope with the challenges, daily losses and continual frustrations of getting older and, indeed, *being* older.

I know one thing. Even when you intellectually know that being happy is a choice—that you can choose to have a good day or a bad day—that you can choose to have a good attitude, the actual "choosing" itself is so much easier said than done. As Susanna Wesley once wrote (actually about trying to write in spite of all those children), there are days when making that choice and acting on it is like "rowing against wind and tide."

This is what I want to say to you on such a sun-sprinkled, beautiful day: Faith is key. Yes—it is. Study after study has shown that those individuals able to understand that the ultimate course of their lives is not in their hands, but in the control of the One who created DNA, have a formidable advantage allowing them to more successfully confront and navigate the demands of growing older.

Oh, sure—don't start. You're right. There are hundreds, maybe even thousands, of unanswered questions: the problem of evil in the world, the problem of suffering, how humans can be so cruel and murderous to each other. Those are big questions, that's for sure, and I can't answer them. And, for the first time in my life, as I contemplate leaving my fifth decade, I don't much care that I can't. The fact that strong faith extends our lives, and contributes greatly to making those extra years healthier and happier, is proven. Harvard knows it. And so do I.

Udall on Growing Old

Morris Udall is one of my heroes. Not for his political beliefs, but for the creative way he wove the words of his speeches and writings to give life to those beliefs. Like Presidents John F. Kennedy and Ronald Reagan, he used beautifully crafted expressions that caused his words to remain in our memory long after they were spoken.

Congressman Udall gave a speech, in 1975, to the National Council on the Aging. Reading the entire address today makes the 1976 presidential candidate sound like a prophet. Among other things, he spoke of age discrimination, of a failure to address the real health needs of the elderly by ascribing all their illnesses to "old age," of older Americans being easy targets for scams, frauds and other crimes, and he suggested that the president appoint a White House advocate for aging Americans.

In the address, "Public Policy and the Future of Aging," Congressman Udall said that society has developed two basic stereotypes of the aged in order to justify our neglect—serenity and senility. On the one hand, he said, our images of old age are idealized. We can visualize Normal Rockwall paintings showing "beloved and tranquil" grandparents. We picture the serene and gracious white-haired matriarch dispensing her wisdom from the family kitchen, and the matching patriarch dispensing wisdom from the front porch rocker. Of several things not quite right with that picture, there's also the fact that no one is really listening to all the wisdom being dispensed! On the other hand, said Udall, the opposite image disparages the aged. Old age is viewed as irreversible decay, decrepitude and serious loss of mental powers. A Harris poll, conducted apparently around that time, found that younger people regarded the aged as "inept, ineffectual, physically depleted and waiting for death." Older people, Udall said, are seen as "rigid, querulous and resistant to change; narrow and superficial in intellectual activity; and almost universally senile."

These images and ideas are self-perpetuating because, in truth, many elderly persons have, for instance, Alzheimer's disease, probably called senility in 1975. Many have become bitter because of the loss of their spouse, or because it's so hard to hear, or because they can no longer read easily. These situations cut them off from society, and any self-esteem they once had is continually and continuously undermined. When I'm with my mother who—while getting on in years—is still feisty, goal-oriented, determined and never willing to give up, it's striking how often people ask questions or make comments concerning her as though she's not in the room. It's no wonder that so many seniors lapse into what Udall called "patterns of despair."

Because Udall's address was given almost thirty years ago, there's unintended comic relief to partially balance the bleakness. For instance, here's the quote about prescription drugs: "One of the most basic of health costs to the elderly is for prescription drugs—which are only covered by Medicare if the individual is institutionalized. Many, therefore, must pay $20–$30 a month in drug bills." If you're over 65, and your prescription drug bills are less than $30 per month, I would certainly like to hear about it. In fact, I'm sure many people would like to find out how you do it!

Congressman Udall, a member of the Basketball Hall of Fame because of his play with the Denver Nuggets in 1948 and 1949, died in 1998 at the age of 76, from Parkinson's disease. The disease had caused him to retire from the national stage in May 1991. In the address that is the topic of today's column, he wrote: "Older Americans fear, above all, institutionalization...." Sadly, even though he was an honored sports figure, a committee chairman in the House of Representatives, and a candidate for president in the 1976 Democratic primaries, he could not, himself, avoid that most feared condition. His last days were spent in a nursing facility.

F-U-N (Seniors—Society's FUN Faction)

> Although common, depression is not a normal part of the aging process. We have an epidemic of depression in older people. More than six million Americans 65 and older suffer from depression...depression reduces life expectancy, creates other health problems and can even lead

to suicide. (Rodrigo Munoz, M.D., chief of Behavioral Health, Scripps Mercy Hospital)

They say that depression is rampant in the elderly. They say that one of the reasons is, as people grow older and are subject to the decline and losses of age, they feel they are no longer "needed." Being needed by someone, it is said, is very high in the hierarchy of human needs. Abraham Maslow includes it in his list of the "love needs." We need to feel loved (nonsexual) by others, to be accepted by others. Performers appreciate applause. We need to be needed.

It's true that most healthy adults are, in fact, needed by their spouse, by their boss, by their employees, by their infants, their Girl Scout, their high school graduate. They are needed to pay for the wedding, to spoil the grandchildren and, finally, to care for their own parents.

One suggested solution for the depression caused by not being needed is to create opportunities and "life scapes" to help people feel needed again, in a different way. This is achieved, in some cases, with phenomenal success. Becoming a Foster Grandparent is a well-known example, and one that has a dual outcome, for even children need to feel needed.

Some seniors cannot bring themselves to pursue or cooperate with these opportunities. Perhaps they are ever hopeful that their situation will change and they will be able to do all the things they once did and won't have to resort to participating in opportunities for seniors. Some just cannot move past it. They won't volunteer at the senior center, or consider assisted living, or join a senior's choir because "old people" are there. They find something somehow demeaning about the entire situation, so they won't learn adaptive skills to match their current capabilities. So, unneeded, they waste away, full of sadness and regret, feeling misunderstood and unloved.

Well, I'm ready to propose a whole new approach. Frankly, I think "un-needed" just needs a better PR man, and I volunteer! We will stop the poor-pitiful-Pearl approach and celebrate the status of being unneeded! What, you ask—are you saying being unneeded is a good thing? Exactly! It certainly can be. Despite how some people may feel right now, unneeded is not the same as being useless. It is not the same thing as being ready for the trash heap. It is not synonymous with being put out to pasture. Indeed not. Not in a million years. Consider this:

Unneeded is *restful*—There is no excuse not to nap in my favorite easy chair.

Unneeded is *creative*—Finally, I can write my memoirs.

Unneeded is *freedom*—I don't have to adjust my life by someone else's schedule.

Unneeded is *hope*—There is time to imagine unlimited, wondrous future events.

Unneeded is *adventurous*—So much to see and do, and finally enough time.

Unneeded is *inspiring*—Watching others lead by the example we have set.

Unneeded is *beautiful*—Time to sit still and enjoy the sunset, or the sunrise.

Unneeded is *loving*—Time to sit back and watch someone you love bustling about.

Unneeded is *leisurely*—I can lollygag as long as I want.

Unneeded is *freeing*—No one expects much from me.

You know, for every other challenge life sends us, we have clichés. For instance: if life gives you lemons, make lemonade. Or: if someone is rubbing you the wrong way, turn around. But, for the sadness caused by being unneeded, we just shake our heads in sadness and defeat, and offer no answers.

This, I say, is a new day. Maslow taught that humans also have a desire to belong to groups: clubs, work groups, religious groups, family, gangs, etc. That need to belong is also in the category of "love needs." So, if you are reading this and feel unneeded and unloved, you have a choice. Feel sad and depressed and let those feelings eventually destroy your physical health, or Unneeded Friends of Senior Moments, unite! Contact someone you think may also feel unneeded and start a club! If those "red hat ladies" can do it, so can you! If you have physical limitations, you may have to use the phone or e-mail. That's okay. Just do it.

Band together as friends and fellow-sufferers and challenge the world. Here is a suggested name for your new undertaking. The Fabulous UNs: Unbelievable uses for the UNder used! You can see that "Fabulous UNs" has an acronym of "FUN." So, we can also call the Fabulous UNs "The FUN Faction."

There is no end to where you can go with this. Come on. Turn those lemons into lemonade. Make it fun, admirable, sexy and desirable to be Unneeded—a Fabulous UN.

Author's Note

Nothing, they say, is new under the sun. All that I know about seniors and the practice of elder law, I learned from others who came before me, from extensive reading, and from my own experiences. In acknowledging those who have helped me most, I run the risk of omitting others who have contributed to my knowledge with their writing, their lectures, and their advice. To all of them I offer my apologies if I have not named them, and my gratitude for all they have contributed to my work with seniors and to this book.

With the advent of the Internet, it becomes more and more difficult to separate public information from copyright-protected information. The weekly "Senior Moments" column attempts to share voluminous helpful information for readers, and to direct them to resources for even more information. Every effort is made to ensure that proper credit is given to sources, and that information is accurate and up-to-date. The author apologizes for mistakes or omissions in this area.

Finally, information such as names and addresses can very quickly become outdated, so please let us know if any of the information has changed and/or if you know of new or important services for seniors. I welcome comments about the book and suggestions for future editions. Readers can contact me through the firm's Web site, www.byrdandbyrd.com.

Acknowledgments

I know how the winners feel on Academy Awards night. To try and begin to name the persons who have had an impact on the existence of this book is a daunting task.

First of all, very, very special appreciation to Josie, my legal assistant. Her friendship, loyalty, dedication and understanding of what is required to effectively advocate for seniors is priceless. She has typed and re-typed, nudged, suggested and persevered. It is not an overstatement to say that without her, this book would absolutely not exist.

The University of Baltimore School of Law—they took a chance on a 50-year-old, first-year student who never really and truly actually learned to "think like a lawyer" in spite of their heroic efforts, and especially to Leslie Metzger, Eric Easton, Byron Warnken, and Charles Teifer.

The staff and attorneys at BYRD & BYRD, LLC, not only co-workers but friends.

My beautiful mother, my number one fan. Our struggles as she has attempted, very grudgingly, to learn to grow older have served as a laboratory and proving ground for my work with clients. Our stories allow clients and readers to know that I truly understand what they are experiencing. Although one column is completely devoted to her, she has served as the anonymous inspiration for many columns. On occasion, she has said, "why didn't you just go ahead and say my name?"

Everyone at Smart Marketing, especially Mark Merenda, who never quit believing there was a book somewhere.

Jay Poynor, uncle extraordinaire, agent and emmy-winner, book-writing encourager, friend and counselor. As a teenager, I never wondered what "cool" was. I knew. It was my uncle Jay.

John Rouse, Editor, *Bowie Blade-News*, epitomizing everyone's idea of what a newspaper editor should be like, he took a chance and gave

313

me the opportunity to write the column in the first place, and to Sandy Stewart, and all my generous friends at the newspaper.

Debbie and Jason, my children and much more—my friends.

My clients, whose stories consume my thoughts, sometimes break my heart, and inspire me to try harder because they need my help, and believe I can help them.

NAELA (National Academy of Elder Law Attorneys) whose members and staff have nurtured me, mentored me, educated me and inspired me from the beginning of my elder law adventure.

Members of the Maryland/D.C. NAELA Chapter, and the MSBA Elder Law Section, especially Jason and Laurie Frank, Morris Klein, Cathy Stavely, Ron Landsman, Nomiki Weitzel, Anne DeNovo, Karren Pope-Onwukwe, Camilla McRory, Stephanie Edelstein and Ben Woolery—excellent attorneys all and friends in the trenches.

Lynn Gemmell, generous literary editor extraordinaire, whose efforts never fail to make me sound better than I really do and whose encouragement, exhortations and empathy comfort me in the most frantic of times.

And a very special thank you to Tom Begley Jr., Esquire, of Begley and Bookbinder, Moorestown, New Jersey, a real elder law hero, who took the time to read this book and write comments about it for the Foreword. Tom is a well-known lecturer, TV and radio commentator, and author, having written books on Elder and Disability Law and Estate Planning. He is a Certified Medicaid Planning Attorney and a Fellow of the National Academy of Elder Law Attorneys. Tom is listed in *Who's Who in American Law* and *Who's Who in America*. Visit the Begley and Bookbinder Web site at www.njelderlaw.com.

> *"…with many counselors, there is safety."*
> Proverbs 11:14 (NLT)

About the Author

Jacqueline D. Byrd worked on Capitol Hill for the House of Representatives for more than 25 years, ending her career as the director of support operations in the House Office of Non-legislative and Financial Services. She began law school in the fall of 1995, and practices law with her husband, Toby, in the firm of Byrd & Byrd, LLC, in Bowie, Maryland.

Jackie is a member of the National Academy of Elder Law Attorneys and limits her practice to areas of Elder Law, including wills, powers of attorney, trusts, Medicaid, guardianships, and asset preservation.

Jackie is a public speaker and enjoys giving informational lectures to community organizations. She is currently the Recording Secretary of the Maryland/D.C. chapter of the National Academy of Elder Law Attorneys and serves as program chairman for the governing council of the Elder Law Section of the Maryland State Bar Association.

In the spring of 2004, Jackie received the President's Award of the Prince George's County, Maryland Bar Association for her work with Karren Pope-Onwukwe in founding the Elder Law Section. She has also been designated Outstanding Chapter Member of the Maryland/D.C. NAELA Chapter. As an alumnus of the University of Baltimore School of Law, she received a Dean's Citation as Founding Editor-in-Chief of the Administration newsletter, *The Official Reporter*.

Jackie was named as one of Washington D.C.'s top elder law attorneys in the December 2004 issue of the *Washingtonian Magazine*.

She is the proud grandmother of triplets born in July of 1999 and of their baby brother born February, 2005. In her free time, she enjoys spending every possible moment with them. She also loves reading, playing piano, movies and traveling.

You can read more about Jackie at the firm's Web site, www.byrdandbyrd.com